T0247564

The History of the Schaumburg-Lippe-Bückeburg Carabinier and Jäger Corps

G.W. Düring

Translated and Edited by James R. Mc Intyre

The History of the Schaumburg-Lippe-Bückeburg Carabinier and Jäger Corps
by G.W. Düring
Translated and Edited by James R. McIntyre

Cover image by Albert Knotel
This edition published in 2024

Winged Hussar Publishing is an imprint of

Winged Hussar Publishing, LLC
1525 Hulse Rd, Unit 1
Point Pleasant, NJ 08742

Copyright © Winged Hussar Publishing
ISBN PB 978-1-958872-52-9
ISBN EB 978-1-958872-53-6
ISBN HC 978-1-958872-63-5
LCN 2024941618

Bibliographical References and Index
1. History. 2. Germany. 3. Seven Years War

Winged Hussar Publishing, LLC All rights reserved
For more information
visit us at www.whpsupplyroom.com

Twitter: WingHusPubLLC
Facebook: Winged Hussar Publishing LLC

Contents

Acknowledgements

First, I need to thank Vincent Rospond, who has supported my work since we first crossed paths. Likewise, he has shown incredible patience with my delays while I tried to nail down certain facts and arguments.

Since this work is a translation, I need to thank John Peters, my high-school German teacher who introduced me to what has become a life-long interest in the language, and languages in general. This work is the fruit of the seeds you planted Herr Peters.

I need to thank, as well, Alex Burns, Ken Bunger, the late Dean West, and all the members of the Seven Years' War Association who have supported and contributed to the organization's journal over the years. Their assistance is especially important as I discovered the original volume on which the present translation is based while doing research for a special issue of the journal on Schaumburg-Lippe-Bückeburg in the Seven Years' War. The positive comments and feedback from that issue spurred me to do further research and translate the work that forms the core of the present volume.

In addition, I would like to thank Boris Brink for his wonderful and engaging correspondence as well as the source materials he so willingly shared with me on the army of Schaumburg-Lippe-Bückeburg. These materials aided me in pinning down some aspects of the experience of the Carabinier and Jäger Corps during the conflict.

Finally, but certainly not least, to my family, wife Catherine, daughters Jessica and Zayne and son Nathanael, you put up with me through a prolonged interest in a state that measured barely thirty miles across. You supported and never detracted, though I am certain at times you probably questioned my sanity privately. Thank you and all my love!

G. W. During
Translator's Introduction

The following is a translation of the history of the Schaumburg-Lippe-Bückeburg Carabinier Corps in the Seven Years' War. The first question which might arise is why translate the history of such a small unit? At its peak, the corps numbered under two hundred men, and it hailed from a state which was barely thirty miles wide. The diminutive size of Schaumburg-Lippe is part of the reason. This work is meant to provide insight on the experience of one of the minor participants in the Seven Years' War. Likewise, it is meant to offer some insights on the fighting in western Europe during the conflict. There have been some excellent studies of the fighting in this theater. Sir Reginald Savory's classic work, *His Britannic Majesty's Army in the Seven Years' War* remains without doubt the pre-eminent study.[1] Savory, however, covers so much territory in his work that many of the smaller states are easily lost in the discussion. Likewise, many of the other English language works tend to focus on the British contingent and neglect the important contributions of the various German states. Thus, the following translation highlights the experience of one contingent in Anglo-German force which served first under William, Duke of Cumberland, and then under Duke Ferdinand of Brunswick-Luneburg for the duration of the conflict. In addition, it provides new insights on the development of light troops during the eighteenth-century. The history of Carabinier Corps offers a number of accounts of the small actions that occurred alongside the major clashes. Consequently, it highlights the role of small war, or as contemporaries would have known it *petite guerre* or *kleine Krieg*. Lastly, the following gives some indication of how a smaller state with extremely restricted means sought to maintain a military in keeping with the trends established by the larger, more powerful contemporary states.

Beyond the translation itself, this work includes a short description of the military forces of Schaumburg-Lippe. Its purpose is to situate the Carabinier corps in the slightly broader context of its parent

[1] Sir Reginald Savory, *His Britanic Majesty's Army in Germany during the Seven Years' War*. Oxford: Clarendon Press, 1966.

military force. In addition, there is a biography of the monarch who established the corps, Graf Wilhelm zu Schaumburg-Lippe-Bückeburg. These works originally appeared in the *Journal of the Seven Years' War Association*, which it is my honor to edit. Finally, I included a translation of a brief biography of Captain Johann von Monkewitz who served as commander of the Carabinier Corps from April of 1757 through the remainder of the conflict.

KÖNIGREICH
HANNOVER

STEINHUDER
MEER

Buchholz Loccum

Hagenburg

Wunstorf

Windheim Sachsenhagen

KÖNIGREICH
PREUSSEN

Stadthagen

Rodenberg

FÜRSTENTUM SCHAUMBURG-LIPPE

Bückeburg KÖNIGREICH
HANNOVER

GRAFSCHAFT SCHAUMBURG
(zu Kurfürstentum Hessen)

Steinbergen

Rinteln Oldendorf

Varenholz

Weser

FÜRSTENTUM
LIPPE-DETMOLD

Hameln

Schaumberg - Lippe

The Army of Schaumburg-Lippe-Bückeburg in the Seven Years' War

It stood among the smallest of the German states of the Holy Roman Empire, even though it was composed of an amalgam of several territories. However, during the Seven Years War Schaumburg-Lippe-Bückeburg under the leadership of Count Wilhelm zu Schaumburg-Lippe-Bückeburg (r. 1748-1777) contributed a very effective force to the western army under the overall command of Count Ferdinand of Brunswick-Wolfenbüttel. While recent historians have criticized the army, Graf Wilhelm's army stood as a balanced force, and as will be seen below, was in many ways quite innovative for its day.[2] The following will argue that while Schaumburg-Lippe's contribution to the coalition was small, it was indeed quite significant.

In order to adequately examine the Army of Schaumburg-Lippe, it is first necessary to provide some context by discussing the state which produced it. As noted, Schaumburg-Lippe was one of the more diminutive states of the Holy Roman Empire. Not quite thirty miles wide at its widest extremity, it occupied an unfortunate geographical position of being surrounded by Hanover to the north and east, Hessen-Kassel to the south and Prussia in the east. Wilhelm's father, Graf Albrecht Wolfgang understood the precarious security position of his state and worked to build friendships with England, Hanover and Prussia. In the end, however, these alliances remained unwritten on Albrecht's death. Wilhelm, therefore, followed a foreign policy which sought to solidify them.[3]

His desire for more permanent alliances with his larger neighbors could be interpreted as one reason for his focus on the military. If

---

[2] The chief modern critic of the Schaumburg-Lippe forces and their count is Stuart Reid. See Stuart Reid, *The Battle of Minden: The Miraculous Victory of the Seven Years' War.* Havertown: Frontline, 2016. See also *Frederick the Great's Allies.* Gery and Sam Embleton, illus. Oxford: Osprey Publishing, 2010. For biographical information on the count, see Charles E. White, "Scharnhorst's Mentor: Count Wilhelm zu Schaumburg-Lippe and the Origins of the Modern National Army." in *War in History.* 24, 3 (2017): 264.
[3] Ibid, p. 266.

Schaumburg-Lippe possessed a capable army for its size, that was one more asset the count could bring to the negotiating table. Likewise, it served to enhance the defense of his small state, both positive outcomes for a ruler in his geo-political position. The military reforms Graf Wilhelm enacted resulted in his creating one of the first truly national defensive forces of the period.[4]

Count Wilhelm began organizing the army of Schaumburg-Lippe-Bückeburg as it would take the field during the Seven Years' War about a year after he came to the throne. He developed the force over the course of the years between the end of the War of the Austrian Succession and the outbreak of the Seven Years' War, (1748-1755). During this time, the young count routinely traveled to Prussia to confer on military matters with Frederick II.[5]

On ascending to the leadership of his state, the first unit Wilhelm formed for his national defense force was an infantry regiment of eight companies which eventually totaled nearly 800 men. Interestingly, one of the earliest histories to address the Army of Schaumburg-Lippe-Bückeburg in the Seven Years' War, G.W. Düring's *Geschichte des Schaumburg-Lippe-Bückeburgischen Karabinier und Jäger-Korps*, asserts that the regiment was composed entirely of grenadiers.[6] If this is true it would have constituted a truly unique and potentially innovative force. It is likely, however, that Düring was in error. Interestingly, Düring noted that the grenadiers carried two one-pounder falconers with them.[7]

These were light cannons based on a medieval design.[8] It is more likely that they carried some form of amusette. These were essentially extra-heavy muskets first suggested by Maurice de Saxe in his *Mes*

---

[4] White, "Scharnhorst's Mentor," p. 264. This point should be taken with some circumspection. While White makes a good case for the fact that Graf Wilhelm's army was composed, at least initially, of the residents of his state, there is no indication of any nationalist sentiment among the troops given in his research.

[5] Ibid, p. 266.

[6] G.W. Düring *Geschichte des Schaumburg-Lippe-Bückebourgischen Karabinier und Jäger-Corps*. Berlin: Ernst Siegfried Mittler, 1828, 1.

[7] Ibid.

[8] I would like to gratefully acknowledge George Nafziger's help in confirming the origins of this word.

Reveries. Given the time in which Wilhelm came of age and his military interests, specifically the artillery, it is more than likely that the count had read Saxe's work and may have taken the idea into the service of his own state. While the specific details of the weapon carried by the grenadiers remain unclear, it is certain that the unit was "the most fully trained and practiced corps in the army."[9]

Demonstrating his awareness of current trends in military development, Wilhelm's regiment included a company of light infantry as well.[10] As with other similar forces in European armies of the period, these men would be taught to fight in more open order and to utilize aimed fire as opposed to the volley fire of the regular line infantry. In addition, he added a very innovative corps, the Carabinier, in 1753.

An artillery contingent was added by Graf Wilhelm in 1750. The artillery unit eventually grew to two hundred men.[11] The count held a fascination with artillery, so this part of the contingent was fairly large. It included a miners and engineers as well as artillery.[12] It has been suggested that Graf Wilhelm "stands out as one of the greatest military innovators and artillerymen of his age."[13] It is often repeated that in the creation of this corps, neither cost nor effort were spared. The corps of miners was composed of one hundred men.[14]

In addition to the regular army units described above, Graf Wilhelm created a national militia in 1751. The men were drilled on Sundays during the spring and autumn. The Count undertook several measures to make service in his national militia an attractive option for his people. First and foremost, the men were paid, it was not a voluntary force. Secondly, they were presented with an official uniform as opposed to having to wear their own clothes. Additional incentives in-

---

[9] Düring, *Geschichte*, p.1.

[10] White, "Scharnhorst's Mentor," p. 266. On the development of light infantry in the mid-eighteenth century, see James R. Mc Intyre, *The Development of the British Light Infantry, Continental and North American Influences, 1740-1765*. Point Pleasant, NJ: Winged Hussar Publishing, 2015.

[11] Düring, *Geschichte*, p. 1

[12] Ibid, p. 2.

[13] White, "Scharnhorst's Mentor," p. 268

[14] Düring, *Geschichte*, p. 2.

cluded pensions and humane treatment from their officers. In the realm of the militia officers, Graf Wilhelm sought to promote from within and rewarded traits such as bravery, leadership and initiative whenever he perceived them.[15] The militia, as it was officially reorganized in 1751, served to provide a force for home defense. [16] While it is not clear from the sources, it could provide a pool of trained manpower to draw on when necessary.

One aspect of the count's force that set it apart from those of its neighbors lay in the fact that it was composed almost entirely of men from his small state. In addition, the Graf did not take part in the Soldatenhandeln practiced by many of the other petty German princes of his day.[17] Instead, he relied upon local recruitment to provide the manpower necessary for his army. As a result, some credit Count Wilhelm with being among the forerunners of the nation in arms concept.[18] Certainly, such an assessment holds some validity. Still, as is often the case, the count's military reforms were not completed before his forces were drawn into a major conflict.

At the outset of the Seven Years' War, Graf Wilhelm contributed a contingent to His Britannic Majesty's Army which consisted of one infantry regiment and a corps of artillery which included engineers and miners. Wilhelm's was the only contingent in the Allied army to possess the latter force.[19] The regiment itself was comprised of seven line companies and one of grenadiers. In addition, he provided a regiment of dismounted jäger and a squadron of mounted grenadiers. A company of

[15] White, "Scharnhorst's Mentor," p. 265.

[16] Ibid, pp. 266-7.

[17] This was the infamous soldier trade, so named by many nineteenth-century German historians of the nationalist school who decried the practice of many of the petty princes of the eighteenth century who "sold" their troops in order to finance luxurious and superfluous projects within their states. Representative of this school would be Friedrich Kapp, Der Soldatenhandel deutscher fürsten nach Amerika. Ein Beitrag zur Kulturgeschichte des Achtzehnten Jahrhunderts. Berlin: Verlag von Julius J. Springer, 1874. For a very useful corrective, see Peter H. Wilson, "The German "Soldier Trade' of the Seventeenth and Eighteenth Centuries: A Reassessment." The International History Review. p. 18, 4 (November 1996): 757-792.

[18] White, "Scharnhorst's Mentor," pp. 269-70.

[19] Düring, Geschichte, p. 2.

artillery and a staff of engineers rounded out his force. It took the field with twenty-nine 3-pounder battalion guns, four 8-, two 12- pounder canon, three howitzers and four heavy mortars.[20] The large size of the artillery contingent reflected the count's aforementioned fascination with this arm of the service.

This small contingent was attached to Hessen-Cassel brigade in the Allied army.[21] Sir Reginald Savory notes that "it was small but efficient and trained under the personal supervision of the Graf."[22] He maintains that at the start of the war, the main duty of the infantry contingent was to escort the guns.[23]

This force comprised an element of the army that was beaten at Hastenback, then forced to abide, albeit briefly, by the embarrassing Convention of Kloster Zeven. It returned to the field under the command of Prince Ferdinand of Brunswick. In June 1758, the Schaumburg-Lippe- Bückeburg battalion composed one section of the right wing of the army under the command of Duke Ferdinand himself.[24] Under his leadership, it took part in the dramatic reversal of fortunes in the west which included the engagements at Krefeld and Lutterberg and culminated in the battle of Minden on August 1, 1759. In this engagement, the Bückeburg light artillery which included ten 6-pounder guns served in the sixth column under Lieutenant General von Wutginau. Not engaged in the great turning point battle was the Bückeburg line battalion which was under Lieutenant General von Wangenheim on his far right (once again occupying a post of honor). They provided an escort for the artillery.[25] Likewise, the Bückeburg regiment of heavy artillery served in

---

[20] Digby Smith, *Armies of the Seven Years War: Commanders, Equipment, Uniforms and Strategies of the 'First World War'*. Stroud, Gloucestershire: The History Press, 2013, p. 154.

[21] Ibid.

[22] Sir Reginald Savory, *His Britannic Majesty's Army in Germany during the Seven Years' War*. Oxford, Clarendon Press, 1966, p. 457.

[23] Ibid.

[24] See George F. Nafziger, "Army of the Duke of Brunswick-Luneburg, June 1758" Online source: http://usacac.army.mil/cac2/CGSC/CARL/nafziger/758FAG.pdf . Last accessed August 12, 2018.

25   Nafziger, "Anglo-Allied Forces at Hille, Battle of Minden 1 August 1759" 1-2.

Wagenheim's Corps at Minden while the Bückeburg Jäger brigade of 500 served under Major Fredricks.[26] The Schaumburg-Lippe-Bückeburg contingent took part in the fighting at Marburg Castle as well.[27]

The Schaumburg-Lippe-Bückeburg contingent continued to serve as a component of the allied army through the remainder of the conflict. As of 10 May 1760, the Bückeburg light artillery brigade, consisting of nineteen 3-pounders was with the army under Ferdinand. In addition, there was the Second Bückeburg Artillery Division which consisted of four 12-pounders and six mortars and the Jäger Corps made up a contingent of the light troops.[28] They took part in the siege of Münster as well.[29] Contingents of the army fought at the battles at Vellinghausen and Wilhelmsthal as well as the sieges of Minden, Warburg and Wesel. In addition, elements of the force took part in the double siege of Kassel.[30] The infantry battalion served in the siege of Kassel from 19 February to 28 March 1761.[31] Likewise, a Schaumburg-Lippe-Bückeburg contingent took part in the battle of Hamm.[32] Clearly, the various components of Count Wilhelm's army were quite active in the Seven Years' War.

Turning to the uniforms of the Schaumburg-Lippe-Bückeburg contingent. The hair of the infantrymen was powdered, rolled and queed. The uniforms were cut following the Prussian style. Badges of rank fol-

---

Online resource: http://usacac.army.mil/cac2/CGSC/CARL/nafziger/759HAJ.pdf . Last accessed August 13, 2018.

[26] Nafziger, "Anglo-Allied Army 1 August 1759" 2-3 Online source: http://usacac.army.mil/cac2/CGSC/CARL/nafziger/759HAD.pdf . Last accessed, August 13, 2018.

[27] White, "Scharnhorst's Mentor," p. 268.

[28] Nafziger, "Anglo-Allied Army, 10 May 1760." 2-3. Online source: http://usacac.army.mil/cac2/CGSC/CARL/nafziger/760EAH.pdf . Last accessed August 13, 2018.

[29] White, "Scharnhorst's Mentor," p. 268.

[30] Düring, *Geschichte*, p. 1

[31] Nafziger, "Anglo-Allied Siege Forces of Cassel, 19 February-28 March 1761." Online source: http://usacac.army.mil/cac2/CGSC/CARL/nafziger/761BAE.pdf . Last accessed August 12, 2018.

[32] White, "Scharnhorst's Mentor," p. 268.

lowed the Prussian format as well.[33] This is not surprising and may have been more than purely military fashion. Graf Wilhelm worked throughout his reign to promote industry in his small state, but by the outbreak of the Seven Years' War he had enjoyed only moderate success.[34] Thus, the uniforms his men wore into battle may have been provided to them by Prussia as part of the conditions of the alliance. Further research on this point is necessary.

Officers wore a silver gorget crowned with the cipher "W" when on duty as a designation of rank. In addition, they wore waist sashes, however, the specific colors of these remain unknown.[35] The basic head covering of the Schaumburg-Lippe-Bückeburg line infantry was a plain tricorn with a white pompon and hat cords. The coat was a dark blue collarless, double-breasted coat with dark blue lapels and red cuffs and turnbacks. The buttons were brass.[36]

The waistcoats were white, as were the breeches and belts, though all had brass fittings. The gaiters were black.[37] The lid of the cartridge box was black with a crowned 'W' on the badge. The men were armed with a musket and brass-hilted saber in a black leather sheath. The uniform of the grenadiers differed only slightly from that of the line infantry in that they wore brass-fronted caps with a shield bearing the crowned 'W' cipher, brass headband and dark blue backing with a white pompon.[38]

Drummers wore dark blue swallow's nest on their shoulders, with white braid as decoration and five white braid chevrons, pointing up, on each sleeve. The drums themselves were brass with red, white and blue striped hoops.[39]

---

[33] Smith, *Armies of the Seven Years' War*, p. 154.
[34] White, "Scharnhorst's Mentor," pp. 261-2. The possible connections with Prussian manufacturing described above warrant further research.
[35] Smith, *Armies of the Seven Years' War*, p. 154.
[36] Ibid.
[37] Ibid.
[38] Ibid.
[39] Ibid, 156.

Figure 1 A jäger, a grenadier, musketeer a bombardier and an engineer of the Schaum-burg-Lippe-Bückeburg contingent of Ferdinand of Brunswick's army of the Seven Years' War.

In addition to line infantry and grenadiers, Schaum-burg-Lippe-Bückeburg contributed two specialized formations, the Jäger and the Carabinier. The first were uniformed in dark green, single-breasted coats with yellow collars and cuffs. The cuffs were rounded, with brass buttons and the coats featured dark green turnbacks. The green alluded to the origins of the Jäger among the game wardens of the state.[40] They wore buff waistcoats and grey breeches, with black boots and belts and armed with rifles as well as Hierschfanger (sword bayonets). The latter stood as a means for the Jäger to defend themselves if attacked by regular infantry or cavalry during their long reloading

---

[40] For a very useful discussion of the origins of the Jägers, as well as their development in several German states, see Thomas M. Barker and Paul R. Huey, "'Military Jägers, Their Civilian Background and Weaponry." In *The Hessians: The Journal of the Johannes Schwalm Historical Association*. 15 (2012): 1-15.

process.[41]

Without doubt, the second group were the most unique unit in the army of Schaumburg-Lippe, the regiment of Carabinier. This unit was organized in 1753, built around a core of some eighteen mounted Carabinier.[42] The following year the corps Wilhelm augmented the corps by adding approximately fifty foot Jagers as accompanying infantry.[43] The count created the unit with the specific intent that it serve in the role of a light corps petite guerre. Jager were often recruited for this purpose in the various states of the Holy Roman Empire.[44] Some sources place the numbers for the original establishment as high as some seventy-five mounted and fifty infantry troops.[45] It is clear that by 1756, the mounted contingent consisted of some eighty-seven troopers.[46] The count took a very personal interest in the Carabinier and Jager corps as he held the post of regimental inhaber throughout the unit's service in the Seven Years' War. During the conflict, the day to day command of the Carabinier devolved on Major Johann Casimir von Monkewitz from April 1757. The major formerly served as the equerry of Wilhelm's stables.[47]

The foot Jager were commanded first by a Major von Buttlar, from 1754 until 1760 at which point command transferred to a Major von Lindau.[48]

By the time of the diminutive state's involvement in the Sven Years' War as part of the Allied army in the west, it had grown to 110 mounted troops and ninety foot Jager. Wilhelm maintained 25 of the mounted Carabinier at his personal disposal and the Liebcarabinier

[41] Ibid, 1-2.
[42] "Bückeburg Carabiniers" Online source: https://www.kronoskaf.com/syw/index.php?title=B%C3%BCckeburg_Carabiniers Last accessed 11/11/23.
[43] Ibid.
[44] Ibid.
[45] Richard Knötel, Herbert Knötel, and Herbert Seig, *Uniforms of the World: A Compendium of Army, Navy and Air Force Uniforms 1700-1937.* New York: Charles Scribners and Sons, 1980 reprint of 1956 translation, p. 238.
[46] "Bückeburg Carabiniers" Online source: https://www.kronoskaf.com/syw/index.php?title=B%C3%BCckeburg_Carabiniers Last accessed 11/11/23.
[47] Ibid.
[48] Ibid.

company.[49] While the conflict certainly consumed significant manpower, and the Carabinier and Jager especially so due to the mature of their actions, Wilhelm replaced the losses through soldiers he personally selected from other units.[50]

Their uniforms constituted one exceptional aspect of the unit. These consisted of black steel helmets with a brown bearskin turban. On the front was a green plate, bearing the inscription, "Pulchrum mori saccurrit in extremis."[51] Smith has their coat as buff colored leather with red collar and cuffs, while Knötel gives it as "black leather turned up with red."[52] Similarly, Smith gives the other uniform details as follows: "The breeches were buff leather as well with an elk hide tunic."[53] Alternately, Knötel presents them as

To begin with, black laméd pauldrons were worn on the upper arms. The breeches were of yellow leather.[54]

Both sources agree that the Carabinier wore black steel cuirasses and armor on their upper arms. Concerning their equipment, their cartridge boxes were black leather as were their sabretaches. Both bore the crowned brass "W" insignia.[55] There sabers had brass hilts and were carried in steel sheaths on black slings. The horse furniture and harnesses were in black as well. The fittings were steel. The men carried a black cartridge bandolier which they wore over their buff carbine bandoliers. The men were issued a green greatcoat as well. When not in use, this was carried over the pistol holsters. Graf Wilhelm insured that all the men of the Carabinier Corps were mounted on black Spanish stallions. The unit was issued one Liebstandarte and one regimental standard.[56]

---

[49] Ibid.

[50] Ibid.

[51] Translated as "The prospect of a glorious death is a help in time of danger." Quoted in Ibid.

[52] Smith, *Armies of the Seven Years' War*, 156, Knötel and Sieg, *Uniforms of the World*, p. 238.

[53] Smith, *Armies of the Seven Years' War*, p. 156.

[54] Knötel and Sieg, *Uniforms of the World*, p. 238.

[55] Smith, *Armies of the Seven Years' War*, p. 156.

[56] Ibid.

The regimental was red with a black border. It bore the crowned 'W' in silver. The cushions of the crown were in a darker red than the field of the standard, thus setting off the crown. Details on the Liebstandarte are unclear, though most accounts have it in white. It is known that the flagpoles were black with silver finals.[57]

Figure 2 Members of the Schaumburg-Lippe- Bückeburg Carabinier Corps. Note the breastplates that were blackened as well as the greatcoats slung over the pistol holsters.

The uniform for the artillery stood as a simple affair by comparison. The main item was the coat, which was of a dark blue. It was single-breasted and collarless with round black cuffs, red lining and white buttons.

The waistcoat was white and the breeches were dark blue, with black gaiters and belts. The hat was a tricorn with yellow pompon and hat cords. The men were armed with short, straight artillery swords.[58]

The engineers, as well as sappers and miners were clothed in the same fashion as the artillery, but with a black collar on their coats. Their boots were black as well. One further factor which served to distinguish them from the artillerymen was that they were all considered officers.[59]

57   Ibid.
58   Ibid.
59   Ibid.

White notes that "No costs were spared in training and equipping these units." [60]

Finally, in his work *Frederick's Allies*, Stuart Reid asserts that "The Schaumburg-Lippe- Bückeburg contingent was reasonably-organized on the presumption that it would only ever take the field as part of a coalition force, and it was felt it could do so more effectively by specializing in artillery than by attempting to field a more balanced 'army in miniature.'"[61] Considering what Graf Wilhelm was attempting to accomplish in his small state, and with the limited resources at his disposal, Reid's assessment seems to fall very far from the mark. Rather, it seems that the Count sought to create a small but balanced force. One that could both successfully defend his county, and one which could form a useful contingent in a larger coalition force as well. Further, in fielding this sort of force, the count would retain some flexibility in how he deployed his army. The elasticity of his army gave Count Wilhelm the ability to utilize it as both a military and a diplomatic tool in furthering the policy agenda of his state.

---

60   White, "Scharnhorst's Mentor," 267.
[61]Stuart Reid, *Frederick the Great's Allies*, p. 33.

Scion of the Military Enlightenment: Field Marshal Friedrich Wilhelm Ernst Graf zu Schaumburg-Lippe-Bückeburg

While the leader of a diminutive state, Friedrich Wilhelm Ernst, Graf zu Schaumburg-Lippe-Bückeburg (1724-1748) stands out as one of the most important subordinates of Ferdinand of Brunswick in the western theater during the Seven Years' War. Beyond his military contributions, in a period when many European monarchs sought to reform their states upon rational and humane lines, the count excelled in this endeavor, making his small state a model of Enlightened thought and practice. The following will examine the life and efforts of Friedrich Wilhelm, often known simply as La Lippe, with special emphasis on his service as Ferdinand of Brunswick's chief of artillery during the Seven Years' War. What will emerge from the following study is the portrait of a monarch who sought, with some success, to discover and follow the course which held the best possibility for securing and enhancing the quality of life for his people and his state.

Friedrich Wilhelm was born in London in 1724 and many believed him to have been an illegitimate son of George II of England.[62] His father, Albrecht Wolfgang, Graf zu Schaumburg-Lippe (1699-1748) made certain the Friedrich and his older brother, Georg, had a proper education. His mother was Countess Margaret Gertrud of Oeynhausen (1701-1726).[63] When Friedrich was only two, his mother died, and both boys were left in the care of their fraternal grandmother, Johanna Sophie (1673-1743). Described as rather "pious and well-educated," she was well-connected in English society as well, serving as maid of honor and

[62] Patrick J. Speelman, "Field Marshal Friedrich Wilhelm Ernst, Graf zu Schaumburg" in Daniel Coetzee and Lee Eystrulid eds. *Philosophers of War: The Evolution of History's Greatest Military Thinkers*. 2 vols., Santa Barbara, CA: Praeger, 2013, p. 92. See also, Sir Reginald Savory, *His Britannic Majesty's Army in Germany during the Seven Years' War*. Oxford: Clarendon Press, 1966, p. 64, n.1

[63] Charles E. White, "Scharnhorst's Mentor: Count Wilhelm zu Schaumburg-Lippe and the Origins of the Modern National Army." in *War in History*. 24, 3 (2017): 258

mistress of the robes to Princess Caroline Elizabeth of Great Britain.[64] One recent biographer of Friedrich Wilhelm noted, "Johanna Sophie had a profound influence on Wilhelm and George. They were educated in the classics and trained in the social etiquette of English court life."[65] As a result of her care, the boys remained in England while their father returned to the continent. Friedrich Wilhelm embraced the English lifestyle, and his Anglophilia would come to play an important role in several of his decisions in later years.[66]

At approximately age five, Friedrich travelled to his ancestral home in Bückeburg for the first time. He spent the next six years in his ancestral homeland. Then, at age eleven, he and his older brother were sent off to school in Geneva, Switzerland. In Geneva, the boys studied arts and sciences, religion, horsemanship, religion, fencing and sketching, in short, all the subjects necessary to create a polished gentleman with a high likelihood of military service as their profession.[67] Likewise, Friedrich became fluent in five languages. First were English and French, then German, Italian and Portuguese. It is interesting and telling that he learned English and French before his native tongue. French, of course, was the international language of the eighteenth century in Europe, while English would help him better communicate with the George II's ministers and representatives. In the autumn of 1740, the boys journeyed to Holland and continued their education at the University of Leiden.[68] They studied music, agriculture and natural law at the university. In addition, Friedrich Wilhelm employed a private tutor to help him continue his studies in mathematics.[69]

At one point in their studies, the brothers journeyed to the Prussian ambassador's residence in the Hague where they met the famed French philosophe, Voltaire, who was busy at the time promoting the *Anti-Machiavel* of Frederick II. The following spring, their formal ed-

---

[64] Ibid, 258-9.
[65] Ibid, 259.
[66] Ibid, 259.
[67] Ibid, 259.
[68] Ibid.
[69] Ibid.

ucation completed, the young men embarked on a grand tour of sorts, making their way to Italy via Strasbourg, Lyons, and Montpellier. [70]

Following their grand tour, Wilhelm journeyed to England on his own. There, he planned to embark on a military career, the foundations of which had been set up for him as the second son. In 1742, he was posted to the Life-Guards. He did not immediately take to the military life, as he often found himself under house arrest for disciplinary infractions. Likewise, he regularly spent himself into financial trouble as well. In Wilhelm's case, maturity came out of tragedy, however, as his brother Georg died in a duel on August 6, 1742. This made Wilhelm the heir apparent to his father as Graf zu Schaumburg-Lippe. He soon experienced his first taste of combat as well. [71]

At the age of nineteen, Wilhelm joined his father on campaign with the Pragmatic Army during the War of the Austrian Succession. This force was under the personal command of George II of Britain and Hanover. While serving in this force, Wilhelm took part in the battle of Dettingen on June 27, 1743. [72] He distinguished himself in the engagement "by his intrepidity and coolness under fire." [73]

Following the battle, Wilhelm, at the bidding of his father left the army and made a second, proper, grand tour. On this expedition, the young nobleman visited England, Saxony, Austria and Italy. Wilhelm may have attempted to join the Royal Navy during his stint in England. If so, any aspirations he had of a career in the British fleet ran aground on the reality of his chronic sea-sickness. [74]

---

[70] Ibid. On the grand tour, see Jeremy Black, *The British Abroad: The Grand Tour in the Eighteenth Century*. Stroud, Gloucestershire: The History Press, 2003. See also, Black, *France and the Grand Tour*. Basingstoke: Palgrave Macmillan, 2003.
[71] White, "Scharnhorst's Mentor," p. 260.
[72] Ibid. On the battle of Dettingen, see Reed Browning, *The War of The Austrian Succession*. New York: St. Martin's Press, 1993, pp. 137-40. See also M.S. Anderson, *The War of the Austrian Succession 1740-1748*. London, Longman, 1995, p. 117.
[73] Edward Barrington de Fonblanque, ed. *Political and Military Episodes in the Latter Half do the Eighteenth Century: Derived from the Life and Correspondence of the Right H. John Burgoyne, General, Statesman, Dramatist*. London: MacMillan, 1876, p. 29.
[74] White, "Scharnhorst's Mentor." p. 260

The trip to Italy was actually against his father's wishes. While there, Wilhelm joined the Austrian Army, serving as a volunteer colonel. He served under the command of Austrian Field Marshal Johann George Christian von Lobkowitz, a Bohemian prince.[75] Such voluntary appointments stood as an important part of the military apprenticeship served by a young officer. They allowed the apprentice to learn first-hand the art of war at the side of an experienced leader. Likewise, if all went well, they could result in an appointment to command under their benefactor either through merit or if vacancies opened during the campaign. At this time, Lobkowitz's star was in the ascendant in the Austrian military, as the previous year he had driven the chief Spanish army out of northern Italy. Wilhelm's observations of the campaign inspired him to compose his first military study, and analysis of the campaign itself.[76] The young man continued his cultural education during his excursion as well. While in Italy, for instance, he learned to play the piano.[77]

Next, the young nobleman traveled to Vienna. There, on September 7, 1746, he applied for a colonelcy in the imperial army. Three days after making his application, he had a formal audience with the Empress Maria Theresa to discuss the possibility. She declined his petition. Ever on the pious side, the empress found Wilhelm's relationship with the actress Elena Brabant and his changing religious affiliations scandalous for a candidate for officer in the imperial service.[78]

Following his failed attempt to gain a commission in the Imperial service, Wilhelm determined to complete his education in the art of war. He returned to the Italian states, this time to Venice. There he visited his uncle, the renowned Field Marshal Johann Matthais von der

---

[75] Johann George Christian von Lobkowitz (1686-1755) An Austrian Field Marshall who served under Eugene of Savy in the War of the Spanish Succession (1700-1714) and against the Turks in the Austro-Turkish War (1716-1718). He served as governor of Sicily and later of Milan. During the War of the Austrian Succession (1740-1748) he was commander of Austrian troops in Italy until losing the battle of Velletri in 1744.

[76] Ibid. On the topic of military apprenticeships and their role in forming young officers in the period, see Christopher Duffy, *The Military Experience in the Age of Reason 1715-1789*. New York: Scribner, 1987, pp. 42-3.

[77] White, "Scharnhorst's Mentor." p. 260.

[78] Ibid, pp. 260-1.

Schulenburg (1661-1747). Schulenburg stood as a good choice for the young man to take as a tutor.[79] His military experience went back to the Austrian war against the Turks in Hungary in 1667-78. Next, he participated in the Great Northern War (1700-21). He even served with the famed Prince Eugene of Savoy in the war of the Spanish Succession (1701-1714). Finally, he had served in the defense of the island of Corfu against the Turks in 1716.

Due to this latter experience, Schulenberg was quite familiar with the Venetian militia. His discussions with Wilhelm on this topic may have served as an inspiration for the young man later when he came to rule the county of Schaumburg-Lippe.[80] On March 14, 1747, the old Field Marshall died, and Wilhelm departed Italy, this time for Britain, where he failed for a third time to secure a commission.[81]

The following year, 1748, while still three months short of his twenty-third birthday, Wilhelm's father, Graff Albrecht Wolfgang died on September 24. Thus, he became the new Graf von Schaumburg-Lippe.[82]

As noted at the outset, the state he inherited was among the smallest of the German States and among the poorest as well. While Wilhelm's father had initiated a number of public works for the betterment of the people, these were not sustainable improvements, and had left the state deeply in debt. Many who could were choosing to leave Schaumburg-Lippe at the time of Wilhelm's coronation. Frequent territorial disputes among the princes of the Holy Roman Empire only exacerbated the distresses of Schaumburg-Lippe.

Up to this point in his life, Wilhelm had spent very little time residing in his patrimony. Once installed as count, however, he grew keenly aware of the woes of his state. Scion of the Enlightenment that

---

[79] Johann Matthais von der Schulenburg (1661-1747) was a Brandenburg-Prussian aristocrat who served in the Imperial and Venetian armies, eventually grand collector of Venice.

[80] Ibid, p. 261.

[81] Ibid.

[82] Ibid.

he was, he sought to reform the state along rational lines.[83] Wilhelm studied the problems of Schaumburg-Lippe then initiated a series of reforms designed to root out frivolous and wasteful spending. In addition, he began selling off or mortgaging state property. The goal of these activities was to reduce his country's national debt, in particular to Hanover.[84]

Further, he closed the borders of his small state to prevent the continued hemorrhaging of people of talent. He forbade foreign agents from impressing his subjects as well. These initial steps gave the young count some domestic stability, however, like his father's attempts at reform, they were not sustainable. Wilhelm next set about launching a series of reforms geared to place his small state on a solid footing into the future.

Among his first steps taken along this road lay in the establishment and cultivation of domestic industries in Schaumburg-Lippe. Specifically, Wilhelm oversaw the construction of a silk factory, an iron mill, and various other foundries and brickyards. He even brought chocolate manufacturing to Schaumburg-Lippe, constructing a factory in 1756 and bringing in experts from Portugal to train his people in the trade.[85] In addition, he sought to expand agriculture in his patrimony by forming farming communities and actually recruiting settlers from other adjoining states to come and farm in his territory. He went so far as to provide these new residents with housing, seed, and tax incentives.[86] Thus, Wilhelm worked diligently to reverse the drain of people from his state, going even further to bring in new settlement.

Clearly a fan of education himself, Wilhelm recognized its value as an investment in the long-term success of his state. He therefore reformed the education system of Schaumburg-Lippe, developing com-

---

[83] Speelman "Schaumburg," p. 92.
[84] White, "Scharnhorst's Mentor." p. 262.
[85] Wilhelm would later serve in Portugal during the Spanish invasion of that sate in the latter stages of the Seven Years' War. From the above, it seems that there existed a previous tie between the two countries. Further research on this connection is necessary before anything concrete can be said regarding it.
[86] White, "Scharnhorst's Mentor." p. 262.

mon standards for his county.[87] Again, the modification of the education system stood as yet another enlightened reform in that the problems were studied logically, solutions devised, and then implemented without being subordinated to the personal interests of the Count or the nobility.

In addition to trying to raise the standard of living for his people, Wilhelm sought to bring more culture to Schaumburg-Lippe. In pursuit of this goal, the count sought out scientists, artists and musicians and convinced them to come to his court. Among the lumieres attracted to Schaumburg-Lippe in this manner was Johann Christoph Friedrich Bach (1732-1795), one of the sons of Johann Sebastian Bach. Even more remarkable stands the fact that Wilhelm labored on these efforts while he served in the army of Ferdinand of Brunswick during the Seven Years' War. Wilhelm's reforms were made more difficult since his state was overrun by the French early in the fighting, and therefore for much of the conflict, Wilhelm served as a count without a state. He actually had to delay plans for attracting cultural lights to his state due to French occupation Schaumburg-Lippe.[88] These efforts led one contemporary to describe Wilhelm approvingly as "A typical representative of enlightened absolutism, noted for his love of chamber music, mathematics, science, philosophy, history, languages, horse-breeding, archeology, and military affairs."[89] Further, many saw him as a "man of great culture and dignity."[90]

Interestingly, in his efforts to bring reforms and improvements to his country, Wilhelm even created representative bodies of a sort which included members from the various interest groups in Schaumburg-Lippe. He organized councils with men from the various important trades such as merchants, craftsmen and famers. Wilhelm's councils were not the beginning of any democratizing process, however, as the role of these groups was purely advisory.[91] Still, it likely helped to bind the people to their sovereign.

---

[87] Ibid.
[88] Ibid.
[89] Klaus Hornung, quoted in Ibid, p. 263.
[90] Ibid.
[91] Ibid.

Unlike many of his contemporaries who sought to mimic the wealth and extravagance of the great courts of Europe, Wilhelm remained on the frugal side economically. To some extent, his thriftiness reflected his personal choice. He was more given to an interest in work and military matters than building luxurious dwellings for himself and his family. It is likely as well that his economy was dictated at least in part by the conditions then prevailing in Schaumburg-Lippe. Still, some commentators go so far as to assert that he was in fact possessed of a "contempt for luxury."[92]

While his economic and cultural reforms in Schaumburg-Lippe certainly earned Wilhelm the approval of Enlightenment philosophes, of overriding importance for the count due to the size and position of his state was its defense. It is in this area that Wilhelm made his most impressive contributions. Wilhelm certainly had need to be concerned with security, the location of his state made it paramount, with Hanover to the north and east, Hessen-Kassel to the south, and Prussia to the west, he was, in effect surrounded by potential foes. Recognizing this dilemma, Wilhelm's father had striven to develop relationships with the surrounding states, and succeeded in concluding informal alliances with England, Hanover and Prussia. Now that he stood at the helm of Schaumburg-Lippe-Bückeburg, Wilhelm sought to formalize these agreements. He labored on the diplomatic front to keep in check any designs Hessen-Kassel might have on the mines in Bückeburg. Likewise, he sought to prevent the Hessians as well as Prussia from recruiting in his diminutive state.[93] In all, Wilhelm's answer to these pressing security dilemmas counts as one of the more creative of his age.

In essence, Wilhelm developed the concept of the nation in arms. He hoped that this would serve the dual purpose of answering the needs of national defense while at the same time, serving as a school for the nation.[94] His hope was that by creating such a nationalized military, it would create enough of a threat to give his neighbors pause should they

---

[92] Ibid, p. 264.

[93] Ibid, pp. 264-5.

[94] Ibid, p. 265.

consider invading his territory. At the same time, given the size and population of Schaumburg-Lippe-Bückeburg, his army would not be large enough to stand as a security threat to those same neighbors. Essentially. It would serve as a purely defensive force. As a recent biographer noted, Wilhelm believed "every citizen is a soldier, and every soldier a citizen, and every nobleman a soldier and citizen."[95] To be sure, Wilhelm did not follow this verse to its logical conclusion. There occurred no expansion of the rights of the people as modern reader might expect, though as noted above, Wilhelm did create various representative bodies in order to keep himself better informed as to the status of the interest groups in his state. All in all, the count did manage to organize Schaumburg-Lippe on a rational footing for its own defense.

Wilhelm started organizing the defenses of his state by dividing it into military districts that provided both men and materials to supply it defensive needs. In essence, he adapted parts of the Prussian canton system to Schaumburg-Lippe. This should come as no surprise, as Wilhelm regularly visited with Frederick II of Prussia during this time. While Frederick did not devise the canton system for Prussia, he did possess a thorough understanding of it.[96] At the same time that Wilhelm built up the military forces of Schaumburg-Lippe, he developed what can be described as a combined arms doctrine in his *New System of Tactics*. This *New System* called for the close cooperation of infantry, artillery and engineers on the battlefield.[97] This system held many similarities to the methods advocated in France during the debate of tactics there.[98] Wilhelm's ideas on warfare are contained in his unpublished *Mémories pour servir à l'Art Militaire Défensif*. The ideas contained in the text fell along two broad lines of thought. First there stood the concern over defensive war. Second, the development of a military state, with a military academy to train the officers of the army.[99] That the

---

[95] Ibid.
[96] See Christopher Duffy, *Frederick the Great, A Military Life*. New York: Routledge, 1985, pp. 21-76.
[97] Ibid, pp. 267-8.
[98] Ibid, p. 268.
[99] Speelman, "Schaumburg", p. 93.

system Wilhelm devised exerted a long-term impact is evidenced in a letter of the Prussian General Gneisenau to a Varnhagen von Ense who had just published a book discussing the Count's military contributions. In the letter Gneisenau observes:

> *You have praised the Count La Lippe highly, yet not as befits his merit. He was far greater than you represent him. I formerly stayed some time in his capital at Bücke-burg and have read his manuscripts in the archive there. All our systems of national armament with its Landwehr and Landsturm, the whole modern method of making war, this man thus thoroughly worked out, in its greatest principles and smallest details he had learned its prac-ticality and taught it. Just think the kind of man he must have been whose genius could thus forecast the vast re-quirements of war, so that their realization in latter days actually shattered the whole power of Napoleon him-self.*[100]

Even with the penchant for effusive praise that marked the Romantic period, Gneisenau draws a clear and explicit connection between the ideas Wilhelm set down in his New System and the eventual Prussian resurgence against the French in the later years of the Napoleonic Wars. No system, however innovative, would give Schaumburg-Lippe the security Wilhelm desired if it were not provided with adequate manpower. Thus, the specifics recruiting the army absorbed a significant portion of the count's attention as well.

As applied to Schaumburg-Lippe, the recruiting and training of the subjects went as follows. At a certain point, men were inducted into the army.[101] After their initial training and service, they were returned

[100]De Fonblanque, *Political and Military Episodes*, pp. 30-31.
[101] The precise manner in which Wilhelm implemented his system remains unclear. It is therefore uncertain if he enacted a military class type system in which he took all men who reached a certain age in a given year or employed some other means of raising a part of his population.

to civilian life. Interestingly, Wilhelm reduced the term of the subject's service to his state, instead replacing it with an annual training program which served both to maintain the reservists in a state of readiness and provide opportunities to select promising candidates for the leadership roles in the regular army.[102] In addition to the national militia, Wilhelm built an army for Schaumburg-Lippe-Bückeburg. The organization and development of this force are dealt with in the previous chapter. In this context, suffice to say that the count took great personal interest in the development of the army, especially the artillery.

Regarding the artillery, Wilhelm's studies at Leiden may have brought Graf Wilhelm into contact with Henri Claude du Frainoy of Luxembourg, who later served as the chief of Schaumburg-Lippe's engineer and artillery corps.[103] However they became acquainted, the Luxembourger quickly grasped the Count's interest in gunnery as well as his fascination with experimentation and innovation in the realm of the artillery.[104] The artillery always fascinated Wilhelm. As a result, he became one of the few ranking nobles in Europe at the time who possessed a real understanding of the arm. Many in the upper nobility spurned this branch as being too technical and requiring more work than courage. Wilhelm sought to make his state independent when it came to providing guns for its army. Thus, he built a weapons foundry in Bückeburg. He utilized this facility as a laboratory as well, a place where he could experiment with different alloys for his cannons, different powder mixtures, different types of projectiles, breach-loading guns, and armor as well. The foundry at Bückeburg housed a factory for gun carriages.[105] Artillery clearly stood out as the aspect of warfare which caught Wilhelm's fascination the most, and he wrote extensively on the subject. He even predated the reforms of the French artillerist Gribeauval by nearly a decade casting both iron and bronze guns to his own specifications at Bückeburg. All these barrels were bored out with a drill the Count himself devised.

---

[102] White, "Scharnhorst's Mentor," p. 265
[103] White, "Scharnhorst's Mentor," p. 267.
[104] Ibid.
[105] Ibid.

Wilhelm experimented with all facets of the artillery at Bückeburg. He tried developing lighter gun carriages, with the goal of making
his artillery more mobile in the field. He went so far as to examine the
harnessing of the horses to see if teaming them in in pairs as opposed
to in tandem would influence their speed and dexterity while hauling
the guns.[106] A significant reform the Count enacted was replacing the
civilian teamsters for his artillery with soldiers. The former were often
inclined to cut the harnesses and flee at the first sign of things going
badly on the battlefield.[107] Bringing the drivers under military discipline
formed yet another of the count's innovations. The Bückeburg arsenal
should be seen as a further manifestation of Wilhelm's desire to culti-
vate the local talent of his territory. It constituted one of Wilhelm's most
successful ventures as well, supplying guns, powder and other military
equipment not only to the forces of Schaumburg-Lippe, but to many
other Germanic armies as well.[108] He drew the recruits for his regular
forces predominantly from within his domains as well.

The count often promoted the native talent of his state. For instance, during the Seven Years' War, he singled out Majors Römer and
Dufresnap of the Carabinier Corps. Both men led frontal assaults in
most of the sieges the Corps took part in in Westphalia, Lower Saxony
and Hesse. In addition, these officers distinguished themselves in fighting at Harburg, Rothenburg, Minden, Münster, Wesel, and Kassel. They
conducted work on numerous fortifications for the army at locations
near Brenken, Krossdorf, Thresna, Thonhausen and in the camps along
the Diemel as well.[109] Given the contributions of these men, it is clear
why their conduct earned the approbation of their monarch. To this list
could certainly be added the name of Major von Monkewitz, who led
the Carabinier Corps in numerous actions throughout the Seven Years'
War, as well as Captain von Baum who served as Monkewitz subordi-

---

[106] Ibid.

[107] Ibid.

[108] Ibid, p. 268.

[109] G.W. Düring *Geschichte des Schaumburg-Lippe-Bückebourgischen Karabinier und Jäger-
Corps*. Berlin: Ernst Siegfried Mittler, 1828, p. 2.

nate.[110] All of these officers earned the praise of their monarch, and all benefited accordingly.

The Seven Years' War, then, served as the forge which molded the army of Schaumburg-Lippe-Bückeburg. As noted by Patrick Speelman, a great student of Wilhelm's contributions as a military intellectual, his "military thought emerged as a result of his experience in the Seven Years' War."[111] His experiences in that conflict are therefore worth examining in some detail.

Wilhelm would serve in His Britannic Majesty's Army in the west during for the majority of the conflict. First, he served under William, Duke of Cumberland, son of George II, then under Ferdinand of Brunswick-Luneburg. Soo, Wilhelm was appointed *Generalfeldzeugmeister* of the electorate of Hanover and placed in command of all of the Allied artillery.[112]. Along with this post, Wilhelm received the rank of Major General.[113] Most sources agree that he performed very well in this role. It is worth considering that during the majority of his tenure in the Allied army, Wilhelm was a king without a state, Schaumburg-Lippe-Bückeburg being overrun after the Battle of Hastenbeck on July 26, 1757.[114] Hastenbeck led to the humiliating Convention of Kloster Zeven as well, which effectively took Hanover out of the war. On learning of the Convention, George II as well as Parliament began to search for a way out of this agreement, and Cumberland returned to England, superseded by Ferdinand of Brunswick.

Ferdinand quickly set about trying to restore some sense of discipline and esprit d'corps to the men under his command.[115] These efforts began to bear fruit on March 17, 1759 when the town of Minden surrendered after a two day bombardment. Wilhelm commanded the artillery at Minden, and most credit him with excellent handling of that

---

[110] Monkewitz's exploits are described throughout Düring.

[111] Speelman, "Schaumburg," p. 92

[112] Generalfeldzeugmeister is essentially the chief of artillery. See Ibid, p. 268, n. 51.

[113] Speelman "Schaumburg," p. 93.

[114] White, "Scharnhorst's Mentor," p. 268.

[115] On Ferdinand as a coalition commander, see

arm.[116] The great turning point came later that year at the battle of the same name. At the battle of Minden, on August 1, 1759, the Allied army defeated a superior French force. In so doing they demonstrated the capability of the army in the West to sustain the war effort.

In addition to their service at Minden, Wilhelm and his troops participated in the fighting at Marburg Castle in 1759, in the siege of Münster in 1760. On June 21, 1760, Ferdinand ordered La Lippe to undertake the siege of Giessen, which he conducted with great skill.[117] Likewise, he performed well directing infantry at the battle of Hamm in 1761.[118] The small contingent participated in a number of other engagements as well, including Wilhelmsthal and Vellinghausen.

As the war wound down in the western theater, Wilhelm returned to his home in Schaumburg-Lippe. He found a country devastated by several years of French occupation. He immediately set in motion efforts at rebuilding. He did not remain at home to oversee these efforts, however, as he was called away to take command of the Portuguese army as the French and their erstwhile ally Spain sought to open up a new theater in the conflict.[119] The French convinced Spain to enter the war in accordance with the alliance known as the Family Compact. Spain was not in the best position to initiate hostilities.

Neither, for that matter, was Portugal prepared to adequately defend its frontiers. In order to support its oldest continental ally, Britain sent troops and asked for a capable officer to command them. Given the excellent record he had earned fighting under Ferdinand of Brunswick, Wilhelm was appointed Commander-in-Chief of the Anglo-Portuguese army in 1762.[120]

---

[116] Those who praise Wilhelm's efforts include Savory, *His Britannic Majesty's Army*, 149; See also White, "Scharnhorst's Mentor," p. 265; Speelman, "Schaumburg," p. 92. His chief critic is Stuart Reid, *The Battle of Minden: The Miraculous Victory of the Seven Years' War*. Havertown: Frontline, 2016.

[117] Savory, *His Britannic Majesty's Army*, p. 207.

[118] White, Scharnhorst's Mentor," p. 268.

[119] White, Scharnhorst's Mentor," p. 268.

[120] Look for a translation of Wilhelm's account of his activities in the peninsula in an upcoming special issue on the Guerra Fantastique.

Upon assuming his command, Wilhelm had to defend against a Spanish invasion of Portugal. He accomplished his goal through leading a series of marches and counter-marches which always seemed to baffle his opponents. While the Spanish routinely possessed a three-to-one advantage in troops, through careful shuffling of his forces, Wilhelm routinely out manouevered them by placing his forces in well-constructed, defensible positions.[121] Under his leadership, several British officers achieved some measure of fame as well. For instance, brevet colonel John Burgoyne was tasked with capturing the walled town of Valencia de Alcántra on the Portuguese-Spanish frontier. He accomplished this goal after a fifty-mile forced march and directing a cavalry charge that disrupted the Spanish and took the colors of three regiments.[122] For his actions, Burgoyne was promoted to full colonel. He and Wilhelm became close friends as well, with the latter writing an encomium to Burgoyne which was published in the *Gentleman's Magazine.* [123]

Following the conclusion of hostilities in the Iberian Peninsula, the Portuguese Secretary of State and Prime Minister to king Joseph I, Sebastião José de Melo, Marquis de Pombal (1669-1782) asked Wilhelm to remain in Portugal and train the Portuguese Army to a higher standard of professionalism. Wilhelm agreed. Under his direction, the Marquis established a military academy as well as an artillery school. The two men thoroughly reformed the Portuguese Army as well.[124] These reforms included the construction of the Fort de Nossa Senhora de Craça, which Pombal had named Fort de Lippe in the Count's honor.[125]

Wilhelm returned to Schaumburg-Lippe in late 1764, and immediately recommended rebuilding his war-ravaged state. The top priority for Wilhelm stood in the completion of the fortress at Wilhelmstein. This was a massive star-shaped fortress containing four bastions and

---

[121] White, Scharnhorst's Mentor," pp. 268-69.
[122] Andrew J. O'Shaughnessy, *The Men Who Lost America: British Leadership, the American Revolution and the Fate of Empire.* New Haven: Yale University Press, 2013, pp. 126-7.
[123]Ibid, p. 127.
[124] White, Scharnhorst's Mentor," p. 269.
[125] Ibid.

a citadel which mounted 166 guns of 3-, 6-and 12-pounder weights as well as mortars. Situated on the Steinhunder Meer, the largest lake in north-western Germany it possessed an excellent natural moat.[126] The fortress was meant to serve as a final fallback position should his country be overrun as it had been in the Seven Years' War. In addition, Wilhelm saw the fortress as serving as the base from which to launch a campaign to drive any invaders out of his state. It would support the regular troops who would work in concert with the national militia to oppose the invader.[127] Since any attempt to storm Wilhelmstein would require an opponent to come across the Steinhunder Meer, Wilhelm had an observatory constructed atop the citadel. Should an enemy attempt such an attack, they would come under the devastating fire of the fortresses batteries long before they reached the fortress walls.[128]

The construction of Wilhelmstein stood as one of the great engineering feats of the day, and one in which the count took a great personal interest. Wilhelm laid the foundations of the artificial island on which it was built himself in 1761. Much of the population was drafted into service on the construction project, either hauling materials to the shores of the Steinhunder Meer or transporting them out the site itself.[129] It took the better part of two years between 26 August 1765 and 30 March 1767 to complete Wilhelmstein. During that time Wilhelm further constructed an additional sixteen smaller islands in the lake on which he built four outlying bastions facing the four cardinal directions. There were four ravelins and eight curtains which themselves shielded the bastions.[130]

The chief fortress of Wilhelmstein was garrisoned by 250 troops in peacetime, along with their families. These soldiers and their families were brought in on a rotational basis throughout the year. It was planned that the works could safely hold 800 men without their families in time of war. As the fortress neared completion in the autumn of 1766, Wil-

---

[126] Ibid.
[127] Ibid.
[128] Ibid.
[129] Ibid, p. 270.
[130] Ibid.

helm turned his attention to military education and began planning the school for his officer corps.

Once again, the Count took a very active role in the development of this national institution, developing and at times even teaching the curriculum himself. He devised a fairly rigorous schedule for the students. For instance,

> *Two artillery lieutenants under the supervision of the chief of artillery would lecture the students each Monday and Friday for one hour in the officer's quarters. Every Wednesday and Saturday morning from nine to noon officers, senior officer candidates, and cadets from the artillery corps would attend mandatory study halls in the library. No one was excused from these classes unless they were sick, on duty, or on special leave.*[131]

Wilhelm himself often appeared without prior notice during examinations and took over the proctor's role himself.[132] One of the officers produced by this rigorous curriculum was the famed Prussian officer of Hanoverian descent, general Gerhard von Scharnhorst. Scharnhorst attended Wilhelm's school in his youth and by his own account it played a significant role in his professional development.[133]

Clearly, the security of his small state dominated the Count's thinking in the years following the Seven Years' War. He sought to prevent his state and people from ever again suffering the ravages they had during the recent conflict. Unfortunately, on his death in 1777 his throne remained vacant until the Imperial Court of the Holy Roman Empire approved the succession of his Wilhelm's cousin Philip Ernst zu Lippe-Alverdissen (1723-1787). The new sovereign did not understand Wilhelm's reforms and modified them to his own tastes. Thus, much of the efforts of Wilhelm's later years disappeared within a decade of his death.

---

[131] Ibid, p. 272.
[132] Ibid, pp. 276-7.
[133] Ibid, pp. 282-3.

G. W. During

Finally, it is clear that Wilhelm was a soldiers' soldier. When it came to the national defense, he spared no expense from his meager treasury.[134] His expenditures were all to strengthen the defenses of his small state. As noted above, one of main facets of his military thinking was a focus on defensive war. As one recent historian of his ideas observed,

> He understood war from the perspective of a small, vulnerable state and believed the only just war was a defensive one. He drew upon his experiences in Germany and Portugal and outlined the defensive principles. The army had to occupy 'fastened landscapes,' or strong points to retard the enemy's progress.[135]

They went on to note, "Through maneuver, the enemy could be dislodged from your country and routed by militia forces that fought to defend their own land."[136] It seems that Wilhelm developed this last idea based on his experience of the fighting in Portugal. There he observed as "frontier peasant forces drastically curtailed the Spanish invasion."[137] Building on the knowledge gained while fighting in the Portugal, Wilhelm proposed to garrison the borderlands of Schaumburg-Lippe with "militia-farmers." These were his to occupy what the counter termed contrées fortifies, which were essentially fortified townships. Some were constructed to the south-west of the Steinhunder Meer and included smaller forts and covered positions to protect the colonies (Wilhelmsteiner Feld).[138] In essence, the defense of his realm would be akin to the military border in Croatia.[139]

---

[134] Ibid, p. 267.
[135] Speelman, "Schaumburg," p. 93.
[136] Ibid.
[137] Ibid.
[138] White, Scharnhorst's Mentor," p. 270.
[139] Ibid. On the military border in Croatia, see Gunther E. Rothenberg, *The Military Border in Croatia, 1740-1881: A Study of an Imperial Institution.* Chicago: University of Chicago Press, 1966.

To be successful in this form of warfare required a highly trained officer corps. Thus, Wilhelm's keen personal interest in his military academy. His ideas on domestic security for his state were not the limit of Wilhelm's contribution. As evidenced above, he stood as one of the great innovators in the realm of artillery during the eighteenth century to the extent that he is often placed in the same league with Gribeauval.

Building on his reputation as a military intellectual, the academy Wilhelm founded was truly without parallel. Likewise, he took a profound personal interest in the institution, interviewing each candidate personally as part of the admissions process.[140] However, little information concerning the man himself has been presented to this point. Given his activities in his youth, he had little time to find a spouse. As the Seven Years' War wound down, this all changed.

Perhaps the best insight into Wilhelm's character is provided by his former pupil, Gerhard von Scharnhorst. The latter wrote,

> *Seldom have there been united such entire goodness of heart with so many fine qualities of mind. He never left the distressed without relief, nor the widow and orphan without care for their condition. Every expense of his small court was reduced, in order that he may enjoy the happiness of making others happy. Towards those about him he was very agreeable and courteous. In his school, he was at once organizer, inspector, benefactor and friend. He made many a young man happy, and his lessons are already bearing fruit.[141]*

A more apt and thorough tribute would be difficult to find.

---

[140] White, Scharnhorst's Mentor," pp. 278-9.
[141] Scharnhorst on County Wilhelm zu Schaumburg-Lippe-Bückeburg, quoted in De Fonblanque, *Political and Military Episodes*, p. 31.

G. W. During

The History of the Schaumburg-Lippe-Bückeburg Carabinier and Jäger Korps

Introductory Note

The doctrine of little war is herein disclosed through the examples of the excellent arms of this corps during the Seven Years War.

The Prince, who was the most gracious, and the keeper of the archives at Bückeburg proved most helpful in providing many valuable papers. Count Wilhelm of Schaumburg-Lippe-Bückeburg's estate did not possess any papers. The same diary of the Bückeburg Carabinier Corps, along with other documents relating to this corps and of the services rendered by it in the Seven Years' War, are in the original letters of Count Wilhelm, Duke Ferdinand, and the Hereditary Prince Karl von Braunschweig, and in reports by the chief of the Bückeburg Carabinier Corps to Count Wilhelm.

According to the author, these papers contained much of interest concerning Little War, which at that time was conducted so energetically that, even at present, our military writers use examples of the bold partisans in the era of the Seven Years' War as models.[142] The part of the Lippe-Bückeburg Carabinier Corps, however, makes worthy contributions to these examples, although none of the writers who wrote about the Seven Years' War (except Tempelhof, who mentioned them on only one occasion, specifically discusses the Bückeburg Jäger) have given them even a nod. Notwithstanding, their deeds at the time resounded loudly enough for them still to be rehearsed in the mouths of the people

[142] Translator's note: While this author mentions only George F. von Tempelhoff, *Geschichte des siebenjährigen Krieges in Deutschland.* 6 vols. Berlin: Nach. D. Ausg.,1783-1801. There were other theorists who drew on the Seven Years' War for examples of partisan warfare as well. See Carl von Clausewitz, *Clausewitz on Small War.* Christopher Daase and James W. Dais, eds and trans. Oxford: Oxford University Press, 2015, and Johann Ewald *Thoughts of a Hessian officer about what he has to do when Leading a Detachment in the Field.* James R. Mc Intyre, ed. trans., (Point Pleasant, NJ: Winged Hussar Press, 2020).

of Westphalia, Hesse, Waldeck, etc. This is all the less surprising to us, since only in the courtyard of Count Wilhelm are there any monuments, and these without even mentioning one of his great services rendered during the Seven Years' War. Likewise, Archenholz did not even seem to have known that a Count Wilhelm von Schaumburg-Lippe-Bücke-burg was present.[143]

If, as now, the Anglo-Saxon writers could have overlooked the truly great man, it would be well to demand that they should know something of these troops and their doings in six campaigns under Prussia and England's flags, especially as regard for the truth stands as one of the main demands on a historian.

Those who write about this period of history have their reasons why they all do so in the same way. They meant to publicize the deeds of the great, which they offer under the pen, and which seemed to be obliging to us somehow. Still, the deeds of the men, in six active and glorious campaigns, their blood and aspirations, must find its place in history.

From this point of view, the author received permission from his most illustrious prince to write the history of the exploits of the Bücke-burg Carabinier, with an introductory overview of the whole Bücke-burg Auxiliary Corps, in the Seven Years' War. Your Majesty deigned to grant this permission as you found it appropriate to preserve a memorial to the glory of the troops of your great ancestor.

The image of a rich warrior life portrayed in these pages is a picture which is not projected out of the imagination, but merely in the peculiar color of its own, which corresponds to the eye of the inner martial soul. With great love the author undertook a work which he dared to hope would not be unwanted, but instead would be particularly welcome to the warrior.

What is given here is the image of the Little War in its most peculiar attire. -War is the science in which one has never exhausted all the possibilities; Small war is the element in which large plans are found

---

[143] Translator's note: Here the author is referring to Johann Wilhelm von Archenholz, *Prussia and the Seven Years' War, 1756-1763*. Translated from German by F.A. Caty. Frankfort: C Jugel, 1843.

on the first occasion to develop. A water which is so fond of challenging the inner energy and ability that boldly carries the brave swimmer![144]

The purpose of this work is, in part, to lend fresh strength to the great outcry of the warrior heart, filled with deeds, when the thunder of the skies has subsided, and the mundane concerns of everyday life more and more threaten the bend of the bow. Then is the time when great memories and examples of a certain time can fire the warrior's spirit anew. And how, even in writing down of this story, one is given up to a fresher, bolder outpouring of the imagination, glowing only for the true warrior life. It kindles anew the desire to consort with fellow warriors.

It certainly will not be unwelcome to the friends of the fatherland that it was anxious to preserve the memory of a small, brave house from extinction in the whirlwind of the present. Glorious was the course which the little Carabinier and Jäger Corps plotted by their great Count, and how courageously they went through six campaigns! The leaders of the allied army in Westphalia, Hessen, etc. saw the troops of this house as invaluable. Most of all by the fact that wherever it was needed, wherever a service was required, or whatever skill was required, the Carabinier and Jäger Corps gave its full efforts. In effective and punctual fulfillment of whatever mission, one could always count on the Bückeburg Carabinier Corps.

But with what has been said, we should not underrate the glory of any other group, we hope that, by reading our present account, it will

---

[144]Translator's note: During's description of Little War, kleine Krieg, petite guerre or partisan warfare, all of these terms were in use by contemporaries, is much in line with the other commentators of the period. For instance. John Graves Simcoe notes "The Command of a light corps, or, as it is termed, the service of a partisan, is generally esteemed the best mode of instruction for those who aim at higher stations; as it gives an opportunity of exemplifying professional acquisitions, fixes the habit of self-dependence for resources, and obliges to that prompt decisions which in the common rotation of duty subordinate officers can seldom exhibit, yet without which none can be qualified for any trust of importance." while Johann Ewald declared "In this part of the war an officer is often left to himself, has to do on a small scale what a general does on a large scale." See Johann Ewald, *Treatise on Partisan Warfare*. Robert A. Selig and David Curtiss Skaggs, trans. New York: Greenwood Press, 1991, 64 and John Graves Simcoe *Simcoe's Military Journal: A History of the Operations of a Partisan Corps, called The Queen's Rangers, Commanded by Lieutenant Colonel J.G. Simcoe, During the War of the American Revolution.* 1781, 7-8 respectively.

be shown that our Carabinier contributed along with the forces of other powers against the enemy. They bought through so much blood and exertion the honor and the glory for which these men sacrificed which will be remembered as long as there are names on the mountains.

Any accusation of partisanship should therefore be abolished, and no one will interpret it badly if, with all the fire which is at our disposal, the story of the Bückeburg black horsemen and Jäger, and the great leader, the count, is here and now given a feeble tribute. This account pays Count Wilhelm reverence by naming the men worthy of his support and trust. In the lists of our former engineer and artillery corps in particular, names are recorded which will always see the pride of our troops! Let us also see among them the highly praised name of Scharnhorst, who served for four years in Wilhelm's school of artillery as a junior officer.

The sons and daughters of the men, whose honorable warrior life we have striven to rescue from the dust of oblivion, lived around and beside us. The author was very happy to note that their work retained much of its glory, though he tried to take a critical approach to their deeds. It would have been very desirable that there had already been an account before and during the times of the actors to put facts to light in the present, which now, after the earthly shells of these worthy sons of the Fatherland were lying in dust, are entrusted to this weak writer's pen! For life also wants its splendor!

Though, when you, my worthy, brave comrades, marched on earth, the land to which you belonged, the rulers who followed the generous Wilhelm, and the great leaders among you, had done you full justice; Each of you, though so human, was worthy of merit, the better part of the warrior still strives for a higher goal-it is called posterity.

Do not draw your last weary breath, lying on the earth's breast, bleeding for your duty and the Fatherland on the battlefield, to the death! Not with the three cheers that thundered over your grave, when, after the end of the war, you slept well in your home! Your name, your glory in the history of the Fatherland, shall be still in the history of worthy deeds of every time and every nation!—I would like to keep your wreaths fresh and green in their leaves, in the breast of your grandchildren, relatives, friends, and country folk, and if I allow myself a wish, it is only "that my fate also falls along the same path you walked through!"

Introduction

The corps, dispatched by Count Wilhelm of Schaumburg-Lippe in 1757 to the army of the Duke of Cumberland, later to the Duke of Brunswick, consisted of a regiment of grenadiers, an artillery company, an engineer and a miner corps, and a corps of troops on horseback and on foot who bore the name of the Carabinier Corps. The strength of the whole corps amounted to about 1,600 men.

The Grenadier Regiment, raised in 1751, consisted of eight companies, and carried with them, two one-pounder falconers, during the course of the whole of their campaigns, which rendered excellent service on several occasions. The count expended great energy in drilling this regiment, so that it was truly the most fully trained and practiced corps in the Allied army and served with great distinction during the whole war. Its service in the Seven Years' War included participation in the battles at Hastenbeck, Krefeld, Lutterberg, Minden, Vellinghausen, and Wilhelmsthal, as well as the sieges of Minden, Warburg, Wesel, and the double siege of Kassel.[145] The conduct of this regiment, due to the unfortunate coincidence of the partnership with Lutternberg, was praised by the colonel of this regiment, as it remained in the most perfect order, when the latter was completely abandoned by the Allied troops. Likewise, by the exceptionally good order and slowness of its own retreat, under the command of its colonel von Bohm (afterwards one of the Portuguese lieutenant generals, and finally a vice-king of Brazil), completely secured the further retreat of the army and, on the other hand, the consequences on the retreating enemy cavalry declined.

The artillery, engineer, and miner corps were created in 1752, and neither cost nor effort were spared in their development either. Count Wilhelm had a great deal of interest in procuring and training

[145]Translator's note: In referring to the double siege of Kassel, the author appears to have in mind the Allied army siege of the town which lasted from 17 February until 28 March 1761. The siege was disrupted by a successful French sortie on the night of 6-7 March. The Allies resumed their operation on 10 March, thus the idea of a "double siege."

officers for these corps. Several members of these services were singled out for special distinction during the course of the war and were concerned with the most important and honorable missions. For example, Majors Römer and Dufresnap led direct attacks in most of the sieges in Westphalia, Lower Saxony, and Hesse. They performed this same function at Harburg, Rothenburg, Minden, Münster, Wesel and Kassel; In addition, they conducted work on many of the fortifications of important positions of the army, for example near Brencken, Krossdorf, Thrensa, Thonhausen, in the camps on the Diemel.

The Miners' Corps consisted of 100 men, and remarkably, constituted the only troops of this type in the army in Westphalia and Lower Saxony at the beginning of this war.

The artillery, together with the train, varied in numbers between three and four hundred men. They served the guns which Wilhelm sent to the army. The other part of the artillery contingent consisted of Hessian and Brunswick artillerymen. According to the existing inventory, it counted in cannon 29 3-pounders, 4 6-pounders, 2 12-pounders and 3 18-pounder cannon, 3 howitzers and 4 heavy mortars. This artillery sang in the battles and engagements at Gohseld (where the Bückeburg Artillery Major Stort was the chief of artillery of the armed forces to the hereditary prince of Brunswick) Bergen, Minden, Krefeld, Vellinghausen, Brückersmühle, Wilhelmsthal, Lutterberg etc.[146] Just as in the case of the Allied army scarcely a single battle of any importance occurred in which the Bückeburg Artillery did not play a role, for which reason the losses sustained by them were very important in these campaigns.

The artillery of the light infantry corps, commanded by General Luckner, was furnished by Bückeburg, and here, too, it often had an opportunity to distinguish itself. One such incident occurred when, after the last clash at Lutterberg and the retreat had taken place, the Bückeburg artillery-lieutenant Wieting, who served on the left wing with 28 artillerymen, and commanded two 12-pounder guns. His battery came under heavy attack by the enemy cavalry. The cannons were forced to retreat in the most unfavorable terrain and could not be carried any fur-

---

[146] Translator's note: Brückermühle is also known as Amöneburg.

ther. The artillerymen, however, did not shrink from the duties entrusted to them, and fired until a large force of enemy cavalry fell upon them, and killed the officer. Of the 28 men in the contingent, some of them were killed and some wounded.

The heavy, as well as a part of the light artillery, accounted for the different detachments mentioned concerning the Grenadier Regiment, and distinguished itself here also by its praiseworthy conduct. On the 7th of March 1761, when the besiegers had been driven out of the trenches and some of their batteries, the Bückeburg artillery-lieutenant Brameyer and his men decided to die with the battery entrusted to them, as they never surrendered to the enemy, and kept up their fire until (with the exception of a few) all were killed or wounded by bayonet wounds and gunshots next to their guns, while they were still struggling with handling the guns.[147] Lieutenant Brameyer, on the following day, died for duty and fatherland of the two wounds he had been received in the hand, and a gunshot wound.

In 1762, when Count Wilhelm went to Portugal as Generalissimo, a division of Engineers, Miners, and Artillery followed him. These troops also served with honor. Several officers of the same received a position as an instructor in the artillery and engineer's school erected by Count Wilhelm in Fort St. Julien. The instruction was first given in French, and later in Portuguese. The fort of Schaumburg-Lippe at Elvas was rebuilt under the special direction of Bückeburg's chief engineer, Etienne, according to the orders of Count Wilhelm.

When Count William had returned to Bückeburg, Etienne retained the direction of the construction, and completed it.[148] In this case, which was certainly very interesting and almost unheard of to every engineer and artilleryman, the trenches of the works which were 36-40 feet in length and must have been raised in the marble-like rock by the laying of important mines.

The Carabinier Corps whose history during the Seven Years War is contained in the following leaves, was raised in 1753, and original-

---

[147] Translator's note: Here Düring is referring to the 1761 siege of Kassel. See note 2 above.
[148] Etienne was Wilhelm's architect.

ly consisted of 75 horsemen and 50 Jäger.[149] Count Wilhelm, one of the best and most daring horsemen of his time, employed everything to bring this little corps as close as possible to the ideals of a horseman, and to produce a troop which could overcome any obstacle.

The elite team of officers and men formed a close-knit family. Numerous decrees lead to an increase in the corps throughout the war that consisted of equal elements. As soon as one crew had left the depot for the army, therefore, they worked with restless zeal to train new men, and to bring them to the degree of perfection, like those in the field.

Originally, the Corps were mounted on Spanish black stallions.[150] When, however, later, a considerable departure took place, geldings were still available, but mares were not at all to be had. Under the special supervision of Count Wilhelm, the restoration of the riders and horses were worked on, and the former was practiced on horseback. A number of horsemen were trained, who rode with boldness, of which the story below contains a few examples. Often Count Wilhelm was at the head of this group when he went out riding, at other times he went alone. No hedge, no fence, no ditch could hinder them. Count Wilhelm was always the first over. Who of the riders could have stayed behind?

Palisades of not insignificant heights were constructed, to test the men's ability to overcome the obstacles on their mounts. Just like Spanish riders, never was a Carabinier absent at an open posthole to pass through.

Many a horse, indeed, felt the challenge, or rather an exercise of the species -what was the matter? If the horses were to be used for war, better such a faint animal was discovered during peacetime, than later

---

[149] Translator's note: The initial strength of the corps give above agrees with Knötel, Knötel, and Seig, *Uniforms of the World*, 238. Consequently it differs from "Bückeburg Carabiniers" Online source: https://www.kronoskaf.com/syw/index.php?title=B%C3%BCckeburg_Carabiniers Last accessed 11/11/23.

[150] A friend of mine, who knew exactly one of the forestry servants who had participated in the whole of the 7th War as a carabinier, told me that he had asked the foreman Argener whether the stallions were not often disturbed by their unrest, and especially by their neighing. Other expeditions would have betrayed you " The old forester, however, replied: "No, our Spaniards were so fine that no one gave a sound." The stallions, on the other hand, have been very frequent in southern countries, and especially in Spain and Portugal, than in our country.

on, where the rider was abandoned. The most clever and best horsemen were then publicly praised by the Count, and often presented with money. He was concerned about their ability to do ride and maneuver, so he tried the cavalrymen's routine himself, which increased the morale of the Corps. Count Wilhelm was concerned about their ability to do this, so he tried the cavalrymen's routine himself, which increased the morale of the Corps. It seemed they did not know any impossibilities-since even the whole troop, fully armed swam the Weser, inspired by the greatest enthusiasm for their all-loving Count, who himself understood everything that he demanded of his subordinates.

The Count's circumspection was shown in the selection of the officers to this corps, as only those who agreed with his vision of the role of the Corps would be promoted. Foremost among the candidates stood Herr von Monkewitz. Formerly a Freikorporal in the Prussian Army, in 1751, in order to pursue his fortune, took a post in the Corps after he had been part of the battles of Hohenfreidberg, Soor, and Kellersdorf. In the service of Count Wilhelm, whose instinct soon guessed that the man was fit for something better than the drudgery of minor assignments in his service. For this reason, in April 1757, Count Wilhelm ordered him, as a brevet leader of the light troops, to inspect the river Weser from Hameln to Nienburg, which was to become the chief area of operations in the coming war. His report won the satisfaction and approval of the cavalry commander Count Volikommner.[151] M. de Monkewitz, then, took over the command of the Carabinier Corps. First as Major, and later as a colonel, and led them with the greatest care under the Count, and especially under Duke Ferdinand of Brunswick (which is to be found in the Duke's own communications), until the peace returned.

The horsemen of the corps were light, indeed, Jäger on horseback, but their equipment was not that at all. In this respect, they would certainly be regarded more as cuirassier, and it is not really a matter of mobility, but the shock they could deliver, which was like that of hitting

---

[151] Translator's note: Hamelin is a town on the river Weser in Lower Saxony, Germany. It is the capital of the district of Hamelin-Pyrmont and has a population of roughly 56,000. Hamelin is best known for the tale of the Pied Piper of Hamelin.

a wall, since, according to so many contemporary views, the cuirassiers are, at all events, only to be used for shock. Nevertheless, these pages will show that the Carbiniers served and acted as shock troops during the whole seven years of the war and were able to accomplish everything (on some occasions more) than what the boldest expectations of hussars or other troops could demand. As in the case of these historical facts, many a theory and some opinion, which was thought to be heralded may be examined, but I confess to the belief that with a troop, it is easy to do everything which may possibly be ordered by men, as soon as the moral element is increased to the highest potency. If, on the other hand, one can say what one wants, the best lever to bring up this moral element is that which the rider, as well as the soldier of every other nation, must believe from the beginning, he is better than the soldier of another corps. Such an *esprit de corps* in every single regiment of the army can yield only pleasing results. This spirit, however, lived in the Carabinier from the outset, and the influx of men to be absorbed into this corps after the first campaigns had been made, and it had gained a certain reputation, that it still had to reject people. And, like the volunteer Jäger of Prussia in the years 1813-15, people were clamoring to join.

The uniform of the horsemen consisted of a helmet of black-colored leather, with scarlet clothes and jackets, tied in front, so that there was not a single button on the uniform;[152] A yellow frock of fine leather, extending over the knees, as in the customary manner, and boots of half-tanned leather, with a pair of short, spurted spurs, the halves of which were only long enough to fulfill their purpose. They allowed the horseman to spur his horse if he had to retreat from battle but did not stop him from walking. The chest and back were covered by a black, bullet-proof cuirass with scaly bracers, which descend to the elbow, but which, being more of a hindrance than beneficial, was abolished after the first two campaigns.

---

[152] Buttons, Count Wilhelm used to say, no one more than the cavalry, often impossible to rescue her immediately, then he'll try to get him out, and why give him anything that is superfluous. On the other hand, the leather collier proved itself to be very excellent during the course of the Seven Years' War.

A helmet of strong iron plate, tufted with bear skin, with iron armor-chains for the saddle under the halter, and a front and back of reinforced leather. A device stood on a green background on the front of the helmets containing the motto: "Pulchrum mori succurrit in extremis."[153] This helmet certainly did not have the most agreeable form, however, it was quite durable and fulfilled its purpose. The cartridge box, decorated with a W and a crown, hung on the narrow black belt, which ran across the broad armored cuirass support, and held about 40 cartridges. The Carabinier carried the following: a carbine of the same caliber with those of the foot soldiers; a double pistol at the saddle, and with a black saddle-bag, on which a W with a crown, several hooks, a slightly curved Pallasche without cord and straps, thus with a so-called Mameluchian body and semi-iron sheath.[154] If the absence of the hanger or basket had proved to be injurious in the many battles of the Carabinier, there is no trace of this in the highly detailed diaries and records of this corps, which are in the archives. After the campaign of 1758, when an increase of the corps took place, there was a new type of weapon, the personal invention of Count Wilhelm, who at the same time laid a pistol on the blade. These sabers, however, were found too heavy and cumbersome, as they were put into use, and they returned back to the armory, where they are still kept.

The armor of the horses was simple and durable; It consisted in a kind of German saddle, with a high back-piece on the rear, and with its usual fore- and hindquarters; Over it lay a black mantle with red cloth. The mantle was small and round; In front of the gun-holsters, the man's green wide mantle had been strapped under the saddle-blanket. In the left-hand holster are a pair of pistols and an iron chain. The main frame was of strong leather, a chain on the head; The neck was underneath but had no binders since the chain served in the halter. The bridle was a so-called dessau rod.

---

[153] Literally from Latin: Fair to die on the edge. In German, namely in soldier's German, it translates as "A beautiful death beckons in dangers."

[154] Translator's note: It seems here that the author is attempting to indicate that the sword was worn by the troops in something much akin to that used by the Egyptian Mamluks of the Napoleonic period.

The foot soldiers of the corps, carried guns of the same caliber as those of the horsemen and Jäger. They were similar in appearance to the cavalrymen, in that they wore the same head-dress and uniform, but of course the cuirass, the steeled pistols, and the leather breeches fell out of use They wore dressed trousers and shoes with leggings of a gray color. All the garments of the corps had been worked so as to enable the men to sit comfortably, to allow the free use of the limbs, to stand against the weather, and yet to have an appealing appearance. All things which can be very well united.

Stiff and plodding, as were the uniforms of the troops of all the powers at that time, many a man smiled at that of the Carabinier, who were clothed generously among the troops appointed by Wilhelm, according to the above standard. But the enemy troops were well on their way to emulating the Carabinier, and in other armies the expediency of such a uniform could be seen, as it had proved itself after the first campaigns. For, when the mounted and foot-Jäger, like the Carabinies, were organized in Hanover, Brunswick, and Hesse, the uniforms, armor, and so forth were all similar to those of the Bückeburgians, and actually differed only in color of the cuirassier only.

The French army in Westphalia, Lower Saxony, and Hesse, as is well known, had gained a considerable preponderance over the armies which were opposed to it by their number of light troops, and the addition of the Schaumberg-Lippe-Bückeburg Carabinier Corps was very welcome to the Duke of Cumberland. They joined his army under a subsidy treaty with the crown of England, and thereby helped to reestablish equilibrium with regard to the light troops.

It is a historical fact that this corps, from its establishment in the army, succeeded in earning a respectful reputation, and that, as will be shown, these iron men, as the cavalry were called by friend and foe-alike, gave the enemy a greater than usual fear. Duke Ferdinand recognized the Corps' value, as did the hereditary Prince of Brunswick. The following narrative will describe how the Corps, without respite, were ordered from one expedition to another, in the confined spaces of Upper Hesse, Westphalia and the Lower Rhine. In their six-year-long history of continuous marches, battles, and hardships, the loss of men and horses holds great importance for the changes in the Corps' effectiveness. The unit had often been melted down to a few men, so that the enemy would probably have to get rid of that ghost that plagued them for a time. But not less than a fortnight passed, and the Carabinier were again to be found hovering around the extreme fringes of the enemy army, and they carried on their old craft just as boldly as before.

What these repeated efforts at re-equipping and various reorganizations of the Corps cost Wilhelm is easy to understand. Still, the restless zeal to do them always quickly, and yet perfectly, will tell posterity how the Count was true a supporter of the alliance with England and Prussia. Wilhelm's courage and determination are too strong for my weak feather to transform it into an even brighter light. But the virtues of the officers who served in this corps, who, knowing the great spirit of their master, were glowing with a solemn memory of the sacred feeling for the prince and their fatherland.

Just one episode, I beg to be allowed to write, which demonstrates the Count's honor and personal ability to ride. Did I say, "Count Wilhelm was one of the best and most daring horsemen of his time!"

On the 6th of July, 1759, before the Battle of Minden, Duke Ferdinand led the Count against the right wing of the army, in order to see, with him, a captain of the engineers, who had been lavishly passed over. The Duke rode with a considerable suite to the redoubts, where the captain, who built them, stood on the edge of the breastworks, and received his well-deserved praise. Count Wilhelm remained silent and rode, followed by the duke and the suite, about two hundred paces behind the redoubt, but turned his horse against it, and gazed at them for a moment. In the meantime, he was seated while riding at the gallop, crossed the ditch to the parapet, where the captain was standing, greeted him gently, with the hat, and rushed quietly to the rear (not closed) of the redoubt to his headquarters at Petershagen.[155]

---

[155] Translator's note: Petershagen is a town in the Minden-Lübbecke district, in North Rhine-Westphalia.

Chapter 1

The Campaign of 1757

Campaign of 1757. The battles of Harsewinkel and Marten-
feld. Letter of Wilhelm on the battle at Brockhagen; Expla-
nation of Count Wilhelm. Lt. Baum clashes with an enemy
command in Tecklenburg. Carabinier get situated and stormed
a house. Result of the attack. Battle at Grohnde. Battle of Hastenbeck. Retreat via Nienburg against Kloster Zeven; Count
Wilhelm first takes over the cover of the retreat in the right
flank and makes from Nienburg the rear guard with his troops,
took possession of the castle. Battle at Ahausen and Convention of Kloster Zeven. Duke Ferdinand took command of the
army. The hostilities begin again. Bremervörde is occupied.
Lt. Baum invades Vegesack. The enemy goes over the frozen
Mumme, battle at Geilersmühle.

In consequence of the alliance contract concluded with the
Crown of England, the Carabinier Corps, on 26 April 1757, joined the
corps commanded by the hereditary prince of Hessen-Kassel. The Hereditary Prince had his headquarters in Bielefeld; [156] The French had already attacked Lippstadt and the Carabinier (then 60 riders and 40 Jäger
on foot) had to take over the outpost immediately. Lieutenant Baum
of the Corps reconnoitered with 30 horses on the 27th near Rittberg.[157]
He found no enemies to fight, and from this day until the 4 May, daily

[156] Translator's Note: Bielefeld is now a city in the Ostwestfalen-Lippe Region in the north-east
of North Rhine-Westphalia, Germany. The town was initially founded in 1214 by Count Her-
mann IV of Ravensberg to guard a pass crossing the Teutoburg Forest, Bielefeld was the "city
of linen" as a minor member of the Hanseatic League, known for its bleachfields into the 19th
Century. Lippstadt is now a town in North Rhine-Westphalia, Germany. It is the largest town
within the district of Soest. It is situated in the Lippe valley, roughly 70 kilometers east of Dortmund and roughly 30 kilometers west of Paderborn.
[157] Translator's note: Rittberg is now Reitberg. It is a town in the district of Gütersloh in the
state of North Rhine-Westphalia, Germany. It is located approximately 10 km south of Gütersloh and 25 km north-west of Paderborn in the region Ostwestfalen-Lippe. The town is located
on the Ems river.

sorties were undertaken by the corps without coming to blows with the enemy.[158]

On the 4th of May, General Major Count Schulenburg, with a detachment of cavalry and infantry, to which the Carabinier Corps belonged, moved to Monastery of Marienfelde in the Münster area with the intention of raising contributions from the surrounding villages, in order to make subsistence difficult for the enemy who had spread forces all over the vicinity of Münster and up to Wahrendorf.[159] Count Schulenburg, instead of keeping the bulk of his detachment together, and always remaining concentrated divided it into several small squads, and dispatched them around the region. Two Hanoverian officers with 60 horses were sent to Harsewinkel; Lieutenant Baum advanced from there with 12 Carabinier against Wahrendorf, and on the way he heard reliable news that the city around the fortress was greatly invested by the enemy, and that they were already on the way to attack the Schulenburg Corps.[160] Lieutenant Baum retreated against Harsewinkel and advanced his command post and took up an advanced position in order to discover at once the approach of the enemy. It was not long before the vedettes fired, and immediately afterwards French Hussars appeared at all the

---

[158] Translator's note: This was in fact Lieutenant Friedrich Baum. Who may have been born in Haste in 1727. He was the son of a forester and had blond hair and light-colored eyes. The description has led some to postulate that he was an albino. He was 5'1" in height. He began his service to Bückeburg on 22 August 1753, at the age 26. On 15 July 1756, he was promoted to Cornet, and 6 April 1757 saw him promoted to Lieutenant. 3 April 1758, he was promoted to Captain-Lieutenant, and 1760 to Rittmeister, or captain of cavalry. In 1762, he transferred to the army of Braunschweig. In that army, he reached the rank of major on1 August 1762, and Lieutenant Colonel on 20 April 1767. In 1776, he took command of the Dragoon Regiment Prinz Ludwig Erst. He served in the Saratoga Campaign and was cut off by the troops under Colonel John Stark during his raid Bennington, Vermont. The biographical data on Baum derives from Col. Michael R. Gadue, "Lieutenant Colonel Friedrich S. Baum, Officer Commanding, the Bennington Expedition A Figure Little Known to History." in *The Hessians: Journal of the Johannes Schwalm Historical Association.* Vol. 11 (2008): 37-8.

[159] The modern town of Marienfelde is southwest of Berlin and was actually assimilated into that city in 1920.

[160] Translator's Note: Harsewinkel is a town in Gütersloh District in the state of North Rhine-Westphalia, Germany. It lies on the river Ems, some 15 km north-west of Gütersloh. Wahrendorf, now given as Warendorf is a town in North Rhine-Westphalia, Germany, and capital of Warendorf District.

entrances.

Lieutenant Baum, reckoning on the support of the cavalry, led his horse against the enemy, but he was not supported, since the Hanoverian cavalry immediately retreated, and soon collapsed into disorder, so that the enemy, 80 strong, came upon one officer along with only 14 men. The latter were partly cut down and partly captured. The 12 Carabinier closed their front in retreat, and when the opportunity arose kept the enemies' respect by some well-aimed rifle-shots, though he tried to overrun them several times. The whole loss of the Carabinier consisted in one man who was shot.

Count Schulenburg, on the other hand, found his way back from the enemy as well, and returned to Beilefeld the same evening.[161] The enemy attacked vigorously, but by that time captain von Monkewitz, with the remains of the Carabinier, formed the rear guard. This was especially the case in the difficult terrain between Oester and Isserhorst.[162] In defending the defile by the swampy environment of the latter place, Monkewitz gave the enemy a lesson which cooled his ardor for the pursuit a great deal!

Count Wilhelm, always anxious to reward the glorious merit of his troops, gave the greatest praise to the Carabinier, who had been present during the affair, and gave each a gift of money, and ordered, "every one of the 11 Carabinier who fought at Harsmintel was to receive an extra month's salary." Lieutenant Baum received great praise from his master, and two Carabinier, Galenzy, and Harriers, who had been especially heroic, received a gift of two Louis d'Ors. While sophists, philosophers and others smile at this kind of reward, the officer who serves in the field, who knows the soldier knows best how to spur the ambition of the common man. Nor did he offer any different kind of reward to the NCOs and other soldiers at the during the war.

---

[161] Translator's note: Beilefeld is a city in the Ostwestfalen-Lippe Region in the north-east of North Rhine-Westphalia, Germany.

[162] Translator's Note: Oester is a town in the Nordrhein-Westfalen region of Germany. It lies southeast of Harsewinkel and Marienfeld. The author here seems to mean Isselhorst, a town in modern Gutersloh, Detmold, Nordrhein-Westfalen.

Of the affair itself, Count Wilhelm, among others, wrote to Monkewitz's chief,

> *What did the command actually mean, and why was it sent to Marienfelde? My cousin the Count of Schulenburg will find that it is necessary to make a distinction between the Hungarian Hussars with whom he served in Italy, and the Hanoverian dragoons, in a few ways. To give my opinion of the affair, you would not be at a loss for the very least if the Hanoverians only had remained; The hussars would not have attacked them, and the fire of the Carabinier alone would certainly have held them back. I have seen something very similar to this affair at Aschaffenburg: one must not take flight from hussars, if so, it would be for the purpose of luring them into an ambush.[163] The dispositions, as captain von Monkewitz made through the defile, are, in my opinion, inconceivable; at all events I am quite satisfied with this affair, so many officers and their men.[164] If Baum is sent alone with 30 of my Carabinier, I am not worried about any ill result, but if he is under a foreign command, I must confess that I do not have the same confidence.*

On the 9th of May the corps engaged in an insignificant skirmish with the enemy advancing from Wahrendorf, but nothing came out of it on either side; After a few hours of fighting, the enemy retreated to Wahrendorf, the Carabinier Corps followed him to his post before Beilefeld. It remained there until 19 May, while the army occupied a camp near Schlische near Beilefeld.[165]

---

[163] Translator's note: Aschaffenburg is a town in northwest Bavaria, Germany. The town of Aschaffenburg is not considered part of the district of Aschaffenburg, but is the administrative seat. At this time, it formed part of the Archbishopric of Mainz.

[164] To my regret, I have not found them among the papers of Count W.

[165] Translator's Note: This may be the town of Schleich is a municipality in the Trier-Saarburg district, in Rhineland-Palatinate, Germany.

Captain Monkewitz recorded in the diary of the corps: "The little post, which I had the honor of commanding, had to secure the safety of the army, since at that time there were no other pickets at all, so that the patrols of the corps were moving constantly against Münster to observe the movements of the enemy."

On 19 May the Carabinier Corps went to Rittberg under the command of the general Count von Schulenburg, who had been detached with some additional squadrons of cavalry and a division infantry. From there the Carabinier advanced as far as the Lippe and entered Paderborn with the corps of General von Zastrow, who was in the camp.

Count Schulenburg moved back to Bielefeld on the 23rd, and the Carabinier took their old post at Meinersenhof.[166]

On the 25th the Carabinier advanced to Brockhagen, and there met a hostile detachment, which was at once attacked with saber in fist. But as the enemy was not able to stand, it was only possible to wound some of his men and to take one hussar prisoner. The enemy hurriedly made their retreat towards Wahrendorf.[167]

---

[166] Translator's note: This may be the modern town of Meinersen in the municipality in the district of Gifhorn, in Lower Saxony, Germany. It is situated between the rivers Oker and Aller.

[167] As is unfortunately the case with small units of troops, so did the case. The Carabiner Corps were kept on their feet day and night, everywhere, and yet they were not even to produce the small fruits which his activity earned him; And the horse, which was captured on the 25th, together with Equipage, was taken from the Corps, though its indisputable property, upon a higher order. No attention was paid to the distressed complaints of the chief of Monkewitz, and the latter, who was not inclined to take any slight consideration of the kind, found himself therefore to report to Count Wilhelm. Count Wilhelm, equally eager to the rights of a king of England, to whom he was due, was eager to oppress any injustice which might be inflicted on his troops, and turned to the Duke in the matter From Cumberland, to the convention concluded with His Majesty the King of Great Britain, in which it expressly stated: "Trophies and all kinds of booty, in cases where the booty of the Schaumburg-Lippe-Bückeburg is legally made The troops will remain your property, and will not require His Majesty to do so."

The correspondence in this affair seems to be very warm; For, in a letter from the Count to the chief of Monkewiss, it is said, "I beg my paternal master of Monkewitz to have a little patience, for I will not attend to my disposition, so the road to Bückeburg is always open, my people twenty times More labor and trouble than the rest, and if they are ruined in a wanton manner, the army will feel it very much, "and then, moreover," The hussars' horse and Equipage belong to my people who have caught it; The captain of Monkewitz will not allow the corps to be taken by the Corps, together with Equipage. The end result was that the Carabiniers shared the horse, for whose sole purpose, therefore, it seemed to have so great a value, once because it was the

On the 26th of May the army under the duke moved to another camp near Brackwede, on the outskirts of Bielefeld;[168] The Carabinier Corps held outposts along the roads to Münster and Lippstadt. Upon the news that a weak enemy detachment had advanced from Münster to Tecklenburg, and had taken this place, Baum, with 24 Carabinier on horseback and 12 Carabinier on foot, set out to pick up this detachment. Since hostile parties were already fighting beyond Iburg, the march had to be kept very secret.[169] Lt. Baum left at 8:30, marched through the night, and lay hidden in the forest the day after. At nightfall the command continued, and on the morning of the 31st, arrived at Tecklenburg.

Precisely informed of the location of the only sentry, which the enemy had left exposed before the place, the party succeeded in overcoming the noise of the surprise. When, however, the riders burst into the place to surprise the enemy, they were greeted with a heavy fire at a house in which the enemy kept his men out of sight at night. Without thinking long, Lt. Baum dismounted half of his force and rushed with the sword in hand against the house, whose door was broken. The foot Jäger had now also begun their attack and had penetrated the rear of the house. As the enemy continued to defend, there was a very hard fight in a narrow room of the house, until finally the enemy leader called out to surrender. They took 1 officer and 27 men prisoner; 14 men, including two officers, fell or were shot down in the house; Only one man had the opportunity to escape through the window during the scuffle. The Carabinier lost a man killed and had two lightly wounded. Lt. Baum quickly set out with his prisoner and made his return by way of Melle and Herford. He returned to the army on June 2, happy.[170]

---

first prey in this campaign of the Duke of Cumberland, and then the corps of the Karabiner corps were neither a corps for themselves nor a power other than England-in short, in order to gradually merge its existence into the larger mass of troops. We shall see scenes of this kind later on, but all the strength of the Count is put to an end.

[168]Brackwede is located in the region of North Rhine-Westphalia. North Rhine-Westphalia's capital Duesseldorf (Düsseldorf) is approximately 147 km / 92 mi away from Brackwede.

169   Tecklenburg is a town in the district of Steinfurt, in North Rhine-Westphalia, Germany. It is located at the foothills of the Teutoburg Forest, southwest of Osnabrück. Iburg is a town in the Osnabrück district.

[170] Translator's note: Melle is a city in the district of Osnabrück, Lower Saxony, Germany.

On this subject, Count Wilhelm wrote to captain von Monkewitz on 3 June: "Sergeant Brackmann will give you 200 Reichsthalers for the men of the command, which is their reward for their action at Tecklenburg. Those who broke through the door into the house are to get a double share, and I will have a list of those who performed this glorious action. I mean those who captured the gate, for this is a masterpiece of fighting. The lieutenant Baum will have to be made aware that, after this performance, if he is posted at Harsewinkel, I will not be surprised by him accomplishing praiseworthy deeds on all occasions, however beautiful and good-natured. But he would do me an economic favor if he wanted to show me how I could bestow upon him my appreciation for his repeated benevolence, and it would be my intention that he would exhort me, see what he wanted, for I do not think that I can give him too much."

At this point in his letter, Count Wilhelm posed the question, "Is it not possible to increase the bravura and the urge for honorable deeds to the highest degree, if the warlike father of the country himself cares so much about his troops as here?"

A supplement to the affair of Tecklenburg conspired to diminish the fame of the small troop.

At the moment when the fire in the house at Tecklenburg had ceased, and the enemy had surrendered, the Hanoverian Captain-Lieut. … entered.[171] He arrived at the head of two orderlies during the battle, went in the house without notice, when the battle had been committed to-he went to Lt. Baum, telling him: "he had visited the command in vain, Cumberland had been asked to take the lead." Lt. Baum, who was occupied by Mr. v. G. dashed in, gave him the command, and Herr v. G. triumphantly entered the camp near Beilefeld.

History wants truth and in pursuance of it, one will not hesitate to bring to light several scenes of this kind. Which of my warlike readers can not see that this scenario is still common today! At the moment

---

[171] Translator's Note: The name is not given in the original. All that appears is Capitan-Lieut. v. G…It is likely, however, that it is captain-lieutenant von Gerstein. I have left these sections as in the original to preserve the feel of the narrative.

of the decision, when there was the fiercest fighting, you suddenly see figures appear that were not there as long as it was still a light skirmish, or as long as saber and lance work! There is a shriek of victory from troops who did not contribute to making it happen, and sometimes we even see them carrying fresh ammunition into their arms - think a hat full! - At this moment, the commanding general or a higher-ranking officer appears: these ammunition men are the first to wish him luck in the attack, overhear him with details about the battle!! The end is, "he has distinguished himself there very well, and he reaped the reward !! - -"

The retreat of his troops exasperated count Wilhelm to the highest degree, and wrote to captain von Monkewitz:

> *As my officers, in their bravery and dexterity, have no equal, I do not see why my men should be commanded by foreigners? Captain von Monkewitz is expressly commanded never to let any of my subjects march to any place; If a detachment of other troops is commanded, of which the officer has a higher rank, or is older in the service after the patent, there is no objection, but that another officer, of whose troops no one is commanded, is a brave and active (to some extent to the disadvantage of my officers) should be an honor, and the captain, von Monkewitz will, in such cases, forgive me for my express ban and await further action.*[172]

On the 7th of June Count von Schulenburg again made an advance against Brockhagen and Marienfelde, with a strong detachment, to which Lieutenant von Gerstein, with 18 horse of the Carbiniers, was commanded to serve as the advanced guard.[173] The enemy had indeed attacked Harsewinkel and the Abbey of Marienfelde but withdrew as

---

[172] Translator's note: In his convoluted way, the count was ordering von Monkewitz not to place troops of the Schaumburg-Lippe forces, even when in detachment under the command of foreign officers, unless those officers possessed superior rank,

[173] Translator's note: Brockhagen is located in the region of North Rhine-Westphalia. North Rhine-Westphalia's capital Düsseldorf is approximately 138 km / 86 mi away from Brockhagen.

the Schulenburg Corps approached.[174] Marienfelde was defended by them for a short time and was then attacked by Count Schulenburg. The latter, however, did so little to secure his corps, that the deed succeeded, on the night of the 9th, to attack him when he was almost on the march and to throw him out again, with loss, especially after the infantry had stubbornly resisted, two of whom were severely wounded.

On this occasion there were more stories of misbehavior emanating from the command of the Lt. von Gerstein, which at that time was almost inevitable, especially with light troops; but as the church in Marienfelde was plundered by the detachment of Count Schulenburg, so Count Wilhelm ordered every similar case of the kind under his troops to be absolutely and immediately handled with the rope. Count Wilhelm wrote of this affair, among other things, to Monkewitz:

I will hope that my cousin of Graf von Schulenburg, if he intends to visit the monastery of Marienfelde, will not demand the third. The story of the 8th is mine, but it was not unexpected to me. I have already spoken to Majors Brehmann and Reipe eight days ago, who informed me of an ambuscade, which was bad for us. This I have judged, for the most part, from the incautious and hasty manner, as the detachments are sometimes thrown out of the local camp for bad reasons.

The Marshal d'Estrées, however, commanded a strong corps at Rhea, and the detachment of the allied army, which was at Rittsberg, withdrew against Bielfeld, and the latter also retreated against the Weser on the 13th and passed at Rehme.

On this retreat, the Carabinier, served at the most extreme end of the rear guard, which, however, was not disturbed by the enemy, so that on 16th Lt. Baum with 12 Carabinier again proceeded from Cofeld

---

[174]Translator's note: Abbey of Marienfelde is a former Cistercian abbey in the Marienfeld district of Harsewinkel, in the district of Gütersloh, Germany. It was founded in 1185 by monks from Hardehausen Abbey and dissolved in 1803 after German Mediatization, becoming state property and then in 1804 a parish church. The monastic buildings were demolished

against Herford, in order to receive messages from the enemy.[175] This officer returned with the news: "The enemy had not yet touched the place, but he had personally seen the head of the enemy's column against Herford," to which the rest of the rear guards went over the Weser, while the Carabinier Corps went after them. Blotow was detached, in order to set up a post, and to keep a magazine there if possible.

In the evening of the same day the corps was given orders to go back quickly across the Weser, since they had been informed that the enemy was in position to make a significant advance. The army of the Duke of Cumberland invaded the right bank of the Weser between Holzhausen, an area known as the red court, and houses.[176]

On the 18th, the Carabinier advanced back across the Weser to join Blotow, who brought the magazine there to safety, and returned to the right bank of the Weser. On Blotow's return, Lt. Baum was sent with 18 horses to the area of Bielefeld, in order to gain news of the enemy.

The Carabinier Corps, however, under the orders of the Generalmajor von Brunk, moved to Hameln, where he was quartered, and where Lt. Baum was again sent to the corps on the 22nd, after reporting on his reconnaissance at headquarters. He had been driven up to Bielefeld detouring via Uffeln and Ebenhausen. En route he captured two enemy hussars, who had entered the village where Baum intercepted them. Otherwise, Baum learned that the French army was sending out numerous detachments in the Lippische.[177]

On the 23rd and 24th of June, Captain von Monkewitz, with the whole Carabinier Corps, made a march over through Aerzen and Barntrupp, and received a certain assurance that the enemy had a con-

---

[175] Translators Note: Cofeld is located in the region of North Rhine-Westphalia. North Rhine-Westphalia's capital Duesseldorf (Düsseldorf) is approximately 142 km / 88 mi away from Gohfeld. Herford is a town in North Rhine-Westphalia, Germany, located in the lowlands between the hill chains of the Wiehen Hills and the Teutoburg Forest. It is the capital of the district of Herford.

[176] Translator's note: Holzhausen is a village and a former municipality in the district of Stendal, in Saxony-Anhalt, Germany. Since 1 January 2010, it is part of the town Bismark.

[177] Translator's note: Uffeln, North Rhine-Westphalia is nearby to Obersteinbeck and Kälber-Berg. Ebenhausen in Upper Bavaria (Bavaria) is a city in Germany about 326 mi (or 524 km) south of Berlin, the country's capital. The Lippische is the area around the Lippe River.

siderable influence on the territory of Alverdissen and Lemgo.[178] The corps were reinforced at this time by 20 mounted and 25-foot Carabinier from Bückeburg, and spent the rest of the month continually patrolling against the county of Lippe.

On 1 July, Lt. von Gerstein, who had been sent with 12 horses, reconnoitered Aerzen, was attacked by the enemy in superior numbers, and thrown back against Hameln. The Carabinier Corps moved forward, took the enemy, and captured an officer and six enemy infantrymen.

On the 2nd, Lt. Baum with 6 mounted Carabinier moved against Aerzen, which the enemy had once again occupied, attacked the field guards stationed in front of the village, and captured two hussars, who belonged to the Fischer Corps.

The Carabinier remained in Hamlen until the 10th, but patrolled daily against the Lippe. In the meantime, the enemy's army, was strongly advancing against the Weser, by means of the Lippish and Paderborn, until the enemy's light troops and the Carabinier were skirmishing almost daily, but the enemy almost always drew the short straw. The corps, in connection with the Hanoverian Jäger, who had recently been added to the army, on the 21st, near Grohnde, opposed a party of Fischer's Corps, and the dragoons of the Corps, of which on the following day, when the battle was renewed, 1 Col., 3 Caps., 2 Lts. 1 Cornet and 62 Hussars and Dragoons were captured or killed.[179]

[178] Translator's note: Aerzen is a municipality in the Hamelin-Pyrmont district, in Lower Saxony, Germany. It is situated 10 kilometers southwest of Hamelin, and 7 kilometres north of Bad Pyrmont. Barntrup is a town in the Lippe district of North Rhine-Westphalia, Germany. It has an area of 59.46 km² and 8,824 inhabitants (2013). It lies 40 km east from Bielefeld and 9 km west from Bad Pyrmont at the east border of North Rhine Westphalia to Lower Saxony. Lippe-Alverdissen was a county in Germany, ruled by the House of Lippe. It was created in 1613 following the death of Count Simon VI of Lippe, with his realm being split between his three sons with his youngest son Philipp receiving the territory of Lippe-Alverdissen. Following Count Philipp's ascension as Count of Schaumburg-Lippe in 1643 Lippe-Alverdissen became part of Schaumburg-Lippe. Following the death of Count Philipp in 1681 Schaumburg-Lippe went to his eldest son Friedrich Christian while Lippe-Alverdissen was inherited by his second son Philip Ernest who founded the Schaumburg-Lippe-Alverdissen line. Lemgo is a small university town in the Lippe district of North Rhine-Westphalia, Germany, 25km east of Bielefeld and 70 km west of Hannover. It was once a member of the Hanseatic League.

[179] Translator's note: This place is situated in Hameln-Pyrmont, Hannover, Niedersachsen, Germany.

The enemy army, which had hitherto opposed the allied army on the other side at Grohnde on the right of the Weser near Hastenbeck, began to cross the Weser on the 22nd and 23rd. The corps with which the aforesaid bloody invasions occurred seemed to have been destined to ensure this operation on the left flank. The Carabinier, who, with the exception of some wounded, had lost only two dead, held the conviction that the enemy dragoons were ruthless. They believed as well that they would not be able to receive them, and that, as far as they are concerned, the cuirass, over whose burden they had sometimes complained, had no use in combat.

On the 24th and 25th, there was a strong cannonade between the two armies, which, however, produced no result. The enemy merely made a few changes in his position, so that all his troops passed over the Weser. On the day mentioned, a swarm of about 2-300 enemy hussars attempted an attack on the baggage of the army, which had not come near to Hameln. The Carabinier Corps was here, hand-to-hand with the enemy, and had the fortune to drive their whole army out of the field. The allies carried on a considerable fire at a distance with the enemy, many of whom were dead, wounded, and some prisoners lost. As the enemy, however, received a considerable reinforcement in infantry, the corps retreated against Hameln. In this battle, the Carabinier lost a major, Brown, who was thrown down after his horse was shot out from under him, and they had four dead and two wounded.

The light troops of the enemy had at this time declared that they would not give any of the "black men" quarter, and they kept their promises. The Carabinier, on the other hand, returned the treatment in kind. No Carabinier asked for quarter, but he gave it to the enemy. It was only at the end of the ensuing campaign that some agreement was struck, though the mutual exasperation remained strained very much throughout the war.

At the battle of Hastenbeck on the 26th of July, the corps was stationed on the right wing of the army and took no part in the battle, which, as is well known, was decided on the left wing of the allied army. When the army retreated under the cannons of Hameln when darkness fell, the Carabinier, together with Luckner hussars and Jäger, provided the outposts.

On the retreat, the Carabinier Corps served as the rear guards until the army, after a strenuous March, entered the position near Luhden near Bückeburg.[180] The Carabinier Corps marched the same evening to Bückeburg.

Since a further withdrawal of the army from the area of the Weser had already been determined, the 28th was used to send back all the Bückeburg troops to the depots and the unskilled recruits of cavalry to Nienburg.[181] On this and the following day, the allied army passed through Bückeburg, without any trouble whatsoever from the enemy, who seemed to be resting from the shock of Hastenbeck.

Count Wilhelm, on this day, took the Karabiner corps, his company of Liebgrenadiers and the 25 Liebcarabinier under his own command, and indicated to the Duke of Cumberland that he was ready, with this corps, to defend the right flank of the army-the only danger to the retreat. This enterprise was most gratefully accepted by the duke.

The retreat now continued to Rheinburg and on from there to Verden.[182] The Corps of Count Wilhelm marched from Neinburg as the rear guard of the army. On 5 August, Lt. Baum was sent with 9 Carabinier towards Bückeburg, in order to collect news of the enemy. On the 9th this command arrived safely with 2 captured horses taken near Minden, - the riders had been cut down on contact - to the corps, which defended the forward-post of the army near Huttbergen.[183]

---

[180] Translator's note: Luhden is today a municipality in the district of Schaumburg, in Lower Saxony, Germany.

[181] Translator's note: Neinburg is today a town and capital of the district Neinburg, in Lower Saxony, Germany.

[182] Translator's note: Verden an der Aller or Verden Aller or simply Verden is a town in Lower Saxony. It is situated on the River Aller. It is the administrative center of the district of Verden. Verden is famous for a massacre of Saxons in 782, committed on the orders of Charlemagne (the Massacre of Verden), for its cathedral, and for its horse-breeding. Rheinberg is a town in the district of Wesel, in North Rhine-Westphalia.

[183] Translator's note: The area is now known as Döhlbergen-Hutbergen. The district is divided into the two namesake villages, which are located on the western side of the Aller and directly on the Weser, just before the gate of the castle. Huttbergen is divided into large and small mountains. The small village of Rieda also belongs to the district.

The Carabinier Corps, with the Freytag's Jäger and Lückner's Hussars, joined the then Major von Lückner, forming the outposts of the army in the area of Rethem on the Aller.[184] The hostile army, however, had, for the most part, moved from Hameln over Hanover to Neinburg, against the lower Weser. The outposts on either side were opposed to each other. On the 22nd, a hostile detachment of cavalry on the way to Stöcker-Drebber was stopped by the united corps.

When the army retreated, the Hereditary Prince of Braunschweig commanded the rear guard, to which the Carabinier belonged. In the area of Uhausen near Rotenburg, there occurred on the 28th a zealous, hard-fought battle with hostile hussars, in which twelve horses were captured.[185] In the same way, all the light troops had arranged a lively rear-guard battalion, near the Monastery of Zeven, which was fortified on the same day by the French.[186]

The Convention of Kloster Zeven, which was concluded on 9 September, produced a very sad mood in the allied army, especially among the Hessian, Brunswick, Saxe-Gothian, and Bückeburg troops, as they were to be dismissed from the army and sent home by virtue of the second article. This article is as follows: "Auxiliary Troops of Monsgr. the Duke of Cumberland, those of Hesse, Brunswick, Saxe-Gotha, and those of the Count of Lippe-Bückeburg, will be disbanded, and as it is necessary to arrange the march to their respective countries, send from the allies a general or particular officer of each nation, etc."[187] We find in this case that it was quite reasonable for Count Wilhelm not to tolerate his small contingent being merged with other corps. He maintained his control over the troops of his small state and received recognition from the French at the same level as the crowns of Prussia and England.

---

[184] Translator's note: Rethem on the Aller is a town in the Heidekreis in Lower Saxony, Germany. It is situated on the river Aller, approx. 25 km southwest of Bad Fallingbostel, and 18 km southeast of Verden.

[185] Translator's note: Uhausen is now known as Hausen is a city district of Frankfurt am Main, Germany. If the author is referring to Rotenburg, then it was likely Rotenburg an der Fulda, which is a town in Hersfeld-Rotenburg district in northeastern Hesse, Germany lying, as the name says, on the river Fulda.

[186] This is the infamous Kloster Zeven, for which the peace was named.

[187] This section is given in French in the original.

The marching routes for the divisions just mentioned were made by the French; the Hessian Corps set out on the march, and the first detachment had already reached Berden when she received orders to make a turn against Zeven the following day.[188]

The Duke of Cumberland had returned to England when the Battle of Roßbach had been fought with the French and Imperial troops being defeated, and in the allied army there was a dull rumor, as if the fortunes had come again, that Duke Ferdinand of Brunswick was to take command of the army.

The latter, in these days, in which the Brunswick troops under general-lieutenant von Imhof, according to the Convention, were to separate from the army, but were now moved by the new state of affairs to take a different position. The Carabinier Corps went over the east on the 19th of November, and were commanded to march against Bremervörde that evening, but not to enter there until the Hessian troops of Verden and Zeven had also arrived there. The further order was to "begin no hostilities first, but to expect them from the enemy, but then to meet violence with violence."

The chief, von Monkewitz, reported of this march:

> As the evening unfolded, I set out with the Carabinier corps, the Liebgrenadiers, and two light Bückeburg guns, and moved near Bremervörde, but learned that the General von Wutgenau, who commanded the Hessian troops, had not yet entered the place which was occupied by a strong enemy detachment.[189] Lt. Baum had been sent to the place with an orderly to inquire whether General Besager was in the vicinity, and learned that the Hessians had camped near Bevern where he went without being arrested, but when he went round at midnight, he and the orderly were taken prisoner by the French

---

[188] Translator's note, Berden is a town in western German, northwest of Krefeld.

[189] Translator's note: Bremervörde is a town in the north of the district of Rotenburg, in Lower Saxony, Germany. It is situated on the Oste river near the center of the "triangle" formed by the rivers Weser and Elbe, roughly equidistant from the cities of Hamburg, Bremen and Cuxhaven.

at Bremervörde. I received the latter message from a certain spy, and then, on the instructions of the scout, returned to Nieder-Otthausen, and immediately had the incident reported to General von Zastrow, who was in command of the army.[190]

On the 20th, a detached patrol sent the news that a strong column of enemy cavalry was in sight. The Carabinier stood up and came to meet the French, whose leader, when he discovered them, stopped his troops and himself with a trumpeter. Their chief von Monkewitz, for his part, was by now also with the Carabinier and sent for the French officer. The latter said he was sent by the commander of Bremervörde to ask "why the Corps had gone over to the east yesterday, and whether it was known that this was against the convention?" Captain von Monkewitz replied curtly, "he would only do what his general had commanded, without pondering the contents of the conventions." The French did not seem to think Monkewitz was right, but he felt he was ready to retreat immediately back to Bremervörde.

In the middle Major von Luckner with his Hussars met with the Carabinier, and took over the command of the united division, with which he advanced on Bremervörde. General von Wutgenau, at the same time, marched from the other side, so that they now enclosed French command, which consisted of about 50 dragoons, and demanded their capitulation. Since the allied corps had orders to avoid all hostilities, the enemy was allowed to retreat from Ottersberg after Lt. Baum was released together with the Carabinier. Duke Ferdinand of Brunswick assumed command of the army on that same day.

New life had come into the troops with the arrival of the duke. Everything took on a different aspect, and with ruthless activity the duke displaced the enemy from one position to another, so that from the first appearance of the new commander-in-chief, the foe was immediately

---

[190] Translator's note: This may refer to modern Neiderhausen a municipality belonging to a Verbandsgemeinde, a kind of collective municipality – in the Bad Kreuznach district in Rhineland-Palatinate.

thrown on the defensive and kept in constant check. On the course of the great operations of these campaigns, in order not to appear as a mere translator, one has to refer the reader to Tempelhof, and content himself with the figurative representation of what the Bückeburgian Carabinier accomplished.[191]

The corps, in conjunction with Hanoverian hussars and Jäger, was partly advanced against Osterholtz, and partly remained in Bremervörde, patrolling Zeven and Ottersberg. On November 29, Lt. Baum went with 30 horses the town of Vegesack, in which stood an enemy command post, which he cut down and partly destroyed. Lt. Baum had a man wounded and quietly retired to Osterholz.

On the 13th of December, a strong patrol of hostile cavalry lurked in the vicinity of Bremervörde. Captain von Monkewitz had discovered their arrival early enough, attacked killed two men and made four more prisoners. They belonged to the same Dragoon regiment Banfremont, with whom the Carabinier had become so well-acquainted at Hamlen.[192]

On the 14th, the Carabinier, under Captain von Monkewitz, minus a division of the same who stood under Baum near Osterholz. Another detachment served with a part of Lückner's hussars on the Wümme-Zeven.[193] The patrols went as far as Rothenburg, where the French had a stronghold in the old castle. On the night of the 14th, the force of von Monkewitz alarmed the garrison of castle of Rothenburg. The effectives of the Carabinier Corps, including the Leib Carabinier, numbered 108 mounted and 96 foot-Jäger.

When the enemy made an appearance of escaping the castle of Harburg, which was besieged by General von Hardenberg, the Carabi-

---

[191] Here, Düring is referring to Georg Friedrich von Tempelhof, *Geschichte des siebenjährigen Krieges in Deutschland zwischen dem Könige von Preussen und der Kaiserin Königin mit ihren Alliirten als eine Fortsetzung der Geschichte* Lloyd. 6 vols. Berlin: J.F. Unger, 1783-1801.

[192] Translator's note: This appears to be the Beaufremont dragoons, originally raised by Charles Paul de Baufremont, Marquis de Listenois in 1673. It served in both the War of the Polish Succession and War of the Austrian Succession. In the Seven Years' War, it was commanded by Prince Louis de Beaufremont.

[193] Translator's note: Wümme-Zeven was the contemporary name for the modern town of Rotenburg.

nier advanced with a division of the army.[194] Diepenbroick was commanded, according to Burtehude, to thwart this plan. The Allied army, however, had also suffered an insignificant check in the region of Celle, and had retreated to Lüneburg.[195] The enemy, however, gave up the plan, and General von Diepenbroick, on the other hand, marched his troops back to take his former post in the neighborhood of Kloster Zeven. At this time, severe winter weather had begun, and the enemy, who had attacked Bremen, Otterberg, and Rothenburg with about 4,000 men, had drawn up all his power at Bremerburg. On the 28th of December he went over the wilderness the Major von Handverschen who had hitherto covered the river Otterberg with about 300-foot Jäger and a few horsemen (among whom were a part of the foot- and mounted-carabinier of Bückeburg). There arose a very determined attack, as a result of which Major von Müller on Siedersmühlen, and Osterholz had to be abandoned by the Carabinier who had been stationed there. This combat cost the Bückeburg Carabinier Corps 4 Jäger dead and 4 missing.[196]

Since the enemy broke off the fighting at nightfall, the corps did not pursue any further. Watch-master Hirsch from the Carabinier was sent with two men to collect news from the enemy. Towards the middle of the night near Burgdamm, near the village of Lessum, he discovered two enemy sentries before the village.[197] Hirsch sneaked in unseen, picked them off without a shot, and returned with the prisoners to the post at Seidersmühlen.

General von Diepenbroick had received news of the enemy's move against Bremervörde and hastened to Major von Müller to help.

---

[194] Translator's note: Harburg is today a borough of the city of Hamburg.

[195] Translator's Note: Lüneburg also called Lunenburg in English, is a town in the German state of Lower Saxony. It is located about 50 km (31 mi) southeast of another Hanseatic city, Hamburg. Lüneburg lies on the river Ilmenau, about 30 kilometres (19 mi) from its confluence with the Elbe. The river flows through the town.

[196] Translator's note: Siedersmühlen may be Sudermühlen, a town in Lower Saxony.

[197] Translator's note: Burgdamm, or castle dam, is a small town situated in Osterholz, Lüneburg, Niedersachsen, Germany. It is located on the outskirts of Bremen.

Chapter 2

The Campaign of 1758

Battles at Ritterhude and in the suburbs of Bremen. Battle at
Orlepshausen. Bremen is attacked, the enemy pursues Brinkum. Duke Ferdinand advances against Minden. Baum is tak-
en prisoner by the Hussar officer von Luckner at Bergkirchen
after he killed several riders. Minden is won by the Allies.
The attack of Nordhorn in Bentheim. Monkewitz destroyed
a hostile convoy in the Bentheim area. Battle with Plettenberg. Battle with Hauinkel of Wesel. Meeting of sea. Captain
Kiepe with the Leib-Carabinier crosses the Weser and drives
Fischer's corps from the area of Trendelnburg. Kuhner's partisans strike a patrol of two Carabinier. Fight at Hovenstadt an
der Lippe. Brave behavior of the Deputy von Hirsch. Fights
at Rühden and Meschede. Captain Baum exists a fight with
Ahlen.

The Carabinier, now reunited by Monkewitz, were posted on
1 January 1758 against Ritterhude and Osterholz, where the corps remained until the 10th.[198] The enemy had eagerly attacked Osterholz and
Ritterhude. On a daily basis, there were small clashes between the patrols on both sides, with a carabinier falling heavily into the enemy's
hands.

On the 11th, Diepenbroick's corps began to move. Captain von
Monkewitz reported on the continuing incidents as follows:

---

[198]Translator's note: Ritterhude is a municipality in the district of Osterholz, in Lower Saxony,
Germany. It is situated on the Hamme River, approx. 6 km southwest of Osterholz-Scharmbeck, and 13 km northwest of Bremen. Osterholz is a district in Lower Saxony, Germany. It is
bounded by the districts of Wesermarsch, Cuxhaven, Rotenburg and Verden, and by the city of
Bremen.

Battles before Ritterhude and in the suburb of Bremen

Major von Müller, with his detachment, went to the area of Schwanewedel to drive a hostile detachment from Vegesack, with the body grenadiers and foot-carabinier of Bückeburg, together with Lieutenant Baum with 30 horses.[199] *Major von Stockhausen made with me the advanced guard of the Diepenbroick Corps, who directed his march on Osterholz to Ritterhude. Towards the middle of the night I arrived at Ritterhude, where I immediately spotted a sergeant of enemy dragoons and attacked him with his guard; he retired upon his infantry, who, four battalions, was strong in Ritterhude, without being able to touch them. The enemy, on the other hand, drew himself upon the height of the Leßum.*[200] *Major von Stockhausen with his Jäger and my detachment were posted at the end of the village of Ritterhude. The mutual positions were so close to each other that the small rifle balls never missed. Although it was very cold, Stockhausen had to keep the halves of cavalry on horseback and the infantry under the rifle as the enemy seemed determined to do something against us. Toward midnight, the enemy*

---

199   Translator's Note: Schwanewede is a municipality in the district of Osterholz, in Lower Saxony, Germany. It is situated approximately 14 km west of Osterholz-Scharmbeck, and 22 km northwest of Bremen. It belonged to the Prince-Archbishopric of Bremen. In 1648 the Prince-Archbishopric was transformed into the Duchy of Bremen, which was first ruled in personal union by the Swedish and from 1715 on by the Hanoverian Crown. In 1823 the Duchy was abolished and its territory became part of the Stade Region. It consists of 12 smaller villages, that form the municipality of Schwanewede, namely Beckedorf, Löhnhorst, Meyenburg, Aschwarden, Neuenkirchen, Brundorf, Eggestedt, Harriersand, Hinnebeck, Leuchtenburg, and Rade. Vegesack is located about 20 km (12 mi) north from the center of Bremen-city at the mouth of the river Lesum, beside the Weser River (53°10'07"N 8°37'30"ECoordinates: 53°10'07"N 8°37'30"E). Abutting the district of Vegesack to the northwest is the district of Blumenthal, in the southeast the district of Burglesum. Across the river Weser is the Lower Saxony village Lemwerder, connected to Vegesack by a ferry service.

200   Translator's Note: The Leßum is a river in norther Germany. Vegesack is located at the mouth of the river.

made a strong attack on one of our posts, occupied by
captain von Freisenhausen and the Stockhausen Jäger,
and about a hundred strong, the enemy were obliged to
surrender to the Major von Stockhausen.

Although the French were certainly three times as strong as the outposts of the Diepenbroick Corps, their whole power was used for the pursuit of the Carabiniers' post. Major von Stockhausen, and Captain von Monkewitz took the occasion to chastise the enemy for his unscrupulous night-time penetration by impetuously attacking him. They so surprised him by this unexpected attack that he ran in great disorder, and quickly retreated to Lessum in despair, leaving twenty dead, and forty-four prisoners to the generals whose loss was insignificant; the Carabinier Corps sustained merely wounded horses.

The enemy retreated against Burgdamm on the 12th of January, ruined the fortress on the night of 13th, and continued the retreat that day. Since Major von Müller had also expelled the enemy detachment from Vegesack, the Lieb grenadiers and foot-Carabiniers immediately attacked the abandoned castle.

Captain von Monkewitz received orders to pursue the enemy with his cavalry and 100 dragoons. The foe retreated untroubled to the outskirts of Bremen. But Monkewitz succeeded in throwing himself on horseback with the cavalry; some 40 men were cut down in the streets, and 16 dragoons were made prisoners. It was only when the fighting was over that hostile infantry arrived, but too late, for Captain von Monkewitz, with the prisoners and the insignificant loss of one dead and second injured dragoon, retired to the heights of Orlepshausen, where he stopped, reinforced by the Leib-Grenadier and foot-Carabiniers.

Battle at Orlepshausen

To ward off the ravages of the previous day, the enemy made an attack on the position of the corps at Orlepshausen at dawn on the 15th. However, a patrol discovered the enemy's approach early, and General von Diepenbroick, therefore, had at once broken with the bulk of his corps from Gramke and quietly reached Orlepshausen.[201] The local field guards were ordered to hurry back to the Gros after the enemy's sighting, and in apparent disarray. The enemy believed himself made safe thereby and fell into the trap. A strong detachment of enemy dragoons and six squadrons of cuirassiers could be seen hurrying in at the gallop, probably intending to reach the Gros with the pickets at the same time, and now, at about three hundred paces, they were annihilated with such an efficacious grapeshot salvo of four volleys, that at the moment the battlefield was littered with dead and four-wounded riders and horses, and the remnant hastily fled. Captain von Monkewitz had only a moment to dig in with the Carabiniers and dragoons, and chased the enemy beyond his infantry, which, about four battalions strong, had turned out behind the so-called Gröpelinger dam so that it could not be touched.[202] The enemy then returned to Bremen; the corps took up its old position. The Carabinier Corps had a wounded horse; the loss of the enemy amounted to 38 dead and 50 wounded, some severely, who fell into our hands. The dragoons and Carabiniers also captured 16 horses while eating their food. The artillery under the Bückeburg Major von Römer had, according to its report, fired 12 shots.

Diepenbroich's Corps now returned to the cantonment, which the enemy also seemed to do, through the Mumme and Hamme. The Carabinier Corps retained the post at Burgdamm with the Grenadiers, and they met with the enemy almost daily. These clashes always ended with bloody heads on both sides. In this situation, everything was done to capture Bremen. The hereditary prince of Braunschweig traveled to the army and was led, with others, to reconnoiter the suburbs of the fairly firm Bremen defenses by Lieutenant Baum with four Carabinier.

On the 24th of February the hereditary prince made the famous attack of Hona. As the patrols from Bremen, already informed at noon of this incident, withdrew their outposts in a hurry, Captain von

---

[201] Translator's Note: Gramke is a town situated in Vechta, Weser-Ems, Niedersachsen, Germany.

[202] Translator's note: Gröpelinger is a section of modern Bremen.

Monkewitz inferred therefrom that he had planned the clearing of the city, and immediately advanced with the Lieb-grenadiers, Carabinier, and dragoons, the general von Diepenbroick was aware of this. He was not wrong; Bremen had been cleared of the enemy; but the gates were closed, and the magistrate denied Monkewitz the passage. At midnight, General von Diepenbroick arrived with the bulk of his corps at the city and spoke so strongly to the magistrate that he immediately opened the gates. The corps of Monkewitz immediately advanced on the other side to the gate, through which the enemy had departed towards Brinkum and Osnabrück and made prisoners of several enemy stragglers in the suburbs.[203]

On the 25th and 26th of February the corps continued the pursuit of the fugitive enemy, capturing 237 men and 53 horses, and taking part of the enemy's baggage, and on the evening of the 27th, on the orders of General Diepenbroick, they returned to the suburbs of the city gates.

Rothenburg and Ottersberg, on the other hand, were taken away from the enemy, and Nienburg, Verden, and Hanover were evacuated by them.[204] Prince Henry of Prussia had forced him to leave Brunswick and Hildesheim.[205] Duke Ferdinand advanced via Nienburg, Loccum, and Stadthagen, and the Erbprinz, together with Diepenbroick's corps, advanced up the left bank of the Weser on Minden, which was encircled by the Allies on 5 March 1758.[206]

[203]Translator's note: Brinkum is a municipality in the district of Leer, in Lower Saxony, Germany.

[204] Translator's note: Rothenburg ob der Tauber is a town in the district of Ansbach of Mittelfranken, the Franconia region of Bavaria, Germany. It is well known for its well-preserved medieval old town, a destination for tourists from around the world. It is part of the popular Romantic Road through southern Germany. Rothenburg was a Free Imperial City from the late Middle Ages to 1803.

[205] Translator's note: Hildesheim is a city in Lower Saxony, Germany with 104,230 inhabitants. It is in the district of Hildesheim, about 30 km (19 mi) southeast of Hanover on the banks of the Innerste River, a small tributary of the Leine River.

[206]Translator's Note: Loccum is a village situated about 50 km north west of Hanover in the district of Nienburg in Lower-Saxony, Germany. It has been a part of the city of Rehburg-Loccum since 1974. Stadthagen is the capital of the district of Schaumburg, in Lower Saxony, Germany. It is situated approximately 20 km east of Minden and 40 km west of Hanover. The city consists of the districts Brandenburg, Enzen-Hobbensen, Hörkamp-Langenbruch, Krebshagen, Obernwöhren, Probsthagen, Reinsen and Wendthagen-Ehlen. Earlier, there were also the districts

The Carabinier stood on outposts at Hille on the 6th, 7th, and 8th of March, and drove to Gohfeld on Dützen on the last day to watch the enemy's efforts, which seemed to have succeeded in destroying Minden.[207] The Duke of Holstein went on this day with a corps against Lübbecke. The Guards-grenadiers and Guards-Carabinier marched to Bückeburg, where an army of men and horses, trained in the depot at Stade, joined them. For the duration of the war, the number of the corps von Monkewitz commanded was determined at 100 mounted and 100 dismounted Carabinier.

On March 14th the corps marched against Bergkirchen to reinforce this post which had been attacked by the enemy.[208] As the corps approached, the enemy retreated, carrying along a captured officer of the Luckner Hussars. The Carabiniers followed him, and Lieutenant Baum was so happy to rescue the captured officer, knock down some enemies, and take booty of 3 horses. Minden surrendered to the Allies on this same day.

Duke Ferdinand then went through Bielefeld against Lippstadt and Münster, which places the enemy left on 23 March without resistance.[209] The Carabinier and Luckner Hussars covered the march of the army on the right flank, and, after passing through some shantytowns, arrived at Lingen on the 24th.[210]

On the 25th the Carabinier Corps crossed the Ems to Nordhorn in the Grafschaft Bentheim.[211] Here stood an Austrian command of a

---

Habichhorst, Bruchhof, Blyinghausen, Enzen and Hobbensen

[207] Translator's Note: Gohfeld is a place in the region of North Rhine-Westphalia in Germany. Dützen is a small village in the North-Rhine Westphalia region of modern Germany. It is on the road to Minden.

[208] Translator's Note: Bergkirchen is a municipality in the district of Dachau in Bavaria in Germany

[209] Translator's Note: Lippstadt is a town in North Rhine-Westphalia, Germany. It is the largest town within the district of Soest. Lippstadt is situated about 60 kilometres east of Dortmund, 40 kilometres south of Bielefeld and 30 kilometres west of Paderborn.

[210] Translator's Note: Lingen is a town in Lower Saxony, Germany.

[211] Translator's Note: Nordhorn is the district seat of Grafschaft Bentheim in Lower Saxony's southwestern most corner near the border with the Netherlands and the boundary with North Rhine-Westphalia. Grafschaft Bentheim or County of Bentheim is a district in Lower Saxony, Germany. It is bounded by (from the west and clockwise) the Dutch provinces of Overijssel and

captain and 100 men; von Monkewitz attacked it at once, knocked down
a few men, and made the captain, together with sixteen men of the Platz
regiment prisoner. The rest fled across the Vechte.[212]

On the 26th the corps moved against Bentheim. Captain von
Monkewitz reports:

Raid on Nordhorn.

*Four battalions of Austrians and two battalions of
French marched from Ostriesland against Wesel.[213] One
carried a transport of 400 wagons loaded with food,
which made for a very long train. The enemy had spent
the night in Bentheim, moving out two hours before my
arrival. As the enemy could only march slowly along
the rough roads, I immediately decided to go after him.
The foot Carabinier remained on display as a deception
towards the enemy; and a part of the horsemen whose
horses had been ailing from the bishop's incessant req-
uisitions had to remain here. At the village of Gildehaus, I attacked the enemy from the left side with great
shouting, cut down part of the escort, took 200 prisoners and almost all the wagons.[214] But as the terrain was*

Drenthe, the district of Emsland, and the districts of Steinfurt and Borken in North Rhine-Westphalia.

[212] Translator's Note: The Vechte is a river in Germany and the Netherlands. Its total length
is 182 km (113 mi), of which 107 km (66 mi) are on German soil. The Vechte originates in
Oberdarfeld in the German state of North Rhine-Westphalia near the city of Coesfeld and flows
north into the state of Lower Saxony, past the towns of Nordhorn and Emlichheim, across the
border and then westwards into the Dutch province of Overijssel (hence its alternate Dutch designation). There, it flows through the north part of the Salland region past Hardenberg and Om-
men, taking in the water of the Regge stream along the way. Close to the city of Zwolle, the river
suddenly bends north to end in confluence with the Zwarte Water river near the town of Hasselt.
The Vechte is probably the Vidrus mentioned by Ptolemy in his map of Magna Germania.

[213] Translator's Note: Ostfriesland or East Frisia is a coastal region in the northwest of the German federal state of Lower Saxony. It is the section of Frisia in between West Frisia and Middle
Frisia in the Netherlands and North Frisia in Schleswig-Holstein.

[214] Translator's Note: Gildehaus in Lower Saxony is a town located in Germany about 266 mi
(or 428 km) west of Berlin, the country's capital town.

very slippery, the wagons could not easily turn around, and the prisoners also crept in between the wagons, the result was a longer stay than I liked. The enemy now gained time to look over our strength, which did not amount to 70 horses, and had two closed battalions approach the entangled wagons, whereupon the prisoners again took up their rifles and fired at us. By this we were compelled to let our booty go. Nevertheless, it was still possible to bring 17 loaded carts and over 40 prisoners safely to Bentheim. All we had was a heavily wounded Carabinier (named Argener), who on this occasion proved himself as brave as I have been told of him for the whole war; I pursued the enemy, but without being able to harm him until Ahaus, seized the post, and drew the rest of my people from Betheim to me.[215]

As the army of the Duke of Brunswick advanced, troops of the Malakhovsk Prussian Hussars formed the outpost chain. They were first in Coesfeld, then in Schermbeck and Plettenberg.[216] The latter post was attacked by the enemy on April 5. Cornet von Berk made a stand there; however, he had been strengthened in the night by a detachment of Prussian hussars; they managed to drive the enemy back under the guns of Wesel. The Carabinier captured a horse. On the 15th, the entire enemy army had already pushed back across the Rhine, and the Allies had moved to cantonments in Münster. Captain von Monkewitz was giv-

---

[215] Translator's Note: Ahaus is a municipality in the district of Borken in the state of North Rhine-Westphalia, Germany. It is located near the border with the Netherlands, lying some 20 km south-east of Enschede.

[216] Translator's note: Schermbeck is a municipality in the district of Wesel, in North Rhine-Westphalia, Germany. Schermbeck is situated near the river Lippe, approx. 20 km east of Wesel, and 8 km north-west of Dorsten. Its maximum dilatation from north to south is about 12,90 km, from west to east it's about 17,80 km. Plettenberg is a town in the Märkischer Kreis, in North Rhine-Westphalia, Germany. Plettenberg is located to the east of the Sauerland hills. The highest elevation of the city area is in the *Ebbegebirge* with 663 m above sea level, the lowest elevation with 194 m near Teindeln. The city is spread out between the four valleys of the rivers Lenne, Else, Oester and Grüne.

en command of one hundred troopers, with thirty Bückeburgers, and a detachment consisting of the foot-Jäger of the corps, with which he was posted in and around Schermbeck to move on Wesel on the right side of the Lippe. He remained there until 1 May. The now Captain-Lieut. Baum stood against Reeß and Emmerich with the rest of the Carabinier.[217] When Duke Ferdinand, on 28 May, when the army was in motion, came from Monkewitz, who had now also attracted the rest of the Carabinier under Baum, to the division of the Hessian General von Wutgenau, who made a demonstration against Wesel, on the 31st, and then at Ringenberg, in the face of Wesel. The outposts under Monkewitz were at the height of the siege. Duke Ferdinand crossed the Rhine during the night of 2 June. On the 5th General von Wutgenau set off against Reeß, and at night accomplished the crossing of the Rhine on small ships, without being disturbed by the enemy, who, two hours out of it, stood by Xanthen with considerable power in the camp, but became aware of the passage of night.[218] On the 6th von Monkewitz reconnoitered the enemy camp at Xanthen, but on the same night he gave orders to recross the Rhine and to join the Hanoverian general von Spörcken. In the meantime, he (Spörcken) had been very pleased with the arrival of the light troops, as the enemy hussars from Wesel had shown themselves bold enough the day before to ride to his camp.

Battle at Hauinkel

No sooner had they been patrolling for an hour than they saw a strong enemy patrol made up of hussars on the road through Hauinkel

[217] Translator's note: Reeß is a town in the district of Cleves in the state of North Rhine-Westphalia, Germany. It is located on the right bank of the Rhine, approximately 20 km east of Cleves. Reeß is the oldest town in the lower Rhine area, being founded in 1228. Emmerich or Emmerich am Rhein meaning *Emmerich on the Rhine* (Low Rhenish and Dutch: *Emmerik*) is a town and municipality in the northwest of the German federal state of North Rhine-Westphalia.
[218] Translator's note: Xanthen or Xanten is a town in the state of North Rhine-Westphalia, Germany. It is located in the district of Wesel. Xanten is known for the Archaeological Park, one of the largest archaeological open air museums in the world, built at the site of the Roman settlements Colonia Ulpia Traiana. Other attractions include the medieval town center with Xanten Cathedral, many museums and large man-made lakes for various watersports activities.

towards Ringenberg.[219] Captain von Monkewitz approached the enemy patrol with 40 Carabiniers in the direction of Hauinkel, and was happy to ambush them and, after a furious resistance, completely annihilated them by making a lieutenant and 16 horsemen prisoners and cutting down 11 men so that no man escaped.

General von Spörcken moved with a part of his corps to Reeß on the 8th of June, while Monkewitz stopped by the Braunschweig General von Imhof, and did not follow General von Spörcken to Reeß until the evening of 9th, serving as the rear-guard Corps of von Imhof.

At Reeß a bridge had been thrown over the Rhine. The enemy had left the camp near Xanthen and moved into the fixed position of Rheinbergen.[220] General von Spörcken united on 10 June with the Duke's army, which went on to the camp on the Comsbecker Haide. The light corps of Monkewitz served as the advanced guards and in the evening fell on the rear guard of the enemy, who withdrew to Mors after the cannonade at Kloster Kampen.[221] They cut down several enemies and made some prisoners; a Carabinier patrol was surprised on this occasion. The corps of General von Spörcken, to which the Carabiniers belonged, remained standing with the army advancing in Mors to watch Wesel from this side. The Carabinier Corps formed the outposts at Büderich, Offenberg etc., until 27 June;[222] There were small skirmishes almost every day. Captain von Monkewitz, with half of his division, was with general von Imfhof, who stood by the shore on the right bank of the Rhine; Capt.-Lieut. Baum stayed with the rest in Büderich. The detachment of captain von Monkewitz took over the outposts of the small Imhof corps, consisting of only four battalions of infantry and

---

[219] Translator's note: Ringenberg is located in the region of Bavaria.

[220] Translator's note: Rheinberg is a town in the district of Wesel, in North Rhine-Westphalia, Germany. It is situated on the left bank of the Rhine, approx. 10 km (6.2 miles) north of Moers and 15 km (9.3 miles) south of Wesel

[221] Translator's note: Mors or Moers is a German city on the western bank of the Rhine. Moers belongs to the district of Wesel. Kloster Kampen was a monastery in area and the site of a battle between the allies and the French in 1760.

[222] Translator's note: Büderich is a town in northwestern Germany. It lies northwest of Düsseldorf along the Rhine. It is southwest of Krefeld and south of Moers. Ossenberg is a smaller town which has since been absorbed in the city of Düsseldorf.

one weak Hanoverian Dragoon Regiment. It remained in this condition until 15 July without any noteworthy activity, as the enemy behaved and remained quiet after the battle of Kreveldt.[223]

On the 16th, Captain von Monkewitz made a reconnaissance against Wesel at dawn and fired some swan shot at on an enemy patrol of eight hussars, two of whom went down and three he made prisoners.

Cornet von Berk led a sortie against Wesel on the 20th with two Carabiniers and there raided an enemy vidette, which stood near the fortress. At this time, it was reported that the Prince von Isenburg had been driven out of Hesse by the Marshal Broglie and that he had just taken possession of Kassel. At the same time the French army, under Marshal Contades, began to maneuver against Duke Ferdinand, who was in the region of Roermonde and Nuhs, in order to throw troops over the Rhine again.[224]

The French general Chevert, who had been defeated by the Allies at Dusseldorf, had countered by crossing over the Rhine at Cologne, had destroyed the Rhine bridge. He rapidly advanced against Wesel. General von Imhof, who in his position at Meer had covered the bridge of Reeß, the main connection with the army operating on the left bank of the Rhine, and at the same time their hospitals and war-magazines. He expected to be attacked by General Chevert. On 2 August, therefore, he sent orders to General von Zastrow, who was standing near Büderich, to immediately set out with his troops against Reeß, and pass the Rhine there, and attack him. The Rhine was between the two, and General von Zastrow having withdrawn to Reeß, could not reach this place, but had to march down to Grithausen, where he had the troops over-loaded in vehicles.[225] General von Imhof was brought to the fore by this circum-

---

[223] Translator's note: This is the spelling given in the original for the battle of Krefeld, fought on 23 June 1758. Ity is also spelled Crefeld and refers to a town in North Rhine-Westphlen.

[224] Translator's note: Roermonde is a city, a municipality, and a diocese in the southeastern part of the Netherlands. Roermond is an historically important town, on the lower Roer at the east bank of the Meuse river. It received town rights in 1231. Nuhs is a village on the outskirts of Roremonde.

[225] Translator's note: Grithausen may refer to Groothausen which is an old *Langwurtendorf* - a village on an artificially-built ridge - in the municipality of Krummhörn in western East Frisia on Germany's North Sea coast.

stance, and when captain von Monkewitz noticed from a attack made against Wesel, that the corps of Chevert passed the Lippe over the Flam bridge and encamped under the cannons of Wesel. In addition, reports from Reeß said general von Zastrow had not yet arrived. The Carabiniers stayed in a house at Comsfeld until 11 o'clock in the morning and patrolled the night against the abandoned camp by Meer.[226]

On the 5th of August, the engagement occurred at Meer.[227] Captain von Monkewitz reports on how it transpired as follows:

Battle of Meer

At dawn my fresh patrol came back from the Meer, announcing that there was still no sign of the enemy in the area. I reported this to General von Imhof, who informed me that, since General von Zastrow had arrived with the two battalions of Stolzenberg and the one of Prince of Prussia, he thought he would again assault the previous position by Meer, which is why I immediately set out to break up and take the old post again at Wildemannshof.[228] So I marched off, but sent two Carabiniers through Kloster Schledenhorst towards Hauinkel, with orders to stop at about 10 o'clock at the height of Hauinkel and observe from where they should then be disposed of.[229] At about 8 o'clock I arrived at my post, made a patrol against Luhrhase on the way to Wesel, and engaged in a demonstration of my posts. It was 9 o'clock

---

[226] Tranlator's note: What the author gives as Coesfeld is actually Coesfeld, the capital of the district of Coesfeld in the German state of North Rhine-Westphalia.

[227] Tranlator's note: Meer is a town in northwestern Germany. It is north of Göttigen and northwest of Magdeburg.

[228] Tranlator's note: This may be Wildemann is a town and a former municipality in the district of Goslar, in Lower Saxony, Germany. It has been part of the town Clausthal-Zellerfeld since January 1 2015. It is situated in the west of the Harz, northwest of Clausthal-Zellerfeld.

[229] Tranlator's note: This was a Cistercian monastery near Haldern. The monastery was located four kilometres southeast of Haldern. The site of the former monastery is now located in the area of the town of Rees in the North Rhine-Westphalian district of Kleve.

when I was told that a shot had been fired against Hau-
inkel, so I immediately sent coronet Berk with 10 horses
in that direction to investigate. The Dragoon Regiment
von Busch had already reached the camp. General von
Imhof had ordered the day before to place an officer with
fifty horses of this regiment under my command, as I had
complained that it was impossible for me to closely ob-
serve the enemy with my few men and to properly cover
the post. But these 50 horses had not yet arrived, and I
hurried to the commander of the regiment to demand the
detachment. As soon as I reached Colonel von Muller,
a Carabinier brought the news, the patrol sent to Hau-
inkel had returned with the report that the enemy was
in large numbers attacking my posts at Hauinkel. Im-
mediately I sent the Carabinier with the announcement
to General von Imhof, whose troops were just arriving
in the camp; but I for my part went to my people and
led them against Hauinkel. Not long before I spotted the
enemy and judged from the rising dust that Geneal Ch-
evert, with his whole corps, was marching against the
Meer. This conjecture was immediately confirmed by the
sight of 4 squadrons of cavalry and a strong platoon of
infantry by the Captain-Lieut. Baum. I left to report to
General v. Imhof, whereupon he met his dispositions to
receive the enemy properly. In the meantime, I got into
a sharp skirmish with the enemy's advance troops. Soon,
however, the 4 squadrons of enemy dragoons followed
by 1,000 volunteers, drove me back to a detachment of
Hessian grenadiers. The Hessians were at once violent-
ly attacked by the enemy, and, with the greatest effort,
after their captain had been shot dead by Buttlar. They
withdrew with considerable loss. Thereupon I received
orders to divide my corps and, for my part, to go half-
way against our left wing, to observe the road leading

from Wesel through Schledenhorst Abbey to Reeß, while Captain-Lieut. Baum moved with the other half against the right wing, to keep an eye on the path from Wesel to Bislich against Reeß.[230] Underneath, a massive cannon-ade erupted, causing our artillery to inflict significant damage on the enemy.

His intention was to cut us off from Reeß, so that he concentrated his chief power on his right wing in a grove which masked this movement; on his left wing he left only 3 battalions of the Swiss Regiment Salis. General von Imhof, guessing the purpose of the enemy, fell with the Hanoverian Regiment von Stolzenberg with such happy consequences onto the left flank of these Swiss, that they fled after a very hard-nosed resistance. As in the meantime the 2 battalions von Imhof had arrived, and the troops belonging to the Swiss fell, and threw them, this whole enemy left wing had been separated from the part of the corps-which moved ever further to the right-and was forced in the greatest haste to retreat via Luhrhase to Wesel.[231]

The Hessian regiment, Hereditary Prince, had a hard time of it, when, with the advance of our left wing, we came upon the bulk of the enemy who had climbed behind an old Landwehr. The regiment von Tolle, on the other hand, also arrived, and both brave regiments over-whelmed the position of the enemy with such impetuosity that the latter had to withdraw from the wood to Hau-inkel in the utmost haste and disorder. It was a pity that at the moment when the enemy left the wood and had to pass almost an hour and a quarter to gain the way to Hauinkel, there was not enough cavalry to follow him

---

[230] Bislich is a village in the North Rhine-Westphalian region of modern Germany.

[231] Translator's note: Luhrhase is the name of a village that has been swallowed up by the town of Borken in the modern state of Westphalia.

*on hand. However, with the little unit I led, I pursued it
to Hauinkel, and made over 200 prisoners and took 34
horses as booty. The enemy hastily retreated to Wesel.*

On that day, General von Imhof, had the honor of commanding
General Chevert, who commanded 14 battalions of infantry, 4 squadrons
of dragoons, and 1,000 volunteers on horseback, drawn from various
regiments, with 6 battalions (1 of Stolzenberg Hanoverians, 2 Brunswick von Imhof, 1 Hereditary Prince of Hesse, 1 Hessian von Tolle and
1 Saxon-Gotha) and included Bückeburger Carabinier Corps, which
numbered about 400 horses. The foot-Jäger of the Carabinier Corps,
while marching along the road from Wesel past Schledenhorst Abby
to Reeß, were given little to do, they had only one wounded man. The
Regiment of the Hereditary Prince suffered the most; it lost its colonel
von Schotten and the captain von Buttlar. It also counted 8 wounded
officers and 300 corporals and enlisted dead and wounded. The battalion
of Stolzenberg, which made the difference, lost only 13 men. The enemy
lost over 400 dead, about as many prisoners, 11 guns and many ammunition wagons. Two cannons and two ammunition wagons fell into the
hands of the Carabinier in front of Hauinkel, whose entire loss consisted of only three dead and two wounded horses. The corps remained
at Meer on the 6th and 7th of August, while the baggage of the army of
Duke Ferdinand began to cross the Rhine. The army itself followed this
movement on the 9th and 10th.

Count Wilhelm, on the other hand, had departed with this body:
Carabiner to the army of the Prince of Isenburg, and wrote among other
things to captain von Monkewitz on 21 August from Eimbeck: "Twenty
Carabinier who are with me have so frightened the whole Fischer Corps
that it fled at the highest speed; the manner in which this happened I
shall rejoice in telling the captain." Unfortunately, the author found
nothing in the papers about this most interesting event. What has been
preserved as legend is the following:

Attack on Hummen

Captain Reipe, who led the Leib-Carabinier, was stationed between Moringen and Abelpsen against Münster, and was given the task of going in the direction of Beckenhagen across the Weser, in order to indicate where possible, whether the enemy was moving against the Paderborn and Hörter.[232] At Bursfelde he crossed the Weser and made his way across Rheinhardt's forest towards Trendelnburg.[233] The inhabitants and charcoal-burners whom he met said that in the area, apart from a few hussars, nothing had yet been seen of the enemy. In Sababurg he learned that every afternoon an enemy patrol from Hofgeismar over Hummen rode against Trenddelnburg, but always their movements were accompanied by complete ease, since the Allied army no longer stood on this side of the Weser, and the patrol merely seemed intent to bring together a magazine in Trendelnburg, to hold the post their hostage and lay contributions there.[234]

Captain Reipe decided to pick up the patrol wherever possible, and lay down at noon the next day, after spending the night in the Rheinhardt forest, concealed in a hiding place near Hummen. A dismounted Carabinier had to go to the edge of the forest, where the route could be overlooked, to await the arrival of the patrol. Hardly half an hour had passed when the Carabinier reported the approach of the patrol, ap-

[232] Translator's note: Moringen is a town in the district Northeim, in the southern part of Lower Saxony, Germany. The town consists of the center Moringen and eight surrounding villages. Abelpsen is location of the modern concentration camp of Bergen-Belsen in lower-Saxony, Germany. Beckenhagen is now known as Eckenhagen in northern Germany. Hörter is near Paderborn. See Paderborn.

[233] Translator's note: Bursfelde is a village, now administratively joined with Hemeln as Bursfelde-Hemeln, in the northern part of Hann. Münden in the district of Göttingen, Lower Saxony, Germany. The village lies on the east side of the Weser River. Trendelnburg, now given as Trendelburg is a town in the district of Kassel, in Hesse, Germany. It is situated on the river Diemel, 29 km north of Kassel.

[234] Translator's note: The Sababurg, first called the Zappenburg, then Zapfenburg and today, after the Brothers Grimm fairy tale Sleeping Beauty Castle, is the ruin of a hill castle in the legendary Reinhardswald, a forested upland that runs through the North Hessian county of Kassel. Sababurg is also the name of a district of the town of Hofgeismar in which the castle is found. Hofgeismar is a town in the district of Kassel, in northern Hesse, Germany. It is located 25 km north of Kassel. Hummen is a small village in the vicinity of Hofgeismar.

parently ten horses strong. Everything concerning the ambush was set; from the concealed points one could see just about the distance of 20 steps. In the short exchange of fire, the enemy patrol approached without looking back, and Reipe now burst out of his hiding place like lightning. The enemy tried to turn around; but Reipe had already blocked the way for him. Then a corporal shouted: "Donnerwetter, sir, there are still some men!" Without thinking, Reipe rode around the horse, noting that the supposed patrol was actually the advanced elements of a column of Fischer's corps still in the defile.

The party we cut off was sloppy in their attempt to escape to Hummen and did not bother any more about those who were left behind. Reipe, however, plunged into the fore of the superior hostile column of riders, because they could no longer dodge, so they started off with furious cries. Then the Fischer Corps panicked, one heard no clear orders among them. Everyone drew their horses around and rushed wildly towards Grebenstein.[235] The Carabiniers cut down some in the backcountry, and as soon as the disorder got under way, Reipe, without forfeiting a man, quickly retreated into the Rheinhardt forest, and happily returned the same evening across the Weser.

When, as a result of the events in Upper Hesse and Marshal Contades' immediate superiority, the Allied army was compelled to make a retreat, in order to obtain the reinforcements expected from England, the Carabiniers were with the rear guard, and passed by various easy marches in the withdrawal from Wesel. Meanwhile, Marshal Contades had crossed the Rhine and had taken up a camp on the left bank of the Lippe.

On the 22nd of August, the Carabiniers rode madly on the Cösfeld highway towards Wesel.[236] At daybreak the enemy attempted to attack the corps field guard, which also succeeded in taking two horses from it. He seemed to be content with this, as he hurried from Monkewitz to

---

[235] Translator's note: Grebenstein is a town in the district of Kassel, in Hesse, Germany. It is located 16 km northwest of Kassel on the German Timber-Frame Road. In 1762 it was the scene of a skirmish between British and French troops during the Seven Years' War.

[236] Translator's note: Coesfeld is a Kreis in the northwestern part of North Rhine-Westphalia, Germany, west of the city of Münster. Neighboring districts are Steinfurt, district-free Münster, Warendorf, district-free Hamm, Unna, Recklinghausen, Borken.

Hülse, exhausting the two horses, slaughtering a few more Hussars, and making two prisoners.

Until 6 September the corps was in and around Tungerloh under the command of the general Count of Kielmannsegge and made in this time various strikes and recalls against Wesel and Bockholt.[237]

Kühner: Coup of two Carabinier

The enemy, however, had continued to pull himself up the Lippe, and as they wished to find out whether the enemy army in Hesse had already moved towards Paderborn, two Carabiniers, Salenzkn and Schaper, went through Senne on the 8th against the Lippischer forest with the order, "if possible to collect news of the enemy and thus proceed as far as possible in the direction of Hörter."[238] Familiar with all the boundaries, roads and paths of the area, they arrived at the Wierborner Kruges in the vicinity of Blomberg at midday, without finding anything of the enemy. As they walked around a corner, they saw six French cavalry horses tethered close to the box. The host stood in the doorway, recognized the uniform of the Carabiniers, and jumped at them with the expression: "Men, you must go!" These, however, had quickly made up their minds, and Galenzkh asked the landlord softly: "Do they hide behind or in the front?"

"Back," he replied.

Slowly they both rode up to the house: Galenzkh jumped from his horse, his bridle up, his sword in his fist, receiving a brief instruction to pay attention to the door. Galenzkh drew one of the six horses, while the trembling host told him that the six dragoons were sitting behind a long table in a row, and that the table stood right at the door.

---

[237] Translator's note: Tungerloh-Capellen is in the region of North Rhine-Westphalia is located in Germany - some 273 mi (or 439 km) West of Berlin. Bockholt is situated in Recklinghausen, Munster, Nordrhein-Westfalen, Germany.

[238] Translator's note: The Senne is a natural region of moorland and sand dunes in the Regierungsbezirk of Detmold, in the state of Nordrhein-Westfalen in west-central Germany. It lies to the west of the Teutoburger Forest and has an area of approximately 210 km 2. It borders the Lippischer Forest.

Calmly, Galenzkh now took the pistols, let three balls loose, hung the sword on Faustgelk, gave a brief instruction to the innkeeper, and entered the house behind him with a tense gait. Softly the host opened the door; a look convinced Galenzkh that the enemies were in the position they were in. He cocked the pistols and fired three shots in a moment! - Three enemies collapsed in the blink of an eye, and at the same moment Galenzkh sprang into the room, shouting loudly. One of the enemies wanted to go out of the door beside him, he cut him down, the other two fell to their knees and said: "Pardon!" - what became them? They had to drop their sabers and come to the door, where Schaper was waiting attentively at the exit. As quickly as possible, the two prisoners now had to fix the saddles and again take each two horses by the hand and off they went. On the 13th, these Carabiniers and their prisoners happily returned to the corps, which on that day, was marching on to Lippstadt, they entered Telgte.

On September 16th, the Carabinier entered Lippstadt, and came under the command of General von Hardenberg.

On the 17th, Captain von Monkewitz went out with 18 Carabiniers to familiarize himself with the roads and the paths on the left bank of the Lippe down to Hamm. Colonel von Böhm, chief of the Bückeburg Grenadier Regiment, rode with him, but he would soon regret the decision: for on reaching Hoverstadt a large detachment of about 300 horses of enemy light cavalry was discovered. Captain von Monkewitz thus decided to retreat. But as the enemy had at the same time discovered the Carabinier, and their strength in the open country was overlooked, he plunged upon them. The Carabinier, however, were still very well mounted at the time, therefore the enemy could not do much. Only the colonel of Böhm became entangled to some extent with the enemy; to save him caused so much confusion that the enemy had to fight openly with the Carabinier. Lester, on the other hand, happily cut off, lost only one Carabinier, whose horse became entangled, and took captive a hussar.

Brave behavior of the Sergeant Hirsch

On 21 September Sgt. Hisrsch - we know him already from Burgdamm with four Carabinier from Lippstadt - went to requisition a few carriages from the Colonel Sauerland. He came to Aurüchte, 21/2 hours from Lippstadt, went to the local council; demanded the carriages and also inquired about the enemy, about whom one did not want to let on that they knew anything there.[239] The constable wished that he sent the Carabinier to the village to drive the peasants so that they would quickly be made jumpy. This happened, and Sergeant Hisrch, invited by the builder himself, entered the house and tied his horse to the threshing floor. In the meantime, the matter was betrayed to a nearby enemy detachment, and without the sergeant being aware of it at first, about 100 enemy hussars rode up in front of the house; Hirsch hardly had time to close it. The enemy hussars clamored to surrender, a shot that struck one of their officers was the answer, and Hirsch quickly reloaded the rifle, and made three more shots at the enemy, a mere carbine fire against the great house guard behind which a stag stood, where he at last got a deadly shot, and fell down. Only now did some hostile hussars take off, the seized the sergeant, plundered him, and left him lying dead. On the following morning he was taken to Lippstadt by a detachment of Carabinier, who had been sent to visit him, where he died the third day afterward. The four Carabinier captured the enemy in the village. The enemy understood his craft very badly on this occasion. If he had surrounded the house with some hussars and let them break through the side doors of the farmhouse and let them penetrate through the windows, so the sergeant got way lightly and all the banging against the big door of the house fell away.

On 22 September, the corps received reinforcements of 76 foot-Jäger, increasing its strength to 250 heads, now called the Carabinier and Jäger Corps. At the same time, Count Wilhelm sent to the Captain von Monkewitz and the Capt.-Lieut. Baum for the honorable behavior

---

[239] Translator's note: The village of Aurüchte appears to have since been overtaken by the town of Lippstadt.

shown at the meeting at Meer each a richly ornamented silver sword. To the cornet von Berk he sent a beautiful horse, since his had been lost at Meer, and 200 Louis d'or for distribution to the remainder of the corps.[240]

On the 24th of September a patrol of 20 men from the Carabinier at Effel, between Lippstadt and Rühden, was attacking, but they bravely multiplied, and fired on their several enemies, so that they finally succeeded, with the loss of 1 dead and 4 prisoners, to get through.[241]

Marshall Contades camped in the area of Luehnen, on the left bank of the Lippe, and sent General Chevert against Hesse, in favor of the Prince de Soubise, because, after the unification of the corps of General Oberg with the Prince of Isenburg, he was compelled to retire to Kassel.[242]

General Chevert moved before Lippstadt on 30 September and camped, his light troops extended as far as the Lippstadt first foraging local sheep, then advancing. A field guard of the enemy was bold enough to cling to the heights of Erwitte, where they could be reached by small arms fire from the fortress.[243]

On 1 October, following a local battle, the Carabinier drove out the above-mentioned field guard as well as the enemy light troops in Overhagen.[244] Captain Baum had his horse wounded in this action.

---

[240] Translator's note: Louis d'or refers to gold louis, French coins.

[241] Translator's note: Here, the author seems to be referring to the Eifel mountain region. This is a low mountain range in western Germany and eastern Belgium. It occupies parts of southwestern North Rhine-Westphalia, northwestern Rhineland-Palatinate and the southern area of the German-speaking Community of Belgium. Here, the author seems to be referring to Rahden, which is a town in the far north of North Rhine-Westphalia between Bielefeld and Bremen and between Hanover and Osnabrück. Rahden is part of the Minden-Lübbecke District in East Westphalia-Lippe

[242] Translator's note: This seems to refer to Lünen which is a town in North Rhine-Westphalia, Germany. It is located north of Dortmund, on both banks of the River Lippe. It is the largest town of the Unna district and part of the Ruhr Area.

[243]Translator's note: Erwitte is a town in the district of Soest, in North Rhine-Westphalia, Germany. It is situated approximately 8 km south of Lippstadt.

[244] Translator's note: Overhagen is a town in North Rhine-Westphalia and is southeast of Kirchhellen and southwest of Kuhberg.

General Chevert set out against Hesse on 2 October; but the Count de St. Germain, who led the second division of the corps of Chevert, moved in front of Lippstadt, and only marched on the 5th against Hesse. The Carabinier followed the enemy on their march, disquieting his rear guard, and returned to Lippstadt late in the night with 63 prisoners and six cartloads of captured baggage.

On the 7th of October the corps moved to Benninghausen in the direction of Söst in order to reconnoiter it.[245] Here they encountered a hostile patrol of 1 officer and 20 hussars of the Regiment Turpin, attacked them immediately, took the officer with 10 hussars and caught a few men, and pursued the fleeing remnant to Hovestadt.[246]

Duke Ferdinand crossed the Lippe at Benninghausen on 16 October to receive General de Chevert, who was returning from Hesse, if the latter ventured into the Lippstadt plain. But this man turned against the Köllnische Sauerland and marched over Rühden against Arensberg.[247]

Captain von Monkewitz was ordered to advance with his corps, and 200 horses under his command, against Rühden, to observe General Chevert. On the 20th of October. He made contact with enemy reconnaissance at various points, with some prisoners being made. The corps was badly mauled by a force under Master Hille. On the 21st, 100 horses

[245] Translator's note: Benninghausen is situated in Rheinisch-Bergischer Kreis, Koln, Nordrhein-Westfalen, Germany. The second location likely refers to modern Soest, Germany. Soest is a district in the middle of North Rhine-Westphalia, Germany. Neighbouring districts are Warendorf, Gütersloh, Paderborn, Hochsauerland, Märkischer Kreis, Unna and the independent town of Hamm.

[246] Translator's note: Hoverstadt is situated in Soest, Arnsberg, Nordrhein-Westfalen.

[247] Translator's note: Sauerland, is a region North Rhine-Westphalia , northwestern Germany. It is bounded on the north by the Ruhr River and its tributary, the Möhne, and on the south by the Sieg River and the Wester Forest, a mountainous area east of the Rhine. It lies to the east of the Bergisches Land (plateau) and has historically centered on the city of Arensberg. Its name (meaning "Bitter Land") is allegedly derived from the fierce resistance of its Saxon inhabitants against Charlemagne and the Franks, but it may refer to the relatively poor soil and often rugged hilly terrain. Arnsberg, city, North Rhine–Westphalia *Land* (state), western Germany. It lies along a loop of the Ruhr River, east of Iserlohn Situated between wooded mountains and known as the Pearl of the Sauerland (southern land of Westphalia), Arnsberg is a popular spa and summer resort. The city originated in the 11th century around a castle of the counts of Werl and was chartered in 1238.

from this division were supposed to be part of the General Chevert's column and move on the area of Meschede. On this day the Carabinier and Jäger, who had been captured earlier and exchanged, attacked the corps, which they drove into Lippstadt on the 22nd.

Capt.-Lt. Baum was sent down to the right side of the Lippe on October 23, to collect news, to learn if the enemy was trying something against Munster. On the 24th the report came in from him. The enemy, after a very difficult fight, and at the expense of three Carabiniers, had forced him out of his position and had forced him to retreat to Wahrendorf.[248] At the same time General von Kielmannsegge reported that the enemy was at Herben, where he was encamped, but had returned to Munster. As a result of this news, Duke Ferdinand's army retreated on the Lippe on October 25, and Gen. von Imhof retreated the same night against Münster, around this place against the French General d'Armentieres, who advanced against Contrades' army. Capt.-Lt. Baum was attached to the corps of the general von Imhof and arrived in Lippstadt on 1 November. Concerning the locations of the Carabinier: all detachments outside Lippstadt were pulled into the fortress on the 17th and the army made preparations to go into winter quarters. The enemy had retaken all of Hesse with the exception of Marburg Castle.[249] Marshal Contades had his army on the other side of the Rhine in winter quarters, and his light troops in Bergisch, standing between the Ruhr and the Rhine.[250]

---

[248] Translator's note: Warendorf is a town in North Rhine-Westphalia, Germany, and capital of Warendorf District.

[249] Translator's note: The Marburger Schloss (Marburg castle), a.k.a. Landgrafenschloss Marburg, is a castle in Marburg, Hesse, Germany, located on top of Schlossberg. Built in the 11th century as a fort, it became the first residence of Landgraviate of Hesse.

[250] Translator's note: Bergish likely refers to modern Bergisch Gladbach, is a city in the Cologne/Bonn Region of North Rhine-Westphalia, Germany, and capital of the Rheinisch-Bergischer Kreis.

Chapter 3

Campaign of 1759

The French try a raid on Herneburg. Captain-Lieutenant Baum pursues the enemy. Captain von Monkewitz performs a daring partisan attack. Battle at Lippstadt. The enemy lifts the blockade of Lippstadt and launches an attack on Numburg as a result of the Battle of Minden. Captured letter about the Battle of Minden. Fight at Lünen an der Lippe, Carabinier are sitting down to defend the flood passage until the infantry has moved out. Skirmish at Klein Durtmund. Raid of Dorsten. Battle of Notteln near Münster. Battle at Dülmen.

The Carabinier and Jäger Corps belonged to the corps of the Duke of Holstein and came to Werl for the duration of the winter quarters, from there Cornet von Berk was dispatched to Unna.[251] The corps remained in these cantons until 23 January 1759 and spent that time on the restoration of its manpower and equipment for the next campaign. Reinforcements arrived in camp along with horses, and Captain-Lieutenant Baum went to Bückeburg to carry out the enormous task of recruiting and resupplying the force, but especially to put the remounts in order, as some bad horses had been sent to the corps.

On the 24th of January the corps was ordered to move to Recklinghausen to form the outpost of the Lünen position, which, as Monkewitz quite naively expresses, wished to see quiet.[252] Numerous light troops of the enemy stood in the area of Dorsten.[253] The next support-

[251] Translator's note: Werl is a town located in the district of Soest in North Rhine-Westphalia, Germany. Unna is in the North Rhine-Westphalia district of North Germany and is the seat of the Unna district.

[252] Translator's note: Recklinghausen is the northernmost city in the Ruhr-Area and the capital of the Recklinghausen district. It borders the rural Münsterland. Lünen is a town in North Rhine-Westphalia, Germany. It is located north of Dortmund, on both banks of the River Lippe. It is the largest town of the Unna district and part of the Ruhr Area.

[253] Translator's note: Dorsten is situated on the western rim of Westphalia bordering the Rhineland. Its historical old town lies on the south bank of the river Lippe and the Wesel–Datteln

ing detachment of the Carabinier Corps was in Lünen, which was open and accessible everywhere.[254] Under these circumstances he saw Captain von Monkewitz approaching for ideas about his expedient situation with General von ... commanding Lünen. The latter, however, without taking any notice of the circumstances, replied: "That is none of my business, you should go to Recklinghausen, the duke has ordered." Captain von Monkewitz now turned to General von Imhof, commander of all the outposts. He replied: "It is true that the militia of the Duke see the Carabiniers serving up the outposts in front of Lünen; Recklinghausen alone was never mentioned. It would be foolish to send troops there posturing under the prevailing circumstances. On the contrary, the Duke had expressly ordered that Monkewitz should choose himself the post." According to this, the captain wanted to take Herneburg, where a castle was located, which one could possibly value. Here the corps stood until the beginning of June. [255]

Duke Ferdinand had meanwhile departed in March with the greater part of the army for Hesse. General von Spörcken led the troops in Westphalia.

On 3 March, Kapt.-Lieut. Baum engaged part of an enemy detachment in Buer, and brought in eight captured Hussars de Turpin.[256] On 7 March, two Carabiniers patrolling Mesterholte were captured by the enemy.[257] In addition, at that time the corps still had frequent skirmishes with the enemy. By 3 April, he had captured some 30 enemy hussars, losing only one Carabinier dead and one captured.

On April 13, the Battle of Bergen occurred, after which Duke Ferdinand was compelled to return to Kassel.

Canal and was granted city rights in 1251.

[254] Translator's note: In the original text, the author gives the French Soutien, which I have translated roughly as detached units.

[255] Translator's note: This may refer to the town of Herrenberg, which is a town in the middle of Baden-Württemberg, about 30 km south of Stuttgart and 20 km from Tübingen.

[256] Translator's note: Today Buer is the largest suburb of Gelsenkirchen in North Rhine-Westphalia.

[257] Translator's note: This may refer to Mastholte, which is a city in Germany in the region of North Rhine-Westphalia.

Defense of Herneburg

On the night of 28 April, an enemy detachment near the post of Herneburg tried to invade. In spite of Herneburg's heavy patrolling, they managed to sneak undetected to one of the corps' advanced posts and blast it, killing three Jäger with the bayonet. But as the Jäger gave fire, noise arose in other places; the corps had been on the march through the night. At the first alarm, it was instantly in flight. The cavalry moved out immediately towards the enemy, while the Jäger held the castle. The enemy saw his plan undone and withdrew under the shadow of darkness.

As soon as the day dawned, Capt.-Lt. Baum with 40 mounted troops traced the enemy's trail and caught him between Herten and Buer.[258] Notwithstanding the difficult terrain intersected with hedges and ditches, which the enemy admirably uses, Baum did not hesitate for long, but threw himself resolutely upon the enemy. He fought bravely and was able to break up the enemy force, cut down one part, make 12 prisoners, and chase the remainder all the way to Buer. The enemy hussars immediately seized the escape as they discovered Baum's arrival. The Carabiniers severely wounded two men and injured a horse.

On May 3, Sergeant Hille patrolled with four Carabiniers against Westerholte, and was attacked there by the enemy, on which occasion a Carabinier was taken prisoner and a horse was scared off.[259]

Raid on Buer

On the very same day the enemy had occupied Buer strongly, and Captain von Monkewitz made an attempt at driving him out of it, which was also completely successful. On the 4th at 10 o'clock Monkewitz fell in with 60 horses in front of Buer. These were followed immediately by two peasant carts with 6 horses, with ladders and boards thrown off. At the back of the cart a strong round piece of wood was

---

[258] Translator's note: Herten is a town and a municipality in the district of Recklinghausen, in North Rhine-Westphalia.
[259] Translator's note: Westerholt is a municipality in the district of Wittmund, in Lower Saxony.

attached to give them the look of a gun. Another, also six-horse farmer's cart with some old boxes packed, introduced a miniature car. Forty foot-Jäger surrounded the carts, same as would be expected to guard a regular convoy. That's how we arrived near Buer. The enemy sentinels moved on, after which they gave fire on an enemy rider-evidently an officer-sprang out of the valley and watched the detachment approaching at a respectful pace. About 300 paces from the place, on the right hand of the road, an open field was found.

At the trot, the faux-artillery went away behind the Carabiniers who were forming, in an open field, and proceeded to ride off, by removing the nail in the tree-trunk; the wagon chased back with the horses; the Jäger jumped to the reins of the ammunition cart and drove sideways at some distance the guns. All of this happened in the blink of an eye. Until then, the enemy rider had watched quietly. But now he burst into the town in a hurry, and his work was the signal for the formal escape of the picket in front of the place. That was what Monkewitz had been waiting for. Reining and cheering, he threw himself on the enemy, penetrated the village and cleaved everything that came in the way. The fright and disorder of the enemy were limitless; No one thought of the defense; Everyone and everything crowded on the road to Bröttrup, and the Carabiniers cut down a significant number of the enemy without suffering even the slightest loss.[260] The pursuit stopped only half an hour from Buer. The Jäger had meanwhile - with their faux-artillery - gone back to Bernburg and rejoined Hevten to be able to take up with the cavalry. With 8 officers and 56 men whom his troops captured, von Monkewitz returned to Herneburg on 4 May late in the evening.

With all the other remarks about this truly brilliant feat of arms, one can not but recommend this example of prudence, determination, and proper consideration of the possibilities to each officer of the light troops.

---

[260] Translator's note: Today Bröttrup is a city in the   North Rhine–Westphalia Land (state), northwestern Germany. It lies at the northern edge of the Ruhr industrial region, on the Rhine-Herne Canal, northwest of Essen. Although it was mentioned in the Middle Ages, it remained a small peasant community until coal was discovered there in the latter part of the 19th century.

On the return to Herneburg, Captain von Monkewitz found a reinforcement of 130 of Scheiter's Jäger there, who surrendered to his command and remained there until the 25th of May, during which time nothing substantial occurred. The patrols went against the Ruhr and Lippe, and against Wesel, they exchanged shots now and then with the enemy. The headquarters of Duke Ferdinand had meanwhile reached the area of Unna via Lippstadt.

On 25 May, the hereditary prince of Brunswick took over the command of the forward light troops and established his headquarters in Unna. On the same day the Scheiter Jäger bivouacked in Herneburg but were replaced by the Bückeburg Lieb-Grenadiers and Leib-Carabiniers.

Count Wilhelm had come to the army at Westphalen, and on May 30 visited his troops, which were then quartered in Herneburg. Loud and heartfelt expressions of joy issued from the small gathering when they saw the beloved, even worshiped father of the country in their midst. He bestowed upon the corps his most perfect affection, with its glorious conduct, as proved at every opportunity.

On the very same day the Erbprinz of Brunswick wrote to Captain von Monkewitz: "The same will try to find out: 1) if there is still a camp at Busicjk. 2) where actually the headquarters of Monsieur d'Armentiéres is; this was a few days ago in Dusseldorf, but should, according to my news, be again in Wesel. As soon as you get some certainty about this, give me a message."

Following the news and patrols taken by Captain von Monkewitz, the Erbprinz was moved to undertake an expedition to Elberfeld and set off on the evening of 3 June from Unna with about 3,000 men.[261] The most successful attack carried out by the hereditary prince on the following morning at 4 a.m. is described by Tempelhof extensively and can be read there.[262] The Carabiniers were not present and only Capt. Lt. Baum and four Carabinier served as leaders of the column, as they knew every sidewalk in the country. The Erbprinz showed them his particular

---

[261] Tranlator's Note: Elberfeld is a municipal subdivision of the German city of Wuppertal; it was an independent town until 1929.

[262] Translator's note: See Tempelhoff, *Geschichte des siebenjährigen Krieges.*

satisfaction with the way they had handled their mission.

Meanwhile, Captain von Monkewitz moved with the Carabi-nier and Jäger Corps to Dortmund and stayed there until the return of the Erbprinz on 8 June. The Corps then assumed the rear guard of the Erbprinz forces. It moved on the 13th with the main corps to Rühden. Meanwhile the duke's army began to move against Bühren; they set up a camp there on the same day, and united with the generals of Wutgene-au and Imhof.[263]

The French army under Marshal Contades, who was following this general on foot, also arrived in Stadtbergen on the 13th of June, but crossed the Diemel on the 14th and took up a position with his right wing anchored on the forest, stretching from Dalheim to Meerdorf, with the left in the forest anchored on Essen.[264] The Fischer corps was at Brilon.[265] The Lieb-grenadiers and Leib-Carabinier had separated from the corps on 10 June to serve at the headquarters where Count Wilhelm had his command. The Carabinier Corps united with 4 squadrons of Prussian hussars. A newly arrived Bückeburg battery moved to the Duke's camp on 15 June; the light troops had occupied Rühden on the Elbe, and these days they were making some prisoners in the Kaltenhaard area.[266] Mar-shal Contades elected to take the opportunity for battle offered to him and maneuvered against Paderborn. This prompted Duke Ferdinand to leave the camp of Bühren on 19 June to go back through Lippstadt and make a stand at Rittberg. Captain von Monkewitz commanded the rear guard until Lippstadt and arrived there on the evening of the same day and was commanded to remain with the corps at the garrison of this place.

On 21 June, the enemy showed up near Lippstadt. The von Monkewitz's Corps advanced, engaged with the enemy for a while, and

---

[263] Tranlator's note: Bühren (Low German: Bahren) is a municipality in the district of Göttingen, in Lower Saxony, Germany.

[264] Tranlator's note: Stadtbergen is a town in the district of Augsburg, in Bavaria, Germany. It is situated in the outskirts of Augsburg, 4 kilometres (2.5 mi) west of Augsburg city center.

[265] Tranlator's note: Brilon is a town in North Rhine-Westphalia, that belongs to the Hochsau-erlandkreis.

[266] Translator's note: Kaltenhaard is in Soest, Arnsberg, Nordrhein-Westfalen.

drove them away with only two horses lost. The enemy lost a hussar and three horses killed.

On 22 June, the Corps passed away from Lippstadt. It drove the enemy out of West Kotten, killed an unknown number of men, and made 8 prisoners.[267]

A hostile party had passed over the Lippe during the night and plundered the English hospital in Lipperode. On the 23rd of June a part of the Carabinier had to leave to oppose the enemy. But he had gained such a good advantage that he was not caught up.[268]

On the 25th of June Capt.-Lt. Baum with 16 Carabinier and just as many Jäger of the corps posted at Stromberg, to observe the area between the Lippe and Münster.[269] Until the 29th they were quite restless in Lippstadt; "The enemy, Captain von Monkewitz says, raved about because there were bloody heads every day."

Battle at Lippstadt

On the afternoon of June 30," says von Monkewitz in the corps' diary, "a strong enemy detachment approached Borke, drove out the workers employed there by the engineer from the Bückeburg contingent, Major von Römer, and drove off some of the garrison's cattle. I had to leave immediately with the corps, and the commanding General von Hardenberg promised to support me through a detachment of volunteers. I set off after the enemy in a strong detachment, that my retreat was in any case assured by the detachment mentioned above, but, with all due caution, left the foot-Jäger of the corps between Lippstadt and Lipperode in a good position. The cattle were chased

---

[267] Tranlator's note: West Kotten is now the western portion of Solingen, Dusseldorf, Nordrhein-Westfalen.

[268] Translator's note: Lipperode is a town in Regierungsbezirk Arnsberg (North Rhine-Westphalia).

[269] Translator's note: Stromberg is a town in the district of Bad Kreuznach, in Rhineland-Palatinate, Germany. It is situated on the eastern edge of the Hunsrück.

away from the enemy and thrown back to the Haide of Lipperode. In the meantime, however, a strong division of the enemy between Lipperode and the Lippe had penetrated, and threw back my foot-Jäger, together with the detachment that had arrived at the soutia, for the city. Major von Römer was with me when fire began in our back; I sent a Carabinier to see how it was while we were in the midst of the Haider, Lipperode right in our backs. The Carabinier soon returned with the news that; the enemy had thrown the brigades into the fortress and heavily infested the way with infantry.

Major von Römer and I resolved to make our way back to Lippstadt with our sabers in our fists. The enemy we had before us seemed to have had enough of it and fled towards Mettinghausen.[270] I let Apell blow the horn and commenced the march into the ordeal in due course; but soon we became aware that 300 grenadiers had already reportedly prepared for our arrival and had thus posted themselves behind some ditches and hedges and that it was considered impossible to get through here. Likewise, a group of enemy hussars and dragoons penetrated from Lipperode towards our left flank. Now the horses had to do their best. Strade went over hedges and ditches in the direction of Sauerlage and Kappeln, and though the enemy's cavalry were rather better than ours, they were not able to jump over the empty ditch we followed to the road that leads from Rhede to Lippstadt.[271] We were happy to reach the fortress again, having lost more than 2 dead, 4 wounded and 2 horses.

---

[270] Translator's note: Mettinghausen is a town in the North Rhine-Westphalia region of Germany.
[271] Translator's note: Kappeln is a town in the district of Schleswig-Flensburg, in Schleswig-Holstein, Germany. It is situated on the north bank of the Schlei, approx. 30 km northeast of Schleswig, and 35 km southeast of Flensburg. Sauerlage seems to be a smaller village near Kappeln. Rhede is a municipality in the district of Borken in the state of North Rhine-Westphalia, Germany. It is located near the border with the Netherlands, approximately 5 km east of Bocholt.

Enemy Raid on Stromberg

On 1 July the enemy succeeded in surprising Capt.-Lieut. Baum, who had been posted to Stromberg. The enemy sent out patrols and Baum knew nothing of the enemy's attack, which so surprised one of the outwitted sentries they did not have the chance to get off a shot. The enemy was about 200 men strong, and only with great difficulty did Capt.-Lieut. Baum, succeed in breaking through with 18 men and reaching Lippstadt. At this point he knew nothing of the pardon which had been offered him. The enemy had shot dead two Carabinier and a Jäger, a sergeant, 5 Carabinier and 7 Jäger were wounded, and taken 13 horses.

Battle at Lipperode

On July 14, the day the Lippstadt corps moved to hunt down the enemy patrols who swarmed ever closer. The enemy now stood strong on the right side of the Lippe. They had gained the upper hand by the large number of his light troops deployed in front of Lippstadt, and since the incident at Stromberg the Carabinier had again sustained losses of several men and horses wounded. Captain von Monkewitz positioned himself with the foot-Jäger in Lipperode, Baum with the Carabinier right against the Lippe at a good vantage point. A patrol of 1 corporal, and 4 Carabinier, who were well-mounted, was sent to Mettinghausen. As soon as the enemy discovered the patrol, his strong field guard stalked them. The patrol fled, and so happy was the hapless enemy, that Baum, slipping into their left flank, slashed before the enemy came to their senses. A party collapsed; the other was driven against Lipperode, where von Monkewitz received it. Of the whole field guard, which was forty horses strong, only two men escaped; the officer and 16 riders lay dead in the elector's camp, the rest with an officer fell, partly wounded, into the hands of the Carabinier. The Carabinier and Jäger had 2 dead and 3 wounded, along with 2 wounded horses.

On 17 July, the corps retired at night to watch out for the enemy patrols that used to go against Westkotten and back.[272] Capt.-Lieutenant Baum went with the half of the corps against the former, von Monkewitz with the rest towards the lesser place. At dawn the enemy came upon Baum's party, and attacked them with great determination, and resolve, since, as they learned afterwards, the enemy had received news of Baum's posturing from a peasant. The attack wounded 3 Carabinier and 3 horses. In addition, they caught and forced two Jäger of Baum's to retreat. But as Monkewitz immediately became aware of it when the fire began in the direction of Westkotten. Monkewitz concluded from the time that the enemy was playing the attacker and withdrew himself confidently towards Baum's line of retreat and took it up. Until July 28th, the corps remained on this side outside Lippstadt, where there was daily skirmishing with the enemy.

On 30 July, the enemy General d'Armentieres arrived in front of Lippstadt to besiege the place and completed the encirclement on 1 August. A strong cannonade was also heard on this day in the face of Bielefeld, "about which", says von Monkewitz, "we broke our heads very much, as we had learned of it shortly before the removal to Minden, as the Duke Ferdinand marched in the direction of Stolzenau."[273]

Rearguard battle of Böcke

On the 3rd of August, when it became clear at daybreak that all the enemy's camps had been abandoned, General von Hardenberg gave the order to the captain von Monkewitz to go out at once to ascertain the cause of this apparition. "As soon as," says von Monkewitz, "I approached Lipperode, several French deserters came to meet me, whom I asked about the cause of the sudden departure of their army; they gave me the good news of the victory of our army, which had been won at

---

[272] Translator's note: Westkotten did not turn up in any searches. It may have been a small town or village whose name has since changed or it has been swallowed up by a larger urban area.

[273] Translator's note: Stolzenau is a municipality in the district of Nienburg, in Lower Saxony, Germany. It is situated on the left bank of the Weser, approx. 20 km southwest of Nienburg, and 25 km northeast of Minden.

Minden and Sohfeld the day before yesterday. I immediately sent the deserters to General von Hardenberg and informed him of my intention to engage the enemy a little, where possible. In front of Böcke I met the retreating enemy near Paderborn, and without hesitation entered it, and by the afternoon I continued my descent, taking every opportunity to defeat the enemy, and returned with 109 prisoners, 14 dray horses and 3 covered ambulance cars back to Lippstadt." On 4 August the Carabinier Corps again advanced after the enemy in the direction of Böcke and Neuhaus, and observed its march against Paderborn, with a few more prisoners being made.[274] Since, however, the line of retreat of the large, defeated army under Contades was not yet known, the corps moved back into Lippstadt in the evening.

On the 5th of August, von Monkewitz set out from Lippstadt with twenty horses, and crossed over onto the left bank of the Lippe up to Paderborn, where on the 6th an enemy hospital was taken. Now von Monkewitz marched through the Senne against Bielfeld, after he had learned reliably that d'Armentieres withdrew against Warburg to find out where the defeated Contades might be, but at the same time also to receive certain information about where the victorious Allied army stood.

Late in the night, von Monkewitz noticed many fires burning in the direction of Beilfeld; he now cautiously moved on, uncertain as to whether his friend or foe was there, and finally met some peasants approaching him.[275] Von Monkewitz pretended to be French, which made people frightened, but soon a peasant caught himself and said, "If you send Frenchmen, do not ride against the fires, there is the Erbprinz's army." Pleasurably surprised, von Monkewitz moved on, soon meeting the outposts of the Allies, and was immediately led to the Erbprinzen, in order to report all that had happened in the Lippstadt area. It was very agreeable to the prince to learn that d'Armentieres had withdrawn

[274] Translator's note: Neuhaus appears to be is a municipality in the District of Lüneburg, in Lower Saxony, Germany. Böcke could not be located on any present-day maps, and it is likely that it may have been swallowed up by another municipality.
[275] Translator's note: Bielefeld is a city in the Ostwestfalen-Lippe Region in the north-east of North Rhine-Westphalia, Germany.

magazines of the poor, to be free again. Von Monkewitz received orders to immediately march again to Lippstadt, and on the 9th of August, with all the available crew, to join the corps of the Duke of Holstein in the direction of Paderborn, which also happened. The Carabinier Corps now advanced to the vanguard of the Duke of Holstein, who in the direction of Stadtbergen followed the enemy under d'Armentieres.[276] On the 13th, the corps skirmished with the enemy in front of Korbach, killing several men and horses, and getting some prisoners.[277] The Corps suffered no loss, and on the 14th of August was reinforced by 200 horses and just as much infantry, all placed under the command of the Captain von Monkewitz.

On the 15th of August, he went with half of his command against Eisenberg and Frankenberg, Cpt.-Lt. Baum, towards Nege, where he met with a division under the hereditary prince, who on the 18th drove out the enemy.[278] Since it was now certain that d'Armentieres was in the vicinity of Wolfhagen in order to secure the communications of the French army with Fritzlar and Marburg, von Monkewitz moved on the same day again to near Korbach.[279]

---

[276] Translator's note: Stadtbergen is a town in the district of Augsburg, in Bavaria, Germany. It is situated in the outskirts of Augsburg, 4 kilometers (2.5 mi) west of Augsburg city center.

[277] Translator's note: Korbach, officially the Hanseatic City of Korbach, is the district seat of Waldeck-Frankenberg in northern Hesse, Germany. It is over a thousand years old and is located on the German Timber-Frame Road.

[278] Translator's note: The Netze District or District of the Netze (German: Netzedistrikt or Netze-Distrikt; Polish: Obwód Nadnotecki) was a territory in the Kingdom of Prussia from 1772 to 1793. It included the urban centers of Bydgoszcz (German: Bromberg), Inowrocław (Inowrazlaw), and Piła (Schneidemühl) and was given its name for the Noteć River (German : Netze) that traversed it. Eisenberg is a municipality in the Donnersbergkreis, in Rhineland-Palatinate, Germany. It is situated on the north-eastern edge of the Palatinate forest, approx. 20 km southwest of Worms. Frankenberg is a town in the district of Mittelsachsen, in the Free State of Saxony, Germany. It is situated on the river Zschopau, 12 km (7.46 mi) northeast of Chemnitz.

[279] Translator's note: Wolfhagen is a town in the district of Kassel, in Hesse, Germany. It is located 12 km southeast of Bad Arolsen, and 23 km west of Kassel on the German Timber-Frame Road. Fritzlar is a small German town in the Schwalm-Eder district in northern Hesse, 160 km north of Frankfurt, with a storied history. The town has a medieval center ringed by a wall with numerous watch towers. Thirty-eight meters high, the "Grey Tower" is the highest remaining urban defense tower in Germany.

Raid of Nunburg

On 17 August the corps of the Duke of Holstein marched against Numburg; the light troops were united under the general von Urf. "We're raiding," says von Monkewitz in his report to Count Wilhelm, "the enemy posts from Höringhausen and Sachsenhausen.[280] Although the people resisted like righteous fellows, they were beaten, and 200 were cut down before we reached Numburg. The enemy standing there may well have heard the firing of his outposts, but he had not had time enough to prepare for our arrival, for we rode on as quickly as our horses would carry us. Arriving, one party hunted around the place for the other exits, and the other rushed into the city with the saber in his fist. The enemy fought like mad; but it did not help him, and the 800-strong garrison was reduced to 340 men. A Carabinier of the corps was shot dead, and six horses were killed."

The battalion assembled here was engaged by the royal grenadiers of France, as if von Tempelhof persuaded Marshal Contades by this move against him to make the further retreat against the Wetter, where he secured a firm camp and determined to bring the issue to a decision.[281] The Allied army followed this march; the light troops incessantly harassed the enemy, and on the 24th of August the Allied army took up a camp between the enemy and Munchausen.[282] The Carabinier and Jäger Corps was stationed on the heights before the Wetter, even on the same day lieutenant von Berk hastened to fall into the enemy foragers, to beat them down in the same, and without loss took 8 prisoners, 16 horses, and 3 mules and returned to the corps. A stealthy patrol pushed against Beidenkopf and Laaspe picked up a parcel of French

---

[280] Translator's note: Höringhausen in Regierungsbezirk Kassel (Hesse) is located in Germany about 207 mi (or 334 km) south-west of Berlin, the country's capital town. Sachsenhausen situated in Schwalm-Eder-Kreis, Kassel, Hessen, Germany.

[281] Translator's note: The Wetter is a 69 kilometres (43 mi) long river in the state of Hesse, Germany. It is a right tributary to the Nidda which itself is a right tributary of the Main. After leaving the Vogelsberg mountain range the river flows through the Wetterau, a fertile landscape just north of Frankfurt, which is named after the river.

[282] Translator's note: The community of Münchhausen is found 20 km north of Marburg on the northern edge of Marburg-Biedenkopf district.

documents, among which was found a letter, whose copy Duke Ferdinand and Count Wilhelm delivered immediately, and from which one can see how the French felt the blow of Minden.[283] The letter seems interesting enough to earn a place here, since at any rate what the author says about warfare betrays a very informed view.

Copy of an anonymous letter, dated from Vienna in Austria on the 15th of August, addressed to the Count of Guerchy, Knight of the Orders of the King and Lieutenant General of His Army; at the Camp of Contades.

> *Ah my dear friend! That I was in a cruel situation for three days, and what a stroke of lightning struck us! Two contradictory views spread here; the first, that we have lost a battle, and the second that we have won it; three days pass in this terrible uncertainty and the end is, that we are beaten; I learn it by a letter of four lines. M. de Contades he does not speak to me about you, I have not heard from you, I think you are lost; I have a courier from Versailles, who had left very late after the news of this misfortune, he brought me a little note by which I was told that M. de Guerchy had told us that you were doing well. I am penetrated with his attention; I began to regain courage from that moment, and I urge you to take it back too, and to inspire others and prevent the heads from turning. The great misfortunes of this kind are more in the opinion than in reality! You have firmness and courage, you must communicate them to the Generals and Troops; I avow you that I have death in the heart of this event, so humiliating as it is unbelievable; I did not expect this tribulation and Mr. de Contades plays me a cruel trick. But on the field I made up my mind to fight the storm, not to appear dejected, and to walk with*

---

[283] Translator's note: The town of Biedenkopf lies in the west of Marburg-Biedenkopf district. Ringed by mountains reaching up to 674 meters (2,211 ft)above sea level – the Sackpfeife in the Rothaargebirge reaches this height – the town lies on the upper reaches of the river Lahn. Together with 18 other municipalities, it belongs to the Lahn-Dill-Bergland region.

a head held high.

I was in the evening at Monsieur de Cauniz's, where there were many people, no one dared to say anything to me and they looked at me with a doleful eye; I was the first to speak of our affair, I said that it was a misfortune, but that I hoped it would be repaired, and that we would take our revenge; that in war as in life it was necessary to expect to lose and win, that we were not stunned by setbacks or swings of successes, &c. I saw that it had a good effect. We still have no details; it is to be hoped that one day we will learn how 120,000 men are hacked by a handful of troops, picked up, discouraged, etc. etc. -innovative is one word for the Count of the Lippe; As a superior army allows itself to be shut up and puts itself in the necessity of fighting with disadvantage; how is it left, quiet for 15 days, seeing how to make arrangements for his enemy, and how to be three weeks in a camp without knowing the strong and the weak points of the area. I know that you were, however, superior or you had scattered too much, there is no medium. Finally, what is done is done: this plague bleeds long, but one must try to cure it. You are still double the enemy's numbers, whatever losses you may have made, you must gather and take your revenge; you have 39 Battalions and 70 Squadrons that have not fought. The enemy are weakened by their victory, I see nothing desperate if you do not lose your head. I do not know what the court will do or what it thinks; but that's my opinion.

What I think even more is that Westphalia is a gulf and we will lose all the Armies that will be sent there, because it is not possible to keep communications with Wesel and Dusseldorf on the one side, and with Cassel and Frankfurt on the other. The passion of Mr. de Contades for that side is dear to him and to us too; I do not know if he is convinced now, it seems to me that the lesson was pretty good. You know how much I've been fighting over this winter; there is neither little nor big here who has not been surprised that we have been yet strengthened in this ugly country, and who did not know the inconveniences - they were predicted and represented from the beginning of the campaign. In a word, it was to the Landgrave of Hesse and to the Elector of Hannover that we had only to march in the country of Hannover, to besiege Hameln with 25,000 men, and to cover it with 80,000. This place taken, everything is done. You are the masters of the whole country of your enemies, and if they still hold the two places of Lippstadt and Münster, you then take them at your ease at the end of the campaign, or rather they fall of themselves. In truth it is obvious, as two and two are four; but in the name of God, do not lose heart, and do not believe that your campaign is lost, it is only so long as it is sown.

From the 16th

We learn at the moment that the King of Prussia passed the Oder on the 11th of the evening and that on the 12th, he attacked Saltikov and Loudon together, that he was beaten and obliged to retreat after a very obstinate fight, which lasted seven hours; but I thought that in the circumstances in which we are there was not a moment to lose in order to spread it in the empire and especially in our army. I do not reflect on it, however humiliating it may be, to be defeated by the Russians- - we must overcome the national feeling and agree that this event is very happy. The example of the Russians who have just won two battles in three weeks must give effect to what seems to me to be the troops and the Generals. If we had

won the unfortunate battle of Minden, or if we had not
given it, peace would have been morally safe this winter.
Farewell my dear friend.

How correct, how aptly the author portrays the theater of war and the line of operations, which should have been envisaged by the French army chiefs alone. The really anxious concern with which, moreover, the destruction of Hameln by the French was practiced in recent times gives, in our opinion, a very great weight to the words of the author. Should not those hints of a warning of the importance of Hameln as a fortress still be seen today? - - it seems to me that way!

General von Tempelhof chose the above-described line of operations for the enemy in the circumstance in which he found himself. However, and his criticism about it seems unjust, and frankly confessed, his tears over the more correct operation of the French do not seem to make sense to us, though we may like to humbly suggest that the view expressed here may be erroneous. But "to have a cry for yourself is pardonable," says Count Bismarck.

On the 26th of August, the commander von Monkewitz received the following order from Duke Ferdinand:

Captain von Monkewitz, with the Carabinier under your
command, and Jäger Corps to the west, to the corps
d'Amrée of the lieutenant general von Imhof. He arrives
from Münster today. So, direct your march and take the
shortest and best route. You can take the 4th day as a rest
day and have to march 3 to 4 miles. The 15 Carabiniers,
who were arrested on the march from Lippstadt, come to
you and march on to Münster. You must, therefore, send
the direction of your march towards it, or, in case you
reconsider it yourself, take it back to Westphalia.

Münchhausen, 26 Aug. 1759.

According to this order, on the following morning the corps embarked on the march and crossed through Stadtbergen, Fürstenberg, and Westkotten to Lippstadt, where it entered on 1 September, leaving behind the wounded and sick horses. The corps then marched via Stromberg to join the corps of the General von Imhof.[284] He was just about to begin the siege of Münster. At the same time, General d'Armentières near Wesel was moving across the Rhine, advancing towards Münster, and compelled General von Imhof on the 6th of September to withdraw to Telgte.[285]

After General d'Armentières had thrown a significant reinforcement into Münster, he moved back to Wesel on the 12th. General von Imhof moved again before Münster; the light troops followed the march of General d'Armentières but found no opportunity to undertake anything against the life of the general who now occupied a camp at Schermbeck. The Carabinier and Jäger got to the post in Haltern, which the enemy attacked on 16 September with a powerful detachment.[286] However, he was so violently repulsed that he hurried back to his camp.

On the 17th of September, it was reliably assumed that the bulk of the enemy had passed across the Lippe and spread out against Recklinghausen. As a result, the Carabinier Corps made an attack on the Haus-Seithen with the command, in case of an attack, to rendezvous at Dülmen.[287]

On the 22nd of September, the corps, joined by another division of Hanoverian cavalry, marched to Lünen under the command of Major von Bülow, adjutant of Duke Ferdinand, to capture this post, which was

---

[284] Translator's note: Fürstenberg is a town in the Oberhavel district, Brandenburg, Germany.

[285] Translator's note: is a town in the Warendorf district, North Rhine-Westphalia, Germany, on the river Ems 12 km east of Münster and 15 km west of Warendorf. Telgte is famous as a place of pilgrimage, the Marian pilgrimage from Osnabrück to Telgte.

[286] Translator's note: Formerly Haltern am See, Haltern is a town and a municipality in the district of Recklinghausen, in North Rhine-Westphalia, Germany. It is situated on the Lippe and the Wesel–Datteln Canal, approx. 15 kilometres (9 miles) north of Recklinghausen.

[287] Translator's note: Dülmen is a town in the district of Coesfeld, North Rhine-Westphalia, Germany. Dülmen is situated in the south part of the Münsterland area, between the Lippe river to the south, the Baumberge hills to the north and the Ems river to the east. South of Dülmen the Ruhr area is located.

carried out by the Jäger, while the cavalry should continue to reconnoiter in search of the enemy.[288] Hardly out of Lünen, however, a strong detachment of the enemy, charged our own and threw them back to Lünen. The Jäger steadfastly maintained their position until the cavalry had finished, and preparations had been made to break off from the bridge, though the enemy was terribly fierce. Half of the Carabinier cut off to cover the Jäger assault over the bridge and maintained such an effective rifle fire that it took some time to take the bridge. On this occasion, four Jäger were wounded by our own Carabinier Corps, Sergeant Brinkmann was wounded, and six Jäger were captured. Two enemy riders were captured by the Unfrings, but many were also driven off and wounded. The corps took up the post at Borke.[289]

General d'Armtières began to make all sorts of preparations on the right side of the Lippe, and to make movements which seemed to be only intended to devastate the county, even extending up to Unna. General von Imhof was thus compelled to divert his attention from the blockade of Münster and to weaken his forces there. This, however, was what the enemy wanted him to do. On 28 September General von Imhof withdrew against Recklinghausen and confessed that he was going back to Wesel.

On 28 September the Carabinier Corps, united with Hessian Hussars under Count Görß Lümen, and on the following day moved via Bork to Olphen, but on a recent march, decided to go back to Lünen. For von Bülow had learned that the enemy had left a strong detachment at Hörde, three hours from Lünen on the right bank of the Lippe and decided to do something about it.[290]

Battle at Little Dortmund

---

[288] Translator's note: Lünen is a town in North Rhine-Westphalia, Germany. It is located north of Dortmund, on both banks of the River Lippe. It is the largest town of the Unna district and part of the Ruhr Area.

[289] Translator's note: Bork was, until 1975, a village in the southern neighborhood of the town of Selm in the district of Unna in the North Rhine-Westphalia district of German. In 1977, it was annexed to Selm.

[290] Translator's note: Today, Hörde is a district in the city of Dortmund.

"On the 20th of September, after midnight," Captain von Monke-witz says in his diary,

> I got up and arrived at Hörde just before dawn; but the enemy had recently marched off against Little Dort-mund; We immediately followed suit and caught up with them before this place. Here was a rather difficult defile, which the enemy had already passed on our arrival, but had posted against our arrival with about 150 infantry, supported by just as many cavalry. The enemy was in no better position to get through the defile; I was the most senior officer after Bülow, and therefore received orders to force the defile with the Carabiniers. It was early, and I was so happy to engage the infantry and throw it against their outpost. But because the pass was very difficult, and my men were still struggling with the enemy, I could not immediately form myself properly to get to the enemy cavalry in order. But it went as well as I wanted. But as the enemy now spotted the lead troopers of the cavalry, and saw his infantry redeemed, he did not think he would come under a second attack, but quickly withdrew from the affair. We were indeed going to follow. But the enemy held such good composure that we could not harm him. However, he lost in the defile some 30 men who were cut down, and 3 officers and 64 men who were made prisoners. The rest of the blasted infantry escaped to Bockum in the difficult terrain.[291] The Carabiners had 4 dead and 6 wounded men and horses in this battle.

In the meantime, Bülow was leading this expedition, d'Armen-tierères went to Flasheim, because the water there at the time was very

---

[291] Translator's note: Bockum is situated on the Ruhr Heights hill chain, between the rivers Ruhr to the south and Emscher to the north.

shallow across the Lippe. He marched in the greatest haste across Dülmen towards Münster, where he ejected the very weakened force of General von Imhof, and threw fresh troops, ammunition and food into the place, and then moved back via Kösfeld against Wesel.[292]

The Carabinier Corps now made various raids, both against Wesel, and in the County of Mark. On 9 October they went to Rauschenburg and seized the post, while von Monkewitz with twenty horses cut through the Lippe and proceeded to Herneburg, where he received the reliable news that General d'Armentières had arrived at Bockum in the County of Mark, and only a detachment of 300 men left infantry in Dorsten.[293] Captain von Monkewitz now returned to Olphen and made the General von Imhof aware of it.[294]

On 10 October and the Karabiner Corps and in particular the Captain von Monkewitz and Kapt.-Lieut. Baum were recognized for their glorious conduct in the affair of the 30th in the Orders of the Day by His very Christian Majesty, thanks to the Duke Ferdinand, and at the same time the corps was ordered to move to Dülmen, where it was placed under the command and at the disposal of Major von Bülow.

Raid on Dorsten

On the 11th of October the corps arrived in Dülmen, where at the same time Major von Bülow arrived with two battalions of infantry and a detachment of Hessian hussars.

---

[292] Translator's note: Kösfeld is about six kilometers northwest of Coburg.

[293] Translator's note: The County of Mark (German: Grafschaft Mark, French: Comté de La Marck colloquially known as Die Mark) was a county and state of the Holy Roman Empire in the Lower Rhenish–Westphalian Circle. It lay on both sides of the Ruhr river along the Volme and Lenne rivers. Rauschenberg is a town in the north of Marburg-Biedenkopf district in Hesse, Germany.

[294] Translator's note: Olphen or Olfen is a town in the district of Coesfeld, in North Rhine-Westphalia, Germany. It is sometimes called the "Gate to the Ruhr Area".

Major Von Bülow," says von Monkewitz, "disclosed to me that he had made an attack on Dorsten as a result of my report of the 9th; Since our people were now acquainted with all the passes through the long time that we spent fighting here, I ought to join him with half of the corps, while Baum and the rest and 30 hussars go to Great Beckum this evening.[295] The following day I was destined to move to Wesel to visit this place from the right side of the Lippe, so that we would not be disturbed in our business from there. On the 12th of October, before dawn, we arrived at the bridge over the Lippe near Dorsten; some of Scheiter's grenadiers sneaked up close in the bushes; they had the order to sneak up on our sentinels and knock them down, but in no case give fire. Carefully and slowly, we followed with the majority. We found that we could cross the bridge at four, so had broken off, and I had the honor of seeing the Borderste with the Karabiners; the infantry followed me closely, the Hussars included. A reserve, which included our foot-Jäger, remained in a good position between the enemy and Holsterhausen.[296] Our infantry had orders, at any rate, if the passage over the bridge succeeded in securing and defeating such, then the rest should quickly rush into the place and help us where it was necessary; Ferener should also blow up the Hussars in the city, while the infantry would be busy securing the bridge. Everything went as I desired!

The grenadiers quietly pushed down the two sentinels in front of the bridge; but a hostile post of some men, standing at the bridge in an old sepulcher, gave fire and went to go back to close the gate and the barrier. But as the shots had fallen, one carried went over the bridge and

---

[295] Translator's note: Beckum is a town in the northern part of North Rhine-Westphalia, Germany. It is about 20 km north-east of Hamm and 35 km south-east of Münster.

[296] Translator's note: Holsterhausen is situated in Recklinghausen, Munster, Nordrhein-Westfalen, Germany.

into the place; The noise soon became general, but the enemy was completely overwhelmed, and did not come to their senses, for in one glance everywhere was swarming with hussars, grenadiers, and Carabiniers; One fell down, which came before the blade, and I believe that in the whole probably around 100 enemy dead were lying around in the place, when the thing was over. Four officers and 86 men were caught, the rest had fled from the gate into the bushes. The command of the Major von Bülow lost only a few 20 men, the Carabiniers lost nothing.[297]

On the 13th, Major von Bülow was attacked by a strong detachment, which had left Wesel late the night before, but retreated so masterfully through Lembeck to Gross Beckum that it was impossible to pursue the enemy and exact any revenge. Major von Bülow lost only 13 men.[298] The Carabiniers lost a horse. Capt.-Lieut. Baum came back to the corps on the same day.

On 16 October, a cordon was drawn from Lüdinghausen via Dülmen and Lette to Kösfeld, to cover the siege of Münster, to which Jezel thought, but had not yet worked.[299] Captain von Monkewitz, on the express orders of Duke Ferdinand, was given command of two battalions of infantry and three squadrons of dragoons, who joined the corps, and moved to Kösfeld to cover the area of Gross-Beckum and Borken. Duke Ferdinand, as well as the hereditary prince of Braunschweig, had now become acquainted and learned the great usefulness, activity, and insight of von Monkewitz, and henceforth we frequently see him at the head of important troop detachments.

Until 17 November the corps under Monkewitz remained in this area, little was going on, except on the 3rd when a Carabinier patrol at Gescher on the way to Sindehohe was attacked and mauled by the ene-

---

[297]This attack, p. 84, is mentioned in Scharnhorst's military paperback, pg. 84.

[298] Translator's note: Lembeck is a village in the north of Dorsten which belongs to Recklinghausen in Nordrhein-Westfalen, Germany. This may refer to Greater Recke. Today, Recke is a municipality in the district of Steinfurt, also in Nordrhein-Westfalen, Germany.

[299] Translator's note: Lüdinghausen is a town in the district of Kösfeld in the state of North Rhine-Westphalia, Germany. It is located on the Dortmund-Ems Canal, approx. 25 km southwest of Münster. It is known for its three castles, Castle Luedinghausen, Kakesbeck and Vischering Castle. Lette is situated in Kösfeld, Münster, Nordrhein-Westfalen, Germany.

my, with 3 Carabiniers severely wounded who fell into enemy hands.[300] The siege and bombardment of Münster began under Count Wilhelm's direction and command and on 9 November the foot-Jäger of the corps moved there.

The corps of von Imhof, to cover the siege of Münster, concentrated in the area of Alt Rorel against Willenbrenning, and von Monkewitz, with the detachment under him, harassed the outposts at Schapdetten.[301]

Battle of Notteln[302]

General d'Armentières, who discharged his barrels to Münster, and then attacked the sentinels, was mocked by the Scheither's grenadiers at Willbrenning on 19 November but was repulsed in bloody fighting. In the afternoon of the same day, the outpost under the command of Captain von Monkewitz at Notteln sustained a fierce attack and threw them back. A detachment he had sent out, however, came to their aid immediately, and after a rather heated clash, forced the enemy back to Dorup, which lost many people through the fires of the infantry.[303] The cavalry was unable to do anything against the enemy in multiple attempts to disrupt them, because the enemy horsemen were always under the protection of the infantry. But after the enemy had retreated through Notteln, he managed to concentrate one of his battalions to act as a rear guard, while the rest of the enemy hastily continued the retreat. The captain made only 39 prisoners, but the exasperation of our cavalry was greatly increased by the long resistance, so that little pardon was given. The Carabiniers had 2 dead and 5 wounded. They lost 8 horses as well.

---

[300] Translator's note: Gescher is a municipality in the district of Borken, in North Rhine-Westphalia, Germany.

[301] Translator's note: Willenbrenning may refer to the modern town of Willingen, which is a community in Waldeck-Frankenberg in northern Hesse, Germany, some 80 km west of Kassel. Schapdetten is situated in Coesfeld, Munster, Nordrhein-Westfalen.

[302] Translator's note: This is actually Nottuln, which is a municipality in the district of Coesfeld in the state of North Rhine-Westphalia. It is Notteln in Low German.

[303] Translator's note: Dorup may refer to a town in southern Denmark. It may also refer to the town of Dorum, a village and a former municipality in the district of Cuxhaven, in Lower Saxony, Germany.

The loss of the whole corps of Monkewitz amounted to 80 and some militia from Notteln, to which the prisoners taken from the enemy were transferred, testifies that the attacking force likely numbered over 300. General von Imhof hurried on to Captain von Monkewitz that night, following the German leader the following day, but unable to bring him to a halt, and Mr. d'Armentières gave up his last attempt to relieve Münster. On the evening of 20 November, the fortress capitulated, and the Bückeburg Lieb-Grenadiers occupied the New Castle on the same evening.

On 23 November the corps went in conjunction with the Hessian hussars to Dülmen, where one section was sent out to act attack the rear guard of general d'Armentières. They found that he had just left the place and carelessly made its way to Wesel. His rear guard was so completely surprised that all of them ran off in a wild flight without putting up any organized defense; the corps and the Hessian hussars cut down a part and made some 60 prisoners.

All the light troops of von Imhof's corps gathered in Dülmen, crossed the Lippe on the 28th, and undertook various expeditions into the County of Mark, which lasted until the 6th of December, but nothing of relevance occurred. The Carabinier and Jäger Corps together with 100 infantry and 40 heavy horses under the Captain von Monkewitz were posted at this time in Recklinghausen, from there patrols proceeded against the Bergisch, and remained there quietly until the 27th of December.[304] On this day the corps went to Kleine Dortmund, united there with a strong detachment under the Hanoverian Colonel von Monron and went over the Ruhr the following day. Captain von Monkewitz led the advance-guard of the Monkewitz's Corps, which had the purpose of collecting contributions in Bergisch, which they only partly carried out.

---

[304] Translator's note: This may refer to Bergische-Gladbach, which is a city in the Cologne/Bonn Region of North Rhine-Westphalia, Germany, and capital of the Rheinisch-Bergischer Kreis (district).

Chapter 4

Campaign of 1760

Winter quarters on the Lippe. March in the county Waldeck. Battle at Krolsen. Battle at the so-called Trappenberge. Major von Bülow attacks the enemy, who is posted in Kolfen, and is in a heated fight. The enemy attacks the Corps at Külte and forces ours to retreat and carries on a haphazard battle with Volkmissen. General von Spörcken is ordered to retire. Battle at Wolfhagen. Von Monkewitz is made a prisoner, but soon exchanged. Battle at Zierenberg. Von Monkewitz destroys an enemy flour transport at Gudensberg. Raid on Marburg and Butzbach. Battle at Winterberg.[305] Battle of a Carabinier with a French officer. Colonel von Jeanneret crosses the Rhine at the same time Orson attacks. The siege of Wesel is lifted. Battle at Gahlen. Battle at Gartrupp.

Shortly before the end of the preceding year, the enemy at Köln and Dusseldorf advanced sharply against the Monrohsche detachment on the left bank of the Ruhr, which is why on 2 January 1760, it retreated over this river.[306] Captain von Monkewitz caught up with the advanced guard in Mitten Posto; General von Imhof was in Dortmund.

As the army of Duke Ferdinand operating on the Lahn was considerably weakened by the detachment on corps, Marshal Broglie seized the corps d'Armentières of the Neider Rhine, and, despite the rough season of the year, seized the opportunity to go over to the offensive, whereby Duke Ferdinand for the moment thought it necessary to leave the district of Roßdorf and concentrate at Marburg. [307]At the same time

---

[305] Translator's note: Winterberg is a town in the Hochsauerland district of North Rhine-Westphalia.

[306] Translator's note: Köln is modern Köln, in the North Rhine Westphalia region of Germany. It is the largest city in that region today.

[307] Translator's note: Roßdorf is a municipality in the district of Darmstadt-Dieburg, in Hesse,

General von Imhof received orders to march through the Köllnische Sauerland with his entire corps to the Duke's army.

The Carabinier and Jäger Corps covered the right flank of General von Imhof during the whole march, and arrived in front of Dillenburg on 15 January, where it joined the corps of the then Colonel Luckner.[308]

The hereditary prince had since returned from Saxony. At this time, the armies of both sides remained in winter quarters. The headquarters of Duke Ferdinand were at Paderborn. General von Spörcken advanced with a strong corps into their cantonments in Westphalia. The Carabiniers and Jäger were assigned to this corps, and on the 20th they left for Westphalia, where, as Monkewitz says, they moved into so-called winter quarters on the 31st of January 1760.

The corps had come very near both glory and dissolution in the most arduous ways, by the march to Hesse and by the rapid retreat in bad weather. General von Spörcken therefore reinforced it with 100 infantry and 50 heavy horses. The outpost line of the corps retreated from Hamm along the right bank of the Lippe to Haltern, and then crossed Dülmen, Kösfeld, Stadtlohn, and Breden, towards the boundary of the hills. Von Monkewitz was in Haltern with his detachment and covered banks of the Lippe facing Wesel. He had to watch his hat especially at night, for the enemy, notwithstanding the constant and sure news that he heard, could in one march move unnoticed from Wesel to Haltern. The soldiers, therefore, remained dressed at night and the horses were saddled, and half of the men had to be always on stand-by; von Monkewitz remarks,

> *I must say that the light troops in winter quarters, like those who come to Haltern, almost always have to watch their hats; as in the middle of the campaign, especially when the enemy is but a bit distant. The scouts can not always be depended on; the patrols can be caught, or,*

Germany.

[308] Translator's note: Moderm Dillenburg, officially Oranienstadt Dillenburg, is a town in Hesse's Gießen region in Germany. The town was formerly the seat of the old Dillkreis district, which is now part of the Lahn-Dill-Kreis.

more often, fail, very often they do not discover anything
of the enemy, go back calmly, announce that they have
not discovered anything, and the next hour the enemy is
on their feet, chasing them, and coming to visit us when
we least expect it.

On 8 April, shortly before midnight, a scout from the vicinity of Wesel reported that at noon on that day a strong enemy detachment with four guns had moved out of the town and taken the road to Schermbeck. The then Major von Monkewitz (promoted at the beginning of this year) immediately reported to Spörcken's command, at the same time informing the commanders of the adjoining outposts and who remained on their rifles all night. But as the enemy did not appear, on the 9th of April, after it was fully day, Capt.-Lieut. Baum with 30 horses moved against Schermbeck, and Lieut. von Berk with an equal number acted against Dorsten, on the left bank of the Lippe, sent forward scouts to collect messages from enemies. The former returned with the report that the enemy had advanced up to three hours distance from Haltern but had there learned through a scout that the whole cordon was compromised and therefore returned to Wesel in a hurry, went over to Galen had gone out and found everything quiet in this area.[309]

Only in June did the two main armies begin their operations again. Major von Monkewitz was in Haltern until then, and used this quasi-rest period as well as possible to provide for the training and the equipment of the corps. The Carabiniers' remounts began to deteriorate significantly at this time irrespective of the number of Louisd'or paid for each horse by Count Wilhelm, so it was no longer possible to have such good horses and, in addition, stallions, to raise them up earlier. Bückeburg, as well as the neighboring countries, already suffered a considerable lack of the necessary requisite mounts for a capable cavalry, as the French, while they lived there, had taken away almost all useful

[309] Translator's note: Galen is the name of an old Westphalian noble family. The Lords of Galen belong to the nobility of the County of Mark. The eponymous ancestral seat of the family is Gahlen, today a district of the municipality of Schermbeck in the district of Wesel.

horses. The requirement for remounts for the cavalry of the Allied army was, because of the great losses, also very significant.

Major von Bülow moved on 1 June with 5 battalions and 5 newly built squadrons of the Legion Britannique to Dortmund, to watch over the French General Count de St. Germain lying near Dusseldorf. On 9 June Major von Bülow replaced von Monkewitz with Hessian hussars in Haltern, joined the corps of the Lieutenant-General, the Prince of Anhalt, and moved with the Carabinier and Jäger Corps to Erwitte, where he arrived on the 12th, to observe here the regions at rest; Prince von Anhalt camped near Lippstadt.

General St. Germain now camped at Dortmund. From then until 4 July, nothing happened. On this day the French broke out - as later revealed - to the county Waldeck. Major von Bülow always accompanied the march of the enemy in order to keep his eye on the light troops. General von Spörcken followed this movement with the bulk of his corps. But Count St. Germain, who operated on the shorter line, already arrived in Korbach on 12 July and united there with the army of Marshal Broglie. The hereditary prince, who arrived with a weak corps in the region of Korbach, could not prevent the union, since General von Spörcken had not yet approached. The hereditary prince, after a fierce battle, was compelled to retreat to Sachsenhausen. On the 12th of July von Monkewitz took over the outpost of General von Spörcken at Mengeringhausen, where Major von Bülow arrived on the very same evening with two battalions.[310]

On the 14th of July it was noticed that Count St. Germain was in motion against Canstein on the right flank of General Spörcken.[311] Major von Bülow rode in the company of the Major von Monkewitz, several other officers and 20 Carabiniers from Mengeringhausen to observe the movements of the enemy. The extremely broken and mountainous terrain made it necessary to get as close as possible to the enemy column. A swarm of enemy light troops covering the march finally challenged

[310] Translator's note: Mengeringhausen is a village and a municipal district of Bad Arolsen in Waldeck-Frankenberg, in Hesse, Germany.

[311] Translator's note: Canstein is a municipality in Germany›s North Rhine-Westphalia state. Canstein is located in the administrative district Hochsauerlandkreis.

Major von Bülow when he came too close and attacked him with great determination. The commander wanted to break off the engagement; but the enemy cavalry was excellently mounted; soon the fighting became general.

Five Carabiniers were cut down and one fell heavily injured into enemy hands. The prince of Waldeck, too, would have been almost crushed; he had ridden out from Arolsen to observe General St. Germain's march as well, and approached the command the moment the enemy attacked it.[312] Major von Monkewitz hurriedly sent a Carabinier to warn him of the danger, and he was happy to escape.

The enemy now encamped at Canstein, and presently Captain Baum was posted with some Carabinier and the foot-Jäger, on the so-called Trappenberg, from where he could watch the enemy position.[313]

On the 15th of July the enemy advanced with vigor against the Trappenberg and threw down Captain Ruth after he put up a courageous resistance, with the wounded Lieut. Hoffmann along with 9 Jäger fell into enemy hands: a Carabinier and 3 Jäger were shot. As the enemy at once invaded Mengeringhausen, Major von Bülow left the line, and returned to Külte; General von Spörcken camped at Volkmissen and the enemy immediately occupied Arolsen.[314] On 16 July, the patrols skirmished with the enemy throughout the day.

The troops moved on 20 July to the camp at Schmillinghausen.[315] On the 21st von Bülow reconnoitered the same area with a detachment of Carabinier, fighting the light troops of the enemy. He lost 11 hussars and cut down some; the Carabiner suffered a wounded horse. The ene-

---

[312] Translator's note: Arolsen or Bad Arolsen is a small town in northern Hesse, Germany, in Waldeck-Frankenberg district. From 1655 until 1918 it served as the residence town of the Princes of Waldeck-Pyrmont and then until 1929 as the capital of the Waldeck Free State.

[313] Translator's note: Trappenberg is a hill in Schleswig-Holstein and has an elevation of 46 meters.

[314] Translator's note: Külte, Waldeck is a municipality in the central German state Hesse. Külte, Waldeck is located in the administrative district Waldeck-Frankenberg. Volkmarsen is a small town in Waldeck-Frankenberg district in northern Hesse, Germany. Volkmarsen lies on the northern edge of the *Waldecker Tafel* (Waldecker Shield (geology)) where it flattens out into the Diemel Valley, some 28 km northwest of Kassel and 7 km northeast of Bad Arolsen.

[315] Translator's note: Schmillinghausen is a municipality in the central German state Hesse. Schmillinghausen is located in the administrative district Waldeck-Frankenberg.

my general visibly maneuvered to avoid the right wing of the Allies, so the enemy was always kept in view.

Battle at Helsen

On 22 July, at daybreak, a considerable detachment under Major von Bülow attacked the village of Helsen, which the enemy vigorously defended. Although stubbornly growing in numbers as reinforcements were funneled in, the enemy were in the end thrown out.[316] The Carabinier made 23 of the enemy prisoners and captured 6 horses. The battle, however, grew protracted and became more and more heated, as successive formations of the enemy arrived, so that in the end the fight became too uneven and Major von Bülow ordered a retreat. Major von Monkewitz commanded the rear guard with 300 Hanoverian grenadiers and the foot-Jäger of Bückeburg. The enemy troops, the Volontaires Royaux, were attacking fiercely, forcing the rear-guard to make a stand and fight. After fierce rifle fire from both sides, the enemy finally saw itself forced to pursue more slowly; but 16 grenadiers and 3 Jäger were killed, and 25 grenadiers were wounded, along with 8 Jäger. Major von Monkewitz had his horse shot out from under him. The battle ended only at nightfall, the detachment of the major of Bülow again occupied the post of Külte.

Count St. Germain left the French army at that time and was replaced by the Chevalier du Muy in command of the reserve of the army at Schmillinhausen.

Battles by Külte and Volkmissen

On the 25th of July, at dawn, the enemy attacked the post of the Major von Bülow with great force, and, after a bloody battle, forced him to fall back on General von Spörcken, who was at Volkmissen. The Chevalier du Muy now defended himself moving in three columns,

---

[316] Tempelhof calls him Colonel; But as I find everywhere, where von Monkewitz mentions this excellent officer Ferdinand, I find the papers that are my submission. Tranlator's note: Helsen is a town in Regierungsbezirk Kassel (Hesse), just to the east of Canstein.

and a very heated battle soon developed. The enemy mainly directed his efforts against the right wing and threw back the 5 battalions of the Legion Britannique there, after much resistance, and with considerable loss. However, General von Spörcken's position was strong enough to defy all enemy attacks, and the battle on the right wing was soon restored by Hanoverian grenadiers. The cannonade by both sides lasted until evening when the enemy withdrew a little. The Carabinier Corps lost two Jäger killed, and a Carabinier was badly wounded in the melee before Külte.

At the request of Duke Ferdinand, General von Spörcken moved late into the evening via Fischbeck to Wolfhagen.[317]

Rear-guard Battle at Wolfhagen

"26 July at 1 o'clock in the morning," says von Monkewitz in his report,

> *General von Spörcken set in motion in two columns. The first took its way through Fischbeck and consisted largely of infantry; the second column, leaving Fischbeck to the right, consisted of the bulk of the cavalry. Behind the first column, four Hessian Grenadier battalions followed, with whom I followed with the corps and three squadrons of the Legion Britannique subordinated to me. Major von Bülow commanded the rear guard.*
>
> *About nine o'clock in the morning we had passed Fischbeck, and advanced against Wolfhagen without being troubled by the enemy. However, when the column had reached Wolfhagen, it stopped itself in the place where the rear guard had to march, while the enemy now advanced quickly through Fischbeck. Major von Bülow, a man of perspicacity whom the enemy respected for his cunning, positioned himself in place from whence he*

---

[317] Translator's note: Fischbeck is a village near Hessisch Oldendorf, Lower Saxony, Germany. Wolfhagen is a town in the district of Kassel, in Hesse, Germany. It is located 12 km southeast of Bad Arolsen, and 23 km west of Kassel on the German Timber-Frame Road.

could fire at the column escaping from Wolfhagen with a gun. The hill was quickly occupied by our rear guard; I took my position on the left wing with the cavalry, where a favorable terrain for this weapon was found. The enemy General de Bair advanced from Landau against the hill with about 2,000 volunteers. The engagement began with a cannonade, but soon included fierce fire from small arms. Both forces made the greatest effort, one to conquer the heights, the other to defend them. Twice I tried to break the attacks with the cavalry, but the enemies held so solid a formation that we could not penetrate. The battle lasted until about 2 o'clock in the afternoon, when a support of two battalions and two squadrons of Hanoverians, of which the latter ones came to me, arrived.

His account continued,

I had had a fever during that time and was miserably depressed; At noon my horse was shot, and I was forced to mount a young stallion, whom I had bought not long before, and who was not quite used to the fire. As the rifle fire continued to grow violently, the horse became more and more restless and unruly, and at last, quite furiously, it swept me between the lines, without being able to remain his master, and at the same time being subjected to the fire of friend and foe alike.
Meanwhile Major von Bülow had seen a weakness in the enemy dispositions. He went to the head of the army, charged into the enemy infantry with our men, came upon the enemy, upon whom a clear defeat was inflicted so that they fled back head over his heels. Our riders followed fresh, and I was always in the fore with my raging animal. I still could not master of my mount. A division

of Volunteers of Flanders came to shame the infantry by making a stand and forced our riders to abandon the pursuit. I was caught out ahead in the midst of the enemy. No one, however, paid any attention to me, since everyone seemed sufficiently concerned with his own safety, and so I would most likely have got away with it, if not at the moment when I was able to throw the stallion around, a small detachment of those Volunteers of Flanders surrounded me and took me prisoner. Being plundered was a matter of course, but nothing upsets me more than the loss of the saber I received from my gracious master for the action at Mer.[318] I was brought to the Chevalier du Muy and then to the Duke de Broglie. Both treated me very nicely, and the next day released me to Duke Ferdinand in Kassel on the condition that I should not serve until exchanged. Our corps, as I learned now, had 8 Carabinier wounded the day before, 2 Carabinier, and 4 Jäger dead, together with 3 dead and 11 wounded horses. I went to Bückeburg now.

General von Tempelhof started this affair, on the 24th of July. However, the author has learned that he has to adhere to the time constraints of the papers available to him.

The movements of the Duke de Broglie against the position of the Duke of Braunschweig, which were undertaken simultaneously with the attack on the rear guard of Spörcken, compelled the latter to leave the camp at Sachsenhausen and to camp at Kalden on 27 July, the left wing was posted to Wilhelmsthal, the right at Liebenau an der Deimel.[319] The Carabiniers and Jäger, under Baum's orders, remained with the Major von Bülow, who stood with a light corps to Westen Teuffels. Of all the

[318] Count Wilhelm replaced this loss with a saber that was just as beautiful.
[319] Translator's note. Kalden in a small village in south-western Germany near the current border with Lichtenstein. Wilhelmsthal is a municipality in the district of Kronbach in Bavaria, Germany. The last location given is most likely Liebenau, which is a town in the district of Kassel, in Hesse, Germany. It is situated on the river Diemel, 25 km northwest of Kassel.

incidents which took place from now until 23 August, when the Carabinier and Jäger were needed, all data is missing, since Baum, it seems, did not keep a journal. All we know is that under von Bülow there was a heated engagement at Marburg on the 31st of July, in which Fischer's enemy light corps were particularly badly handled, and the Carabinier killed 2 and 4 wounded with 2 horses, but the foot-Jäger had only one man lost. (See Tempelhof, chapter 4, page 116 and following.)

Duke Ferdinand, whose wish it was to soon see Major von Monkewitz again at the head of his band, and was even more solemnly requested by von Bülow to accomplish this, since he had had occasion to give the man sufficient value, charged against a French staff officer fought by Luckner, and on 23 August von Monkewitz, in turn, joined the corps, which at that time, still under von Bülow, was on duty outpost at Zierenberg.[320] Indescribable was the jubilation of his people when they saw the faithful companion of so many dangers, in many a battle at the head, and barely twenty-four hours with the corps when he found the blade again.

Outpost battle at Zierenberg.

On the night of the 25th of August the enemy attacked the field guard of Captain Baum, which consisted of a mixed command of 60 horses, in front of Zierenberg, and seemed determined to drive them out. They moved to support; but it was so dark that nothing could be distinguished. Baum had received a company of Hessian grenadiers and fired on the enemy without leaving his post. At last, the day dawned and Bülow arrived. Quickly disregarding the strength of the enemy, and immediately exercising extreme measures, and maneuvering with so much determination that by six o'clock in the morning the enemy was obliged to retreat. A division of it, which was late, was hewn down together. The Hessian hussars under Captain von Riedesel, who were at the same time marching with the Karabiner, lost several men and horses; the Karabiner

---

[320] Translator's note: Zierenberg is a town in the district of Kassel, in Hesse, Germany. It is located 19 km east of Bad Arolsen, and 15 km northwest of Kassel on the German Timber-Frame Road.

got away without much enthusiasm.

Destruction of a flour transport at Gudensberg[321]

On the morning of 28 August, Monkewitz was dispatched with the Carabinier and 100 Hessian hussars to reconnoiter the road from Marburg to Kassel. In the area of Gudensberg he reached an enemy flour transport and fell so unexpectedly on the covering force, which was composed of Fischer's hussars, that they fled wildly. Some twenty wagons were destroyed, and six men were captured, with these prizes and prisoners, the force returned to Zierenberg during the night. On the following day, Captain Baum went with 60 Carabinier to this area, but returned without having encountered anything of the enemy.

On the morning of the 30th of August, the march of a strong enemy corps on the road from Dörrenberg to Wolfhagen was observed, with the probable intention of doing something against the troops of Brunswick, who were encamped at Breuna.[322] This corps, therefore, went back in force over the Diemel. Major von Bülow followed in the direction of Ober-Listingen and advanced with his corps to Welda in Paderborn.[323]

On 1 September von Monkewitz came with the corps to Colonel von Heels, who was camped at Meerhof with some battalions and squadrons to cover the connection between the army and Lippstadt.[324] Major von Monkewitz received his post in Wunnenberg.[325]

---

[321] Translator's note: Gudensberg is a small town in northern Hesse, Germany. Since the municipal reform in 1974, the nearby villages of Deute, Dissen, Dorla, Gleichen, Maden and Obervorschütz have become parts of the municipality.

[322] Translator's note: Dörrenberg is a small town in the North Rhine-Westphalia, Cologne District (Germany). Breuna is a small municipality in the district of Kassel, in Hesse, Germany. It is situated 24 kilometers northwest of the town of Kassel. Its oldest part is the village of Rhöda, first mentioned in the early ninth century.

[323] Translator's note: Oberlistingen is a municipality in the central German state Hesse. Oberlistingen is located in the administrative district Kassel.

[324] Translator's note: Meerhof is located in Hochsauerlandkreis, Arnsberg, Nordrhein-Westfalen, Germany.

[325] Translator's note: Wünnenberg is a town in the district of Paderborn, in North Rhine-Westphalia, Germany. It is situated on the river Asbach, approx. 20 km south of Paderborn.

Raid on Marburg

In the meantime, the plan was made to take Marburg by surprise, and the execution was assigned to the Colonel von Fersen and Major von Bülow. The former moved with 4 battalions, 2 squadrons and the Carabinier and Jäger Corps over Bühren, Brillon, Affinghausen, Wedebach, Dreckmünden and Sachsenberg to Frankenberg, where he united with Major von Bülow on 9 September, whose unit was about as strong. When they met, they made their dispositions as described below.[326]

Colonel von Fersen remained with the main force at Frankenberg; For his part, Major von Monkewitz was detached to Frankenau with 150 horses and 300 infantry, in order to secure the connection against Landau in the Waldeck with the Erbprinz of Braunschweig, who encamped at Warburg.[327] Major von Bülow, with all the light troops, including the Carabinier and Jäger Corps, and four hundred volunteers from Colonel von Heels attached to the Marburg corps, marched on the same day, and on the night of the 10th to the 11th of September, ruined the enemy field-bakeries, and killed a part of the crew. In addition, they captured 8 officers and 72 men. But they challenged the castle in vain.

Raid on Butzbach

Captain von Hattorf of Freytag's Jäger Corps with 100 horses, and Lieutenant von Berk with 30 of the best-behaved Carabinier composed the vanguard which was sent against Butzbach.[328] Here stood two

---

[326] Translator's note: Bühren (Low German: Bahren) is a municipality in the district of Göttingen, in Lower Saxony, Germany. Brilon is a town in North Rhine-Westphalia, Germany that belongs to the Hochsauerlandkreis. Affinghausen is a municipality in the district of Diepholz, in Lower Saxony, Germany. Medebach is a town in the Hochsauerland district, in North Rhine-Westphalia, Germany. Sachsenberg, Waldeck is a municipality in the central German state Hesse. Sachsenberg, Waldeck is located in the administrative district Waldeck-Frankenberg.

[327] Translator's note: Frankenau is a small town in Waldeck-Frankenberg district in Hesse, Germany. Landau, or Landau in der Pfalz, is an autonomous town surrounded by the Südliche Weinstraße district of southern Rhineland-Palatinate, Germany.

[328] Translator's note: Butzbach is a town in the Wetteraukreis district in Hessen, Germany. It is located approximately 16 km south of Gießen and 35 km north of Frankfurt am Main.

squadrons of hostile cavalry, with the utmost tranquility and cheerfulness, expecting nothing less than an attack from an enemy standing far away in Paderborn. It might have been about 9 o'clock in the morning when Hattorf arrived in front of Butzbach and immediately threw himself into the village at a full-out gallop. Some of the enemy riders sought to get on horseback; The allied troops hit them so hard that not a single one managed to escape. Lieutenant von Berk, with some of his men, at the same time came up on the other side of the village to occupy the troops there, and distinguished himself by great prudence and bravado, as evidenced by an erroneous report by Captain von Hattorf. A part of the enemy's army threw themselves into two houses in the market and began a heavy carbine fire against the horsemen engaged in the gathering of the captured horses. Lieut. von Berk parted with a part of his people attacked the one house, which was done in the same way by Captain von Hattorf against the other. Although the enemy bravely fought back, the attackers still penetrated, and the defenders had to jump over the blade. Hattorf returned with 123 dray horses, a few hundred slaughter cattle and 26 laden wagons with food on the same day to Marburg, after he sold the slaughter cattle - which was not to be carried away - to some Jews he negotiated with on the way. 41 men and 1 officer were brought along as prisoners; von Hattorf had lost 13 men and 9 horses, among them 6 Carabinier and 5 horses from the corps.

Major von Bülow retired on 11 September to Frankenberg and from there on 12 to Frankenau back to the Major von Monkewitz.

We now again let the eyewitnesses report on the other incidents.

Battle of Sachsenberg

"I had," says von Monkewitz,

reliably learned from Frankenau that there was an enemy standing near Bergheim on the Eder, and that his march was on the verge of being blocked by mudslides.[329]

[329] Translator's note: Bergheim is a city found in North Rhine-Westphalia, Germany. It is 20 km

I immediately informed the Colonel von Fersen of this, and as he had received a similar message from another aide. He advised Major von Bülow, as evidently our re-treat was greatly threatened to begin the march against the Söllish Sauerland as soon as possible.[330] Major von Bülow, though fully in the confidence of colonel Ferssen, was of a different opinion, as regards the line of retreat, when the Erbprinz, who set out from the Eder to Bergheim to stab Fersen's and Bülow's detachments in the back, was moving rapidly behind him to follow, and to bring them between two fires. Unfortunately, the great army, under the duke of Broglie, made a move against Duke Ferdinand, which threw the whole operation into uncertainty, and at the same time caused the Erbprinz to join me, Colonel von Fersen and Major von Bülow on the 12th of September, at Frankenau; I now moved to Lelbach. Several strong detachments, sent by the large enemy army, were discovered by our patrols in the area of Wildungen.[331] There were a few minor skirmishes with them, with a few prisoners taken. On the morning of 13 September, both Colonel von Fersen and Major von Bülow, following the direction of Duke Ferdinand, gave orders for the fateful return march. The officer who had come to pass on this order had not met anything hostile on his way. The departure immediately took place in the direction of Sachsenberg and Major von Bülow went ahead with me and fifty Carabinier to observe everything.

west of Cologne and the capital of the Rhein-Erft-Kreis.

[330] Translator's note: The Sauerland is a rural, hilly area spreading across most of the south-eastern part of North Rhine-Westphalia, in parts heavily forested and, apart from the major valleys, sparsely inhabited.

[331] Tranlator's note: Lebach is a town in the district of Saarlouis, in Saarland, Germany. It is situated approximately 15 km northeast of Saarlouis, and 20 km north of Saarbrücken. Wildungen is likely Bad Wildungen, officially the City of Bad Wildungen, is a state-run spa and a small town in Waldeck-Frankenberg district in Hesse, Germany.

When we had just passed Sachsenberg, we discovered some strong troops of enemy riders on the way, which we had to take. Colonel von Fersen, on the other hand, arrived at the head of the column and said to Major von Bulow, "I want to attack the fellows, but you are in command." He took command of three squadrons of heavy cavalry and threw them so emphatically at the enemy that at the moment they were thrown over into disorder and fled. Colonel von Fersen pursued, charged into a violent burst of gunfire, which forced him to turn back. The hostile cavalry had settled down again, threw itself on ours and pursued them violently against our right wing. During this process, Major von Bülow had led the whole corps into an advantageous formation. The artillery began to fire at the weakening enemy. At the same time the enemy advanced against us with a very great impetuosity, and especially threatened the left wing, which was leaning against wheels towards a little brook; the right wing was very well supported in the direction of Münden.

After our heavy cavalry had formed, Colonel von Fersen was missed; but when the enemy cavalry was overthrown again, some horsemen rushed after them, and brought the body of the slain colonel, covered by seven wounds, into our lines.

Meanwhile Major von Bülow had hurried to the left wing. The enemy cavalry went through the little Orke Creek and a strong column of infantry followed in its wake. Major von Bülow saw the moment when the enemy's horsemen had partly passed the water and was ready to form, took the Carabinier and two squadrons of the Legion Britannique, and threw himself upon the enemy with such success that he was overthrown by them and with them great loss was driven back in disarray

*over the Orke. The enemy infantry, however, was inex-
orably penetrating the Orke at a point on our right and
Major von Bülow was just about to throw himself into
our flank with us, when we became aware that our center,
also fiercely attacked by enemies, had retreated towards
Hallenberg.[332] This compelled us to give up the advantage gained and, to cover our left wing, it was again advantageous against Hallenberg, and Major von Bülow
was anxious to turn again into the offensive against the
enemy's ever more threatening weapons than to death
was reported by the colonel von Fersen.*

*He now asked me to ride quickly to the com-
mander of the various regiments, and to ask who was
the senior in command and to inform him at the same
time, that, since he, Major von Bülow, knew quite well
the area; His advice would be at your command. I was
received very coldly by the commander; it was a colonel
of the infantry and two colonel lieutenants whom I first
came to. On my commission I received the answer, "they
would probably miss what they had to do; Major von
Bülow should only keep the left wing, if he so wished,
that they had been ordered by the colonel von Fersen and
could not to acknowledge another order." On the right
wing stood Colonel von Dittfurth, who commanded the
cavalry, which was about a thousand horses strong, and
he, without thinking for a moment, said at once: "Inform
Major von Bülow that I am absolutely in the position of
riding under his command, a man like this, I would like
to obey at such a critical moment, even if he would be the
youngest officer in the army."*

*While I was anxious to relay the above order, the
enemy continued to surge around the left wing to evade*

---

[332]Translator's notes: Hallenberg is a town in the Hochsauerland district, in North Rhine-Westphalia, Germany.

it more and more to completely cut off our retreat line via Winterberg to the Fulda Sauerland. Any thought of getting over to the army again was abandoned long ago. When I returned to Major von Bülow, I thought completely of the defensive, that Major von Bülow had to look solely to avoiding our position being completely overrun, which was done with all energy by him. Step by step, the fiercely advancing enemy fought over the ground, and when I returned to him; he had crossed his front with his left wing, and the enemy infantry could not do anything, though the terrain of our cavalry had to fight in was extremely difficult. My report put the brave Major in the greatest indignation, and he answered: 'My God! If the egoism of these gentlemen can not break the spirit of the 3,000 men in their hands, they may bear the responsibility; As far as I am concerned, the little group here either willingly sacrifices my life or willingly sacrifices it to my attempts.'

He blew up in front of the swarm of lords and said succinctly: "Children, keep trust and stay fired, I'll bring you through."

The movements of the troops were, however, very uncontrollable, and as there was no commander-in-chief to direct what was to happen, he became very sure, and Major von Bülow very rightly foresaw that it would soon take a sad turn as the enemy infantry had almost reached the hill of Hallenberg. The Major then asked me again to ride to the captain of the von Dittfurt Regiment and tell him to take the road to Belerburg and so on towards Lippstadt through the Sauerland as soon as the crisis, which was unfortunately to be feared, occurred.[333] No

---

[333] Translator's note: This may refer to Bad Berleburg, which is a town, in the district of Siegen-Wittgenstein, in North Rhine-Westphalia, Germany. It is one of Germany's largest towns by land area. It is located approximately 30 km northeast of Siegen and 35 km northwest of Marburg an der Lahn.

sooner had I discharged my order than I remembered how our infantry, in great disarray, pulled left against the ground behind Züschen, and at the same time pushed the enemy's riders into it, whereupon a boundless confusion arose, the enemy protected almost everything and also fell on the baggage.[334] It was impossible for me to reach my Carabinier, for the enemy's cavalry had already completely separated me from them. I therefore joined the colonel von Dittfurt, who was in charge of Berlin, and although the enemy always followed us, the conduct of our retreat prevented him from any attempt at attack. The night brought an end to the enemy pursuit.

At 11 o'clock in the evening we reached Berleburg, where as much as possible measures were taken to feed the horses for at least one hour quietly, as they were so tired as to be almost falling over with fatigue.[335]

A part of the defeated infantry arrived here at night, and Colonel von Dittfurth immediately declared to the officers, as they arrived, "Whoever is here is under my command, do what I say and not what he wants and whoever does not obey, I will have you cut down, even if you were my own brother! Now, gentlemen, your people gathered, the murmuring and disorder should and must stop."

This strong language from the Colonel, combined with the goodwill of the arriving officers, had a consequence that we were still able to form two rather strong battalions during the night. With some rest, I was able to see what would happen next.

Until around noon on the 14th of September,

---

[334] Translator's note: Züschen, Waldeck is a municipality in the central German state Hesse. Züschen, Waldeck is located in the administrative district Schwalm-Eder-Kreis.

[335] Translator's note: This likely refers to Berleburg, which is a town, in the district of Siegen-Wittgenstein, in North Rhine-Westphalia, Germany. It is located approximately 30 km northeast of Siegen and 35 km northwest of Marburg an der Lahn.

we expected the arrival of Major von Bülow, but since he did not make it, we made our way via Fleckenberg, Meschede, Rühden, and Hirschberg to Erwitte, near Lippstadt, where we arrived on the evening of 16 September without, since the day of the happy affair, being troubled by the enemy.[336] At the same time, we brought with us our experience, along with the Carabinier whom we gathered up on the march.

On the 17th of September, I immediately sat up and went to Stadtbergen, where I found Major von Bülow lying in a terrible state of nervous disease, of which he died a few days later. In him the army lost one of her most distinguished officers, and I, a friend whom I truly will never forget.

Baum reported to me: as he would have to Major von Bülow, the enemy penetrated into the lines of our infantry, and their destruction saw all their troops throw themselves to the ground and behind trees, in order to take part in the plundering of the baggage-which was completely lost. Thus, he immediately recognized the impossibility of retreating to Berleburg, and decided to open the way over Winterberg with his sword in his fist. At Winterberg they encountered a small detachment of enemy infantry, which was thrown over the houses at the first attempt. The retreat continued further on by way of extremely arduous paths over Usseln and Herrinhausen to Stadtbergen.[337]

On this occasion we lost more than 500 dead and just as many wounded and prisoners along with 8 guns,

---

[336] Translator's note: Fleckenberg is a locality in the municipality Schmallenberg in the district Hochsauerlandkreis in North Rhine-Westphalia, Germany. Hirschberg, a part of town of Werstein in the district of Soest, North Rhine-Westphalia.

[337] Translator's note: Today Usseln is part of Willingen, which is in Waldeck-Frankenberg in northern Hesse, Germany, some 80 km west of Kassel. Hemminghausen is another constituent community of Willingen.

ammunition wagons and all the baggage. The Carabi-
nier and Jäger Korps alone lost 19 men and 23 horses,
some of which had to be left behind ailing.

As far as Major von Monkewitz was concerned about this incident, he did not remember the circumstances which probably led to the
loss that had been suffered, nor did he look for the evil mien of the three
officers mentioned above.[338] How it could happen, incidentally, that the
whole incident transpired, in accordance with his duty, becomes superfluous, and would-if one may venture to speculate-find his reason in this
for the fact that the involved were detached from different armies, even
the staff officer belonged to another army. Though he was of a higher
rank, he did not hold the command.

How brilliantly stands out against the narrow-minded wretched-
ness of those three officers against the truly heroic stature of the colonel
von Dittfurth. The ashes of this valiant soldier deserve the tribute of
making his conduct a pattern to each officer in similar cases. The brave
Dittfurth had to see that the officer was very well acquainted with the
area, and that on several occasions he led considerable detachments of
the army had led to fame and glory. That is why he was much more anxious and hesitant in his command at such a critical moment. The man,
like every soldier, should have the matter before his eyes; whether the
one who led them happily to the end, was called Lieutenant, Major or
Colonel, that was the same to him!!

Battle of a Carabiner with a French officer

A single attack, courageously carried out, may still find room to
contribute to the story of the battle described above.

When the cavalry of the left wing retreated to Züschen and saw
the enemy there, an enemy officer with 10 to 12 flankers dashed to the
right and left in front of the Carabinier and seemed to challenge them.

---

[338] The incident is mentioned in the documents of the court whose congress of court 4 vol., Pp.
37 and 38.

Initially, no notice was taken from it, but when the officer was getting more and more outraged, and rushing ahead of his men, a hot-blooded Carabinier with a rifle named Nordmeher turned to the Captain Baum and said; "Captain, shall I?" The answer was a curt yes! -Nordmeher now fired again, parried his horse and road to the enemy officer: "Lord, let your flankers ride back, then we'll see who brings the other down!" He gave his people a signal to push on ahead of them until he was one with the enemy, and now the Carabinier approached too quickly to him. For a long time, both horses were chasing each other in smaller and smaller circles, the Frenchman was a clever, more talented rider, but nothing in the Carabinier gave him any pause. At last, the officer had gotten his left hand off of Nordmeher, and now seemed certain of it, and put a lightning bolt on the carbine; but he was sure of his cause! For at the moment when the Frenchman was about to deliver the fatal blow, the Carabinier had thrown his horse around on the back, and at the same time had pulled the pallash over the officer's face. As he fell from the saddle, his flankers flew in and prevented Nordmeher from bringing the horse of his enemy back to the squadron, which he managed to reach again.

The Hereditary Prince of Brunswick, as we have shown earlier, had set out from Warburg on the evening of 12 September to give support to Colonel von Fersen. But as the enemy was notified of this on the afternoon of the 13th, he exerted all his strength to throw the corps of troops over the houses and set about his own retreat to get to safety before the hereditary prince arrived. This was the reason why half of the defeated and scattered corps was not further advanced by the enemy. After the hereditary prince had taken possession of a part of the defeated troops at Korbach, which he had made, he went back to Marburg.

After a short time, Duke Ferdinand detached the hereditary prince for the Neider Rhine, while he himself stopped at the Deimel to watch the Duke of Broglie, who was in quarters at Kassel. The Carabinier and Jager Corps joined the Army Corps of the Erbprinzen, and united on 23 September at Bredlaar Monastery with 400 infantry and 4 squadrons of Prussian hussars under Lieutenant-Colonel Jeanneret, who took command of the advanced guard. Major von Monkewitz was in command that night. The further march went over Lippstadt, Werl, Unna against Ruhrort, before which places one arrived on 29 September. A standing enemy detachment, however, escaped across the Rhine at our approach and only 22 men were caught in the insignificant skirmish that took place there.

Raid on Rheinbergen and Orson[339]

On the night of the 30th of September, Lieutenant-Colonel Jeanneret crossed the Rhine with his vehicles, and advanced rapidly towards Rheinbergen, where there was an enemy detachment of about 130 infantry and cavalry. Before the enemy knew it, the place was surrounded by hussars and Carabinier. The greater part of our infantry had been left in a good position as a reserve in the direction between Repeln and Barel, and Lieutenant von Berk, with 20 horses and 30 fighters, had been sent to Orson, where there was reportedly a weak enemy detachment.[340]

"There was loud noise," says von Monkewitz in his report,

> *and the enemy cavalry attempted to escape by the Wesel*
> *Gate, against which I had taken with 150 horses. Baum,*
> *who led my advanced guard, rushed towards her, we fol-*
> *lowed in the galop, threw the cavalry back in disorder,*
> *and at the same time invaded. Meanwhile the enemy in-*
> *fantry had lined up in the churchyard, where the enemy*
> *hussars fled. When we arrived there, we were given a*
> *salvo, which required us to give up the attack at the mo-*
> *ment, until the lieutenant-colonel von Jeanneret would*
> *appear to have entered from the other side; I led my 25*
> *Carabinier expeditiously and they threw themselves into*

---

[339] Translator's note: Rheinberg is a town in the district of Wesel, in North Rhine-Westphalia, Germany. It is situated on the left bank of the Rhine, approx. 10 km north of Moers and 15 km south of Wesel. It comprises the municipal districts of Rheinberg, Borth, Budberg, and Orsoy.
[340] Tranlator's note: Repeln here may refer to modern Repelen, which is a part of Dusseldorf. Barel is a part of Oldenburg, Weser-Ems, Niedersachsen, Germany.

*the houses next to the churchyard to entertain the enemy
with well-aimed gunfire. But that was superfluous, because while the Carabinier were barely off. This induced
the enemy infantry, 1 captain and 100 men to intensify
their rifle fire. The cavalry, the enemy's men, fled against
the rich Thor after our persecution was arrested by the
infantry. There they managed to escape happily by and
for money, although that side of us was occupied. But
they had to thank their salvation on the fact that their
force, mostly consisting of deserters of our army, for the
most part was clothed in their old uniforms, so that they
were regarded as friends, and did not recognize this error until it was too late. Except the rider who were hit
we only captured 14 men. Lieutenant von Berk, meanwhile, had been fortunate in the attack on the garrison
of Orson, consisting of 1 officer and 50 men of Fischer's corps. The Carabinier corps had wounded only one
horse in this incident; the Prussian hussars lost 4 men.*

The enemy, expelled from Ruhrort, had, as one learned from the
prisoners made in Orson, drawn across this place to Wesel and left the
officer with 50 men here as the post of warning;[341] however, no one had
thought of the possibility that Lieutenant-Colonel von Jeanneret would
cross the Rhine that same night and follow his enemy on the foot.[342] For
this reason, the officer left behind in Orson had not taken the most ordi-
nary precautions, in order to detect a raid, which was always conceiv-
able, and as the success taught, really took place. He had been literally
taken out of bed with his command. Nor had any thought been taken
of informing the partisan Cambefort, who was in command of Rheinbergen, that the enemy was in Ruhrort, and therefore he too was quite
careless until then, when the hussars and Carabiniers so rudely put an

[341] Translator's note: picket.
[342] Translator's note: Ruhrort is a district within the German city of Duisburg situated north
of the confluence of the Ruhr and the Rhine, in the western part of the Ruhr area of North
Rhine-Westphalia.

end to his rest.

Lieutenant-Colonel von Jeanneret proved by the swift and vigorous decision to cross the Rhine at once and to follow the enemy with his little group on the spot, in order to avoid the first flight which, the unexpected arrival of the Prince on the Rhine had caused the enemy. To take as much advantage as possible that he knew how to lead the war as a true hussar leader. It should be noted that the Hereditary Prince was almost a full day's march back and moved in the direction of Dorsten against Wesel, so could not be counted on to support any of these maneuvers.

Lieutenant-Colonel von Jeanneret now moved to Büderich, with a few more prisoners, and the corps of the hereditary prince encircled Wesel.

On October 4, Jeanneret moved to Alphen and sent a detachment, in which Lieutenant von Berk had 30 Carabinier, against the Maas, which destroyed and burned a hostile magazine in Venloo[343] When the said detachment returned 7 October, Jeanneret crossed through Rhinebergen in front of Dusseldorf. There, in the Linn area, on the 9th of October, there was a fairly lively affair, in which the enemy received 23 wounded and lost 8 horses.[344] The detachment then returned to Rheinbergen.[345]

On 12 October, von Monkewitz, with the Carabinier and Jäger and three hundred men from the corps of Schondes, returned to Spelle via the Rhine, and then posted troops across the rest of the district of Cologne, where the Marquis de Castries, who arrived hurriedly and made an asylum in Wesel for himself observed him.[346] Count Wilhelm, on the

---

[343] Translator's note: Alpen is a municipality situated in the Lower Rhine region, located between the Ruhr area and the border with the Netherlands. Adjacent cities are Rheinberg, Xanten.

[344] Tranlator's note: The town of Linn, mentioned above no longer exists as an independent entity. Linn has been a part of the City of Krefeld, Germany, since its incorporation into that city in 1901. Linn lies with its historic city center within the lower Rhenish lowlands about 5 km (3.1 mi) east of the Krefeld city center.

[345] Translator's note: Rheinberg is a town in the district of Wesel, in North Rhine-Westphalia, Germany. It is situated on the left bank of the Rhine, approx. 10 km (6.2 miles) north of Moers and 15 km (9.3 miles) south of Wesel.

[346] Translator's note: Spelle is a municipality in the Emsland district, in Lower Saxony, Germa-

other hand, was attached to the siege in front of Wesel, and had taken command of the depot corps, as well as all the troops on the right bank of the Rhine. The hereditary prince had crossed the Rhine.

On 16 October, Lieutenant von Berk fought his way across the Rhine with some Jäger, and had captured an enemy detachment in Orson, which had come down to the Rhine on ships that day and raided the Tianan Regiment, shot some of them, and took 4 prisoners.

On the same day, von Monkewitz left the high Waffers for Ruhort with the bulk of the detachment and made a demonstration in the direction of Neumuehle on the right bank of the Imst.[347]

Establishment of outposts to cover the siege of Wesel

We believe that the report by Major von Monkewitz on the measures to cover the siege, included on the following page, should be studied closely, since they can serve as an example to guide the correct actions in similar cases.

The report is from 16 October and addressed to Count Wilhelm. It reads as follows:

> *It is indispensable to post several detachments to the Ruhr, and to watch for signs of patrols. Now that I had Captain von Hattorf at Ruhrort, the Ruhr could only be seen from here, though a small detachment advanced after a while. The enemy could make many moves during the time that further patrols are on their way back, which would be discovered too late by the subsequent patrol. This can only be prevented by the following measures, which I have held up to your Excellency (who, by the way, practiced them). Captain von Hattorf and his detachment go to Mühlheim, reinforce the command there, and send an officer with 30 horses to Kettwich, as a most*

ny. It is situated approximately 20 km southeast of Lingen, and 10 km north of Rheine.
[347] Translator's note: Neumuehle is located in the region of Rheinland-Pfalz. Rheinland-Pfalz's capital Mainz (Mainz) is approximately 88 km / 54 mi away from Neumuehle.

important post.[348] At the Ackner Ferry I posted an officer and 30 horses.[349] If Lieutenant-Colonel Narzhnskh stops at Hattigen and establishes a post with Little Dortmund, without Ew.[350] You can notify enough of the posts early enough. In this way I patrolled the Ruhr to the Ackner Ferry, the officer standing there could see as far as Mühheim, Captain von Hattorf to Kettwich, the other officer to Hattingen, Lieutenant-Colonel Narzhnskh to Schwerte, and his post established at Little Dortmund, beyond Recklinghausen.[351] Since I do not doubt that these orders of Ew. If you are allowed to be groomed, Hattorf will leave for Mühlheim at this moment. And so forth.

As a result of the affair of Kloster Kampf the Erbprinz went back across the Rhine and the siege of Wesel was lifted.[352] Major von Monkewitz and his detachment arrived in Sahlen on 25 October to watch the left bank of the Lippe against Wesel.[353] The Hereditary Prince camped at Kleine Reckum. A detachment of the army, under General-General von Breidenbach, was in Dorsten.

On the evening of 27 October, Major von Monkewitz made a reconnaissance against Kruidenburg, and learned that the enemy had advanced a strong detachment against Drevenack, on the right side of the

---

[348]Tranlator's note: Today known as Mülheim an der Ruhr, it is also described as "City on the River". Mülheim is a city in North Rhine-Westphalia in Germany. It is located in the Ruhr Area between Duisburg, Essen, Oberhausen and Ratingen. Kettwich is now known as Kettwig. Kettwig is the southernmost borough of the city of Essen in western Germany and, until 1975, was a town in its own right.
[349]Translator's note: The Acker Ferry is one of the ferries across the Ruhr.
[350] Tranlator's note: Hattingen is a town in the northern part of the Ennepe-Ruhr-Kreis district, in North Rhine-Westphalia, Germany.
[351] Tranlator's note: Schwerte is a town in the district of Unna, in North Rhine-Westphalia, Germany.
[352] Translator's note: The affair at Kloster Kampfen refers to a clash between the French and a British and Allied army on October 15, 1760. The French won the engagement.
[353] Translator's Notes: Gahlen is situated in Wesel, Dusseldorf, Nordrhein-Westfalen, Germany, its geographical coordinates are 51° 40' 0" North, 6° 52' 0" East and its original name (with diacritics) is Gahlen.

Lippe.[354] Both General von Breidenbach and the officer in Schermbeck were informed of it. General von Breidenbach's force was broken the same evening so vigorously that he had to return to Wesel after suffering heavy losses.

Battle at Sahlen

On the 1st of November, the enemy on the left side of Lippe put up a considerable resistance at Sahlen; however, their movements had been discovered tentatively enough by the patrols, and General von Breidenbach reinforced Major von Monkewitz with 100 horses, 100 infantrymen, and 2 three-pounder cannons to the Soutien. The Major now quietly awaited the approach of the enemy in the proper position. When the enemy party appeared, it was immediately attacked and compelled to retreat. A rather heated fight ensued, which ended with the enemy forced to retreat towards Wesel. Captain Baum pursued, fell in front of the enemy rear guard near Kruidenburg and hit the enemy hard, leaving many dead and taking 19 horses. Von Monkewitz had only 5 dead and 14 wounded from his detachment, among the latter two Carabinier. "The enemy probably did not expect us to have artillery," added Monkewitz in his report. The headquarters of Duke Ferdinand was at Ovelgünne in Paderborn, and Marshal Broglie was constantly at Kassel.[355]

On the 7th of November Marquis de Castries advanced with his entire Corps d'Armee from Wesel. One part camped by the so-called black stone, another by Drevenack.

"I wrote this," says von Monkewitz, "at once, without the privilege of the hereditary prince's order the following day to reconnoiter the encampment at Drevenack, in order to find out reluctantly whether the enemy is crossing bridges over the Lippe."

---

[354] Translator's note: Kruidenburg is a place situated in Wesel, Dusseldorf, Nordrhein-Westfalen.
[355] Translator's note: Ovelgünne is a village and a former municipality in the Börde district in Saxony-Anhalt, Germany.

Reconnaissance action at Sartrupp[356]

On the 8th of November, at dawn, I went out with forty horses and just as many Jäger, half of us and half from Scheither's Corps, over Sartrupp against their fire, and as I soon reached the Lippe, I became aware of two bridges, which were not quite finished yet, but close. The whole corps of Fischer stood ready as the bridges extended. I sent back my Jäger immediately to fill the defile at Sartrupp, through which I had to return, but with the cavalry I awaited the completion of the bridges. These were soon finished, and immediately the enemy cavalry went on, about four o'clock with 500 horses. About 150 horses immediately began to attack me sharply; I withdrew cautiously, but the enemy discovered my weakness, moved at the gallop, soon became entangled with my rear guard, and also captured two horsemen from the corps of Scheither. But these were immediately chopped off by Lieutenant von Berk, and we succeeded in throwing the bulk of the enemy's attack over their horses. Defeating the enemy and going back, we reached the defile at Sartrupp. Now the enemy doubled his efforts; and probably thought we were cornered. My people were duly instructed and went from both wings in columns through the defile. Suddenly the Jäger opened such an effective rifle fire that the persecution did not cease at once, and many horses were seen riding around without a rider, but the enemy also seemed to consider it advisable to pull back from the rifle fire. I kept my position until late in the evening, and then, without being pursued and without losing a man, I retired to Sahlen.

---

[356]Translator's note: Satrup is a village and a former municipality in the district of Schleswig-Flensburg, in Schleswig-Holstein, Germany. It is situated approximately 20 km north of Schleswig, and 15 km southeast of Flensburg.

On the 9th of November, Captain Baum again reconnoitered Sartrupp to see if the enemy on the left side of the Lippe were doing anything. He returned with four men and six horses, which he had taken from Fischer's corps.

Between 9 and 18 November, nothing happened. In the course of the latter day the enemy made two bridges to Bockholt to counter our foraging, with small skirmishes between the patrols daily until the 27th of November.[357] The hereditary prince of Braunschweig-who always encamped at Reckum-occasionally came to Sahlen to see if anything was going to be done against the enemy foragers. But as they were always covered by strong detachments, nothing was attempted.

After the enemy had fully denuded the area by the end of the month, he returned with all the troops, some of them detached, across the Rhine and moved into winter quarters. This example was followed by the Crown Prince taking his headquarters in Kösfeld.

Major von Monkewitz, to whom the battalion of Appelbohm still came from the Legion Britannique, occupied until January 2, 1761, his old known post at Haltern

---

[357] Translator's note: Bocholt is a city in the north-west of North Rhine-Westphalia, Germany, part of the district Borken. It is situated 4 km south of the border with the Netherlands.

Chapter 5
Campaign of 1761

March to Upper Hesse. Battle at Seelheim between Marburg and Amöneburg. Reprisal battle by Hunsdorf in Waldeckschen. Battle at Altenstäde. March of the Carabinier to Aahaus in the Münsterschen. Bloody battle at Darrfeld. Foray against the Imster. The enemy invades Lünen. Lünen is taken again. Lieutenant von Berk raided an enemy unit at Hörde. A Carabinier patrol is blown up by enemies in Diphen. Major von Monkewitz pursues the enemy, who is retreating from Kösfeld, and hauls him from Hiddingstädt. The enemy attacks Dülmen. Combat at Hilftrup. The hereditary prince of Brunswick takes Dorsten. Battle at Albachten before Münster. Battle between Notteln and Havixbeck. Battle at Lüdinghausen.

The campaign was over. All Hesse and a part of the Hanoverian country, including the city of Göttingen, remained in the possession of the enemy.

On 2 January, Major von Monkewitz and his detachment moved to Dortmund to watch the enemy, which began to spread along the Ruhr. The Hereditary Prince of Brunswick moved in this time against the Köllnische Sauerland. Duke Ferdinand soon followed suit to drive the enemy out of Hesse. General von Hardenberg stopped with a few troops in the Munster, to visit the area between Wesel and Düsseldorf. This general took up his quarters in Hamm and posted the Carabinier and Jäger Corps in Lünen, which he invested on 2 February and stopped until the 17th.

The important garrison of Wesel undertook at this time many movements and demonstrations along the Lippe and Ruhr, whereby Hardenburg's Corps were always kept in motion, without that there was anything serious, only now and then did some small skirmishing occur among the patrols. The depletion of the light troops was very trouble-some to the enemy because of this eastern disturbance; but the enemy achieved his intention of masticating the march of the Chevalier de Muy, through the mountains against Frankfurt. On the 24th of February General von Herdenberg was ordered to leave behind a small detachment of observation from Wesel, and to observe with greatness the movement of the Chevalier de Muy, fearing that he would endeavor to pass Kassel through the Sauerland, to attempt to disrupt the siege of that city. General von Hardenberg to this end moved against Stadtbergen and the Carabinier and Jager covered this march in the right flank and arrived on 1 March in Stadtbergen, from where they were advanced to Sierschagen to observe the paths that lead from the Sauerland into Waldeck.[358]

On the 14th of March, General von Hardenberg, having learned nothing of the Chevalier du Muy, set out again to move on Korbach, Fürstenberg and Frankenberg and then to Gemünden, where he arrived on the 13th.[359] On the orders of Duke Ferdinand, whose headquarters were in Schweinsberg, Monkewitz, with the corps and the battalion of Uhlans assigned to him, moved to the north face to guard the area of Gießen,.[360] The enemy, meanwhile, approached, and spread himself in the Busegferthale.

On the 16th of March, the enemy reconnoitered north-facing pickets, where a rather lively skirmishing occurred, in which a Carabinier was shot and three horses wounded. In the late evening von Monkewitz, by Duke Ferdinand's own order, resolved to move to Rohenhaus, to watch Gießen, and to make contact with the post at Holzhausen. Once there, he was to await the arrival of the English Lord Granby, under whose command he would then come. Lord Granby had hitherto been

---

[358] Translator's note: Sierschagen is a town in Schleswig-Holstein.

[359] Translator's note: this likely refers to the Gemünden which lies roughly 22 km northeast of Marburg on the edge of the Burgwald range to the west and near the Killewald range rising to the northeast. The Wohra River crosses the town.

[360] Translator's note: Schwweinsberg here ma refer to Schweinsberg Castle or Schweinsber-ghaus is a fortified house in the municipality of Attinghausen in the canton of Uri in Switzerland. Giessen, spelled Gießen in German)), is a town in the German federal state (*Bundesland*) of Hesse, capital of both the district of Giessen and the administrative region of Giessen. The population is approximately 86,000, with roughly 44,000 university students.

on the right bank of the river Lahn, but on that day he crossed the river and took the posts to Epsdorf, Frauneberg, Schreck and Grosse, and Kleine Saalheim.[361] The great French army, under the Duke of Broglie, stood on both sides of the Lahn between Wetzlar and Gießen, its light troops roaming in the Buseggerthale until Treis on the Lümme.[362]

18 March, the enemy launched a major move directed against the highway leading from Gießen via Rohenhaus towards Marburg. Lord Granby found himself compelled to go over the Ohm while Major von Monkewitz was dispatched with the Carabinier and 100 English horse to Rauerbach and Kunzeldorf to cover the Marburg Regiment, which vacated this place.[363]

On 21 March, Major von Monkewitz was in Seelheim, on the road from Amöneburg to Marburg. [364]

"Since the enemy says was close by," von Monkewitz observed,

> *and even his light troops were on our side, so every eve-
> ning when it was dark, I left the village and bivouacked in
> a good position beside it. This morning a very heavy fog
> had fallen. After the same had completely disappeared by
> 9 o'clock and my patrols had discovered nothing of the
> enemy, I moved to the village to feed the men and horses
> as circumstances allowed. No sooner had the men moved
> to the stable than 3 squadrons of enemy hussars, which
> were later followed by a battalion of infantry, blasted
> into the village, beating us quite comfortably. My Jäger,
> however, when I stood in the field during the day, were*

---

[361] Translator's note: It is likely the author is actually referring to Elsdorf. Elsdorf is a town in the Rhein-Erft-Kreis, in North Rhine-Westphalia. It is situated approximately 5 km south-west of Bergheim and 30 km west of Cologne. Schreck is situated in Rhein-Sieg-Kreis, Koln, Nordrhein-Westfalen.

[362] Translator's note: Wetzlar is a city in the state of Hesse.

[363] Translator's note: The Ohm is a tributary of the Lahn, a river in Hesse.

[364] Translator's note: This likely refers to the area of Seeheim-Jugenheim which is a municipality in the Darmstadt-Dieburg district in Hesse, Germany. The modern municipality was formed on January 1,1977 through the unification of the previously separate municipalities of Seeheim and Jugenheim.

ready to fight at any moment, having posted them in two houses, right and left of the entrance, which completely covered the way. When, therefore, the Bedette, who had been standing in front of the place, had given fire, and the enemy followed his retreat on foot, he was received with such a good fire, that he felt a desire to go on riding. The hussars hastily left the sanctuary to await the arrival of their infantry. In the meantime, the Carabinier were gaining time to back up on the hill towards Nieder Seelheim, where very soon the English Dragoon Regiment of Elliot under Major Erksine joined us. The Jäger continually defended the village with great tenacity against repeated and brave attacks by the enemy infantry. The battle had already taken two hours when the enemy finally moved up three guns and started firing at the houses where the Jäger were standing. Lord Granby was now on his own, and when it was noticed that the enemy, with strong masses of cavalry and infantry, spread out on the hills of Frauenberg, he gave orders that all the troops who were still the same at that time should come under the cannons of Amöneburg. Our Jäger now left the place step by step, and although the enemy pressed hard, he could not harm them. A squadron of hussars, who rushed too boldly when the village was already vacated, was badly injured by the Dragoons of Elliot and the Carabinier. From the corps I lost five Jäger dead and 12 wounded, along with 5 wounded Carabinier and 9 horses of the same unit.

On this day the battle occurred at Grimberg; also the siege of Kassel was lifted.[365]

Major von Monkewitz now had to occupy Stautzenbach with the

---

[365] Translator's note: Grimberg is situated in Rheinisch-Bergischer Kreis, Koln, Nordrhein-Westfalen.

corps and 50 mounted troops, in order to consider the great road from Marburg to Kassel; he detached the lieutenant von Berk with twenty horses and twelve Jäger to Anzefahr.

On the 24th of March, Lord Granby made a further withdrawal and went to Serbitterode. The Carabinier and Jäger made up the rear guard with Hanoverians and English troops. The enemy followed with strong cavalry formations, but without disturbing the retreat. This went on via Frankenberg into Waldeck. The English Colonel Beckwith commanded the rear guard, which on 27 March between Ahlbach and Hunsdorf was so violently and emphatically attacked by the enemy who was three-times superior that it was necessary to intervene in the unequal struggle.[366] Despite the enemy's overwhelming numerical superiority, the pursuit continued, although his results had to be bought with significant losses. Major von Monkewitz places his losses at nearly 300 men. Of the Carabinier, ten remain on patrol, of the Jäger 8, and 28 Carabinier and Jäger were wounded; Moreover, the Carabinier had 7 dead and 18 wounded horses.[367]

The retreat of the army went gradually by the Wadecksche against the Köllnische Sauerland. The enemy was on von Monkewitz heels, and the commanding officer commanded Colonel Beckwith to fight some more of the same type of engagements, of which the most important was on 29 March between Elberberg and Altenstäde, not far from Wolfhagen. The Carabinier lost 5 men and 7 horses.[368]

From Stadtbergen, where they arrived on 2 April, Colonel Beckwith turned left over Kaltenhaard against the monastery, and posted Major von Monkewitz to Upper and Lower Berheim.[369]

---

[366] Translator's note: Ahlbach is a town in Hesse, Germany. Hundsdorf is an Ortsgemeinde – a community belonging to a Verbandsgemeinde – in the Westerwaldkreis in Rhineland-Palatinate, Germany.

[367] Translator's note: In this case, I take the phrase "remain on patrol" to imply that the troopers in question were killed in the fighting.

[368] Translator's note: Elberberyg is a town in Hesse that is east of Waldeck. Altenstadt is a municipality in the district Wetteraukreis, in Hesse, Germany. It is situated in the Nidder valley, approx. 27 kilometers north-east of Frankfurt am Main. Wolfhagen is a town in the district of Kassel, in Hesse, Germany.

[369] Translator's note: Stadtbergen is a town in the district of Augsburg, in Bavaria, Germany.

G. W. During

The Carabinier and Jäger corps had melted together at this time due to attrition from the battles they fought, the relentless winter-weather on the Lippe, as well as by the constant difficulties of campaigning in Hesse. Captain Baum had been away with an illness for a long time; Lieut. von Berk became ill now, and on 5 April he was sent to Lippstadt with the wounded, sick and ailing men and horses. After this departure, only one corporal, a trumpeter, and 32 Carabinier and 53 Jäger from the corps remained with the major; Therefore, the expected replacement from Bückeburg was eagerly awaited.

On 6 April, very early, Monkewitz received the following order from the Crown Prince dated Neuhaus (near Paderborn) the 5 April noon.

The Major is to march immediately into the Münster office Aahaus. They will lead the way with the cavalry; the infantry can follow. Take hold of the Aahaus Post and in consequence have the castle occupied by infantry. Its end purpose is to cover the communication between Holland and Münster, which makes Campfort very insecure. Then seek to observe closely the enemy's movements. Reeß and Emmerich are said to be occupied by enemy infantry. Repeats go to Münster to the supreme La Chevallerie. You will also see in constant communication with Major Düring, who commands in Bentheim.[370]

Signed, Carl, Hereditary Prince.

It is situated in the outskirts of Augsburg. Kaldehaart may refer to Kallenhardt which is a district of Rüthen in the district of Soest (North Rhine-Westphalia). Berheim would seem to refer to Bergheim, see page 78, note 22.

[370] It is the same Major Düring who, as captain, defended the castle of Dillenburg in January 1760, was deposed by Duke Ferdinand, and subsequently (after a fine defense, as cited by Tempelhof) when he was again included in it, on July 15, against the castle free deduction handed over. Forgive me the little vanity of quoting the name of a slip of my family in such a rude affair. The author.

Major von Monkewitz set out immediately. But as the snow was very melted, he felt it desirable for him, wherever possible, to keep the Jäger in the same footsteps, and he encouraged them, in a sincere way, to make quite an effort.

The march went through Söst, Kirchbinken, Hamm, Drensteinfurt to Rorel, where the force arrived on 8 April.[371] Faithfully, the Jäger had kept up with the cavalry to this point; it was not enough for today alone; they therefore had to spend the night here, while von Monkewitz and the 34 riders were still 3 hours further ahead at Havisheck.[372] All the inquiries that had been made on the march agreed that "there was nothing here known about the French."

Battle at Darrfeld

On 9 April, reports Major von Monkewitz in his diary,

I marched with the Carabinier over Darrfeld and to Aahaus, and as soon as I got there I heard the news that a few hours before there was an enemy detachment of about 100 hussars and 120 infantrymen, the latter moved on to the Bauerwagen See. The Jäger were behind us the whole march and came to Darrfeld today. Upon receiving this unpleasant news, I resolved to return to Asbeck, seeing that it would be impossible for me to stay in Aahuas with 34 riders. It was already late afternoon when I passed Asbeck, and now it became known that the aforesaid enemy detachment, probably informed by the previous inhabitants of my advance, was rapidly approaching from the left to cut me off in Darrfeld. It was impossible to dodge their

---

[371] Translator's note: Drensteinfurt is a town in the district of Warendorf, in North Rhine-Westphalia, Germany. It is situated approximately 15 km north of Hamm and 20 km south of Münster. The villages Rinkerode in the north and Walstedde in the south are part of Drensteinfurt.

[372] Translator's note: This may refer to Havixbek is a municipality situated on the north-east edge of the Baumberge in the district of Coesfeld, in northern North Rhine-Westphalia, Germany. It is located approximately 15 km west of Münster.

advance. The enemy hussars already had a way to go, and I had no choice but to get involved with them. So, I went with my 34 men, with the saber in my fist, to the enemy hussars, although they were certainly four times as strong as I was. In the beginning, things went pretty well, breaking through them and clearing the way to Darrfeld. Alone during the battle, the enemy infantry approached, and as the enemy noticed that our horses had been exhausted, and we were without support, he came up more violently and surrounded me formally. It then came to a scuffle, as a result of which I again as well as I wanted to go through and took my retreat against Darrfeld, to where I was aggressively pursued. In Darrfeld I had already met a Jäger who had just entered there, and with them I immediately went back to the enemy, who immediately withdrew and whom we escorted to Asbeck, but which could not help me much, because I had no cavalry to track him. On this occasion I lost three and twenty men and the same, but, without exception, wounded others into enemy hands. As bad as this incident was for us, even the enemy later confessed that our men had fought well, and I am well-advised that our loss would not have been so great by never going to Hesse during the arduous winter expedition. Rest, and very often completely lack of forage added to our sufferings.[373]

In the report made to Count Wilhelm about this unfortunate battle, von Monkewitz says, among other things, that "various people among the prisoners will certainly find themselves gravely wounded because they desperately resisted."

If all that Carabinier Corps had done in the course of the years-long war were given over to oblivion and never mentioned its name in

---

[373] Translator's note: Asbeck is a village northwest of Münster. It is in the Legden region.

history - as it has done so far - it seems to us that this battle would at least be an honorable entry in the history of cavalry. May the rider's heart feel warmed by the story of this battle, and gain the conviction: that, in spite of dilapidated horses, broken bayonets, and in spite of four times superior numbers of enemy riders, it is possible to get through, if the heart is in the right place, and the very iron will to get through. Once there, it does not break with petty calculation and speculation, which, when it is about to be cut in, has to be completely eliminated.

Among those who found a hero's death on that day was the Carabinier Galenzkh. We have had the opportunity to quote this name several times, and may he not mind, if it is remarked yet, how no battle was passed by the corps in which the name of Galenzkh does not honorably appear as he was an exceedingly brave and prudent soldier. Superiors asked him more than once to become a sergeant; but he always refused. He just wanted to serve as a Carabinier! Although he was only one, yet it is the duty of the historian not to abandon his name in obscurity to the Carabinier Corps, but to boldly place it beside those of other distinguished men of that time. He was a Hungarian by birth, deserted by the Austrian Empire, and entered the Carabinier Corps in 1756; Kremitz is indicated as his place of birth.[374]

The difficulties, almost passed, as the cavalry of the corps was now, it would be very gratifying, when on 10 April, Captain Baum and Lieutenant von Berk, with 22 convalescent Carabinier and horses, again joined the corps, which now stood in Burg-Steinfurth. The Hereditary Prince moved his headquarters to Münster on 18 April and immediately gave orders for the Corps to march back to Greve, three hours behind Münster, in order to concentrate and rest the expected reinforcement.[375] The Erbprinz praised the Carabinier on the occasion of the celebrated skirmish of 9 April, and Monkewitz says: "I could not help noticing, with the gentry's expansive narrative of the fight, that they were taking me too far with so few people prehistory and exposed, which the Prince

---

[374] Translator's note: The Kremitz referred to here may actually be the city of Chemnitz.

[375] Translator's note: Greven likely refers to Greven, a medium-sized town in the district of Steinfurt.

also recognized."

Until 29 April, the corps rested; the replacements had arrived, and most of the sick and wounded rejoined the corps. On this day, Major von Monkewitz was again able to move to Lüdinghausen with 75 horses and 83 Jäger, where he himself remained until 12 May.[376]

The chief master of Duke Ferdinand was constantly at Neuhaus near Paderborn. Duke de Broglie was in Hessen with a part of the enemy army, while the greater part of it under Soubise assembled on the Lower Rhine, and formed several camps at Cologne, Dusseldorf, Derdingen, Wesel, Xanthen, and Rees. Major von Monkewitz had gone near Wesel on 1 May saying, "He is looking for my old acquaintances, who, because they were well paid, brought quite accurate and more frequent information."[377]

In fact, Major von Monkewitz was responsible for most of the affairs of the army's informants, as can be seen from an available calculation of the funds used for this purpose.

On 10 May, the Crown Prince wrote to the Major from Münster: "So Dero received letters from today's date; I ask for a provisional and auspicious two hundred thaler to inspire him to seek information quite diligently, so that we receive early information on the consequences of this first movement. From the 12th of May forward I will take my quarters to Notteln, and Lieutenant-General von Pose will come to Lüdinghausen this day, the Herr Major [Monkewitz] will march to Weddern and from there will send word to me as often as possible."[378]

The corps moved to Weddern, but the following day to Lünen, where it remained until the end of May, and during this time made several movements against the Ruhr and against the Wesel in order to collect news of the enemy.

---

[376] Translator's note: Lüdinghausen is a town in the district of Coesfeld in the state of North Rhine-Westphalia, Germany. It is located on the Dortmund-Ems Canal, approx. 25 km southwest of Münster. It is known for its three castles, Castle Luedinghausen, Kakesbeck and Vischering Castle.

[377] Translator's note: It appears from the quote that Monkewitz was going to try and gather intelligence on the French forces from spies he had paid in the area.

[378] Translator's note: Weddern is a village in Dülmen in North Rhine-Westphalia.

The enemy camp, close to Wesel, was considerably strengthened toward the end of the month, which led the Crown Prince to take a truly advantageous position at Schapdetten.[379] The outposts stood to Dülmen, Lette, Kösfeld and Lünen. The last post was retained by the Carabinier Corps. The troops occupying this position had a very arduous task, as it constantly struggled against the Ruhr and also had to observe all the forces on the left-wing of the Lippe up to Wesel.

On the 10th of June, Major von Monkewitz made a most important communication to the Crown Prince, in a letter from that date, in which he thanked the Major for the, "most pertinent news of the operations the whole campaign."

The Prince de Soubise went on 14 June to Wesel on the left bank of the Lippe and united at Gladebeck, not far Westerholte, with General Chevert recently arrived from Dusseldorf.[380] At this news, the hereditary prince immediately moved to the Hamm area, and Duke Ferdinand likewise set out against the County of Mark, leaving General von Spörcken behind in Paderborn to keep the Duke de Broglie occupied. The enemy army camped at Dortmund and Dorstfeld on 17 June, which is why the Lünen post was occupied by 2 battalions of the Legion and the Hessian Jäger.[381] Colonel von Lindau took over the command. The Bückeburg foot Jäger stood in at Bork.

On the 20th of June, Major von Monkewitz gave orders to cross the Lippe with the Carabiner and three squadrons of the Legion at Dorsten, to stab the enemy army in the rear and, if possible, to try something against their communication with Dusseldorf one day after an insignificant engagement in a reconnaissance against Unna, where the enemy had penetrated that day.

Major von Monkewitz crossed the Lippe at Dorsten on the night of 20 June and advanced towards Imster via Gladbeck but found the

---

[379] Translator's note: Schapdetten is situated in Coesfeld in North Rhine-Westphalia.

[380] translator's note: Gladbeck is a town in the district of Recklinghausen in North Rhine-Westphalia, Germany. Westerholt is a municipality in the district of Wittmund, in Lower Saxony, Germany.

[381] Translator's note: Dorstfeld is a city in Regierungsbezirk Arnsberg (North Rhine-Westphalia).

enemy everywhere and so went back across the Lippe, to dare unnecessarily at night what was not to be carried out during the day. On the evening of 21 June, the Major arrived at Bork to spend the night there. That same night he succeeded in robbing the enemy of the post of Lünen, in which 3 to 400 men of the occupation force were partly cut down, partly captured; among the former was Colonel von Lindau. As a result of this incident, Major von Monkewitz, hauling the foot-Jäger to their feet, advanced via Nordkirchen to Herbern, where the remnants of the men from Lünen were found.[382] From here, Monkewitz posted for the provost Kappenberg, to see if the enemy would make something on the right side of the Lippe.[383]

Duke Ferdinand, meanwhile, had advanced to Merl between the hereditary prince and the prince of Soubise on 27 and 28 June. Lünen as it came to be known stood as a true battle.[384]

Battle at Lünen

On 29 June, the Carabinier and Jäger moved with Scheiter's Jäger against Lünen. The enemy had occupied this place with a strong force and broken up the bridge there.

The Jäger, however, soon found fords to cross over the Lippe. The enemy defended himself stubbornly; but the Jäger managed to drive him away after a two-hour battle, and with the considerable casualties of sixty dead and fifty-five prisoners-mostly wounded. The loss of the allies consisted of 23 dead and 64 wounded, of which the Bückeburg Jäger had 2 dead and 9 wounded. The cavalry could only cross the Lippe at Dahlen Haus and therefore took no part in the engagement; but the enemy was pursued as far as Dortmund, and various men and horses were taken from him. Since the enemy received reinforcements from Dortmund, the allied troops returned to Lünen.[385]

---

[382] Translator's note: Nordkirchen is a municipality in the district of Coesfeld, in North Rhine-Westphalia. Herbern is situated nearby to the hamlet Ondrup in North Rhine Westphalia.
[383] Translator's note: Kappenberg or Cappenberg is a part of Selm, North Rhine-Westphalia.
[384] Translator's note: Merl is a village in Rhineland-Palatinate.
[385] Translator's note: Dahlen here may refer to modern Dahlen is a town in the district Nord-

The month of July, the corps was partly in Lünen and Bork, as it stretches along the Lippe to Wesel and kept this area under observation. The opposing armies clashed against each other, and the Duke de Broglie, after having pushed General von Spörcken aside, on 12 July made his union with Prince Soubise at Merl. On 15 and 16 July, the battle occurred at Vellinghausen. The enemy armies separated immediately afterwards. Marshal Broglie went with his army through the Paderborn back to Hesse. Duke Ferinand followed him. Prince Soubise drew against Schwerte on the Ruhr, and this kept the Hereditary Prince in sight.

Major von Monkewitz expressed himself quite vocally concerning the patrols along the Lippe, which never happened with anyone else, and said, among other things: "Every day we roam the area and sometimes go as far as Wesel, in the hope that we will finally do something to provoke our enemies; but everything stays calm there. We hear the bang on the other side of the Lippe and learn everything that goes on, but nothing comes to us from the enemy, and soon it seemed foolish, as if we were completely forgetting the war here."

Towards the end of the month, however, it became a little more lively, as the enemy at Schwerte made frequent attacks against the Lippe. On 1 August Lieutenant von Berk succeeded in raiding a detachment of enemy Hussars de Conflans in the area of Hörde with 20 horses, knocking down some and returning to Lünen with 7 prisoners and 11 booty-horses.

Incidents at Olphen and Hiddingstädt

sachsen, in the Free State of Saxony, Germany. Since 1994, the town of Dahlen consists of the old town with the addition of neighboring villages Börln with Bortewitz, Radegast and Schwarzer Kater (literal translation: Black Tomcat), Großböhla, Neuböhla and Kleinböhla, Schmannewitz and Ochsensaal. Thus Dahel Haus may refer to Dahlen castle, built by Heinrich Graf von Bünau (on land left to him by his heiress wife Augusta Helena von Döring who died in 1728) between 1744–1751, the castle was originally one of the residences of the von Bünau family and latterly of the Sahrer von Sahr-Schönberg family which lost all its possessions due to expropriation and banishment without compensation by the post-war communists in 1945. It was completely gutted by fire in 1973, just after it had been fully restored.

The Hereditary Prince moved to the area of Unna on 2 August and the Prince de Soubise to Dortmund. There were daily skirmishes among the patrols, and the garrison of Wesel began to move, sending a strong detachment to Olphen on the 6th of July, upon which, unexpectedly, very early in the morning, a patrol of the Carabiniers, now in Kassel, in places Olphen pushed himself. Although the patrol turned around at the same time, it had gone too carelessly and had come so close to the enemy that it sustained two Carabiniers killed and arresting three by overpowering them through weight of numbers; Two escaped Carabiniers brought news of this incident to Major von Monkewitz. He hastily sent word to the hereditary prince, and, while the infantry remained -1 battalion of the legion and the Jäger in Kassel, advanced with the Carabiniers and the squadron von Porbeck against Olphen. On the way came word that the enemy had come to Lüdinghausen, which they were now following. The enemy had left Lüdinghausen, after extorting a great deal of money, on the morning of the 7th of August, and took the direction via Elfen and Hiddingstädt to Kösfeld. He was pursued swiftly, and before Hiddingstädt the Carabiniers met with his rear guard, with whom the squadron of Porbeck, who was at the head of the unit, immediately became common, and as the Carabiniers now approached, they had a fatal loss to the enemy, including 20 wounded and a few deaths and 53 prisoners were taken. But as the enemy now formed his rear guard out of infantry, which also held good countenance, it was not possible to do more against him, but one had to be content to consider his march as far as Kösfeld. The Squadron of Porbeck had 5 dead and just as many wounded in this battle, as well as 2 dead horses; the Carabiniers lost 2 dead and 6 wounded, along with 2 horses shot.

The retreat went via Lüdinghausen to Kassel, where Major von Monkewitz sent an order to the Hereditary Prince to occupy Rauschenbach an der Lippe. The prince wrote in this order in relation to the persecution of the enemy detachment: "I hope by now, you will get some of it."

The Prince de Soubise, on the 8th of August, had moved through Dorsten against the Lippe, and more and more strong divisions had already sent them across the river. This induced the hereditary prince to send several troops into the city, to watch the enemy's movements and prevent a raid on Münster. The incidents in the army of Duke Ferdinand, however, compelled the hereditary prince to set out for Hesse and leave General von Kielmannsegge with too few troops in Münster. The Carabiniers stood until 13 August in Rauchenburg.

The enemy had passed the Lippe that night with the greater part of his troops, reached Dülmen. by a quick march, and attacked, and for the most part captured, the battalion of von Porbeck that had been posted there. General von Kielmannsegge therefore withdrew and moved against Münster. The light troops covered this march on the left flank; but one was not troubled by enemies and seized on the 14th of August post of Amelsbühren in front of Münster.[386]

On 15 August General von Kielmannsegge moved through Münster on the way to Schapdetten. But on the following night the enemy occupied the area of Rorel and, after a violent cannonade, compelled the corps to march on to Münster. General von Kielmannsegge now put the greater part of his troops at the disposal of his Colonel de la Chevallerie and went with the rest over the Emsnach to Osnabrücken. Major von Monkewitz remained with the Carabinier and Jäger in Münster and received the command of the whole cavalry (about 490 horses) of the force.

On 19 August, Major von Monkewitz reconnoitered the enemy with the cavalry; It was observed that he set out from the camp at night with a considerable force and marched against Hamm, where there was a weak garrison of the allied troops.

Battle at Hiltrup

On the 21st of August von Monkewitz, accompanied by Captain Baum and a small detachment of Carabinier, went to Hiltrup.[387] He

[386] Tranlator's note: Amelsbüren is the largest district of Münster in terms of area, as the farms Of Sudhoff, Loevelingloh and Wilbrenning are among others. This means that extensive forest areas such as the Davert and the Hohe Ward belong to Amelsbüren.
[387] Tranlator's note: Hiltrup is a suburb of Münster.

succeeded in invading by approaching under cover acting as a hostile transport of food and bringing 23 loaded carts and 26 prisoners into the city. On 23 August, the Carabinier and Jäger returned to the Hiltrup area and engaged in a rather heated engagement with the enemy outposts, shooting 2 Carabinier and a Jäger, and wounding 4 horses.

After Major von Monkewitz had reconnoitered on the 24th of August with the whole cavalry detachment against Albachten and had perceived that the Prince de Soubise set out and directed his march to Hamm, he was commissioned, on the 25th of August.[388] In the morning with the cavalry, the Jäger, 400 infantry and two guns set out to observe the continuing march of the enemy. The Major moved first against Albachten, but found this area completely abandoned by the enemy and now turn left to Hiltrup, where, according to the common people, the enemy should stand. Before Hiltrup they discovered an enemy picket, who at once withdrew to the place when the head of this body appeared. The town was heavily occupied, but Monkewitz attacked it immediately. After a heated battle, the Hanoverian grenadiers succeeded in throwing the enemy out of the village at the point of the bayonet. Beyond it, the riders also fell upon him, scattered him completely, and pursued refugees up to the so-called Salgenhaide towards Albersloh.[389] Here he discovered the camp of the Prince de Soubise. Major von Monkewitz lost only 11 dead and some wounded in this battle, all from the Hanoverian grenadiers. The loss of the enemy was considerable, including about 40 prisoners.

On the 26th of August a part of the cavalry again reconnoitered the camp near Albersloh. The same day the Prince de Conde bombarded Hamm violently, and would soon have forced it to surrender, had not the Erbprinz von Braunschweig, returning from Hesse, hurried to the city on 27 August. The Prince de Conde found it advisable to turn against Schapdetten. Dorthein, on the 28th of August, was also invested by the Prince de Soubise, and moved a camp here, as at Kleine Bergen, behind

---

[388] Tranlator's note: Albrachten is another suburb of Münster. It is located 4 miles south of Senden. It is also 5 miles northwest of Havixbeck.

[389] Translator's note: is one of two districts of Sendenhorst in the district of Warendorf in North-Rhine-Westphalia. Albersloh is divided into the districts/Bauerschafts Dorf, Sunger, Rummler, Berl, West I, West II, Storp, Alst and Ahrenhorst.

Korei. On this occasion a skirmish took place between the light troops of the enemy and the Carabinier, in which the latter had three wounded horses, while against the enemy some prisoners were taken.

On 29 August, the Hereditary Prince had already moved to Dorsten on the left side of the Lippe, had encircled this place, and had captured the enemy's troops on the following day. General von Kielmannsegge arrived in Münster on this day with about 400 horses and a few battalions, coming from the Ems. Major von Monkewitz set out on patrol to go reconnoitering against Old Bergen, where Münster stood up near Fort Charles. The patrols went against Albachten and Roxel.[390]

Monkewitz reports on the incident on the following day:

Battle at Albachten by Münster

Early on the morning of August 30th, after I had posted myself in the night at Alt Rorel, General Graf von Kielmannsegg, with ten strong infantry battalions of the escort and 400 horse, came out of the city and to my post. I reported to the general that a strong enemy corps was continually encamping behind Rorel at the height of the Alten Bergen, and another, just as strong, at Schapdetten. Therefore, it seemed to me to be dangerous to advance further against Albachten, as the enemy standing near Alten Bergen could easily occupy the only line of retreat to Münster. General von Kielmannsegge expressed his doubts that my news concerning the camp near Schapdetten would be correct and said that he had to convince himself of the matter, for after the incidents on the Lippe, and since the Hereditary Prince was already in Dorsten, so too light troops had already passed close to Wesel, and it seemed unlikely to him that the Prince de Soubise would remain in position at Schapdetten. The Hanoverian Hauptmann, Count von Dennhausen, who

---

[390] Translator's note: Roxel is a section of the town of Münster.

was in charge of General von Kielmannsegge's duties as Brigade Major, was, however, in favor of my opinion, and while it was being discussed, the Commandant of Münster sent an officer with the message: "That from the towers of the city one could perceive quite distinctly and definitely the enemy's position at Schapdetten and Alten Bergen, so that the general would not proceed further so as not to expose the troops who are in it as the fortress."

General Count von Kielmannsegge answered that it seemed to him quite improbable that the Prince de Soubise was really still encamped at Schapdetten; rather, he certainly believed that the enemy had made a move against the Lippe and left the camp behind to mask their movement, in that the enemy could attack without the reinforcements engaged the night before in Münster.

"Everything," says von Monkewitz,

now set in motion forward; the Carabinier and Jäger corps, together with the three squadrons which I had under my command, and a battalion of the Hannover Infantry Regiment von Block, composed the vanguard. On the heights of Albachten we came upon a rather strong enemy picket, which was immediately driven back and pursued. They fled in the direction of Schapdetten and we soon found strong infantry hidden behind a defile, which is the first to be encountered in this direction. We awaited the arrival of our infantry. The battalion von Block and the Jäger attacked the defile which was firmly defended and could be taken only after a very hard fight. At this the cavalry galloped and fought hard against the retreating enemy, while our infantry followed swiftly. But scarcely had the defile been completely cleaned, and we were just beginning to form, when we also became aware that we were very close to the enemy camp. The enemy was completely alerted and immediately began to greet us with gunfire.

Count Oennhausen rushed back to the general to report our desperate situation, whereupon orders were issued to go back through the defile, which was not a very easy task, especially since the enemy was now attacking us with all his might. The cavalry went first through the defile, and the battalion von Block opposed the hardened enemy with such calm and determination that he could do nothing about it. However, this brave battalion lost a lot of men. Behind the defile, General Kielmannsegge had taken a suitable position for our reception, the enemy was following suit, and the further the retreat continued in uninterrupted combat. Never in my life have I seen a more beautiful retreat than this, and I must confess that, however unpredictably General von Kielmannsegge had undertaken this expedition, his unshakeable composure and his clear outline made this imprudence far better. He was also supported, in masterly fashion, by the brave commanders of the Hanoverian regiments and battalions. The enemy's very large cavalry tried repeatedly to infiltrate the infantry, but all the attempts were in vain, and since they could not spread out because of the broken terrain, nor could the infantry strike from all sides. They finally gave up their attacks after considerable losses. The enemy was obliged to accompany us with constant cannon fire back to Fort Charles. We lost over 400 men in this affair; I had two Carabiniers killed and three horses wounded; Of the Jäger, eight remained in the defile.

Despite the excellent orders of the general and the great bravura of the Hanoverian Regiments, our situation seems to have become very grave if the enemy encamped at Alten Bergen. Instead of listening inactively they moved straight to Rorel, thereby cutting General von Kielmannsegge off completely from Münster and thus took the most beautiful opportunity to make a decisive effort on the fortress itself, which we were all very afraid of.

On 1 September the Prince de Soubise was induced by the movements of the hereditary prince to leave his positions at Schapdetten and Rorel, and to move against Dülmen. Major von Monkewitz went with the Carabinier against Schapdetten to observe the prince's march; He followed these movements on the 5th of September, when the enemy crossed the river at Dorsten. In those days, some enemy stragglers and 3 baggage wagons were raided. The hereditary prince, however, was opposed to the right-wing on the Lippe by Falsheim, and had united with General von Kielmannsegge at Dülmen, and had returned to Münster on the same day, a position taken by Stever in advance of the front. The headquarters of the Erbprinzen was in Beckum.[391] Major von Monkewitz was in Notteln until 12th of September with the corps and the 3 squadrons of the Legion Britannique assigned to him, and he observed the territories of Kösfeld and Dülmen. The hereditary prince threw some regiments in Münster, reinforced the Hessian general von Oheimb with a few battalions and squadrons, and then went back over the Lippe with the rest of the army to march to Hesse. Major von Monkewitz was given the command of the advanced detachment of about 600 cavalry of the garrison of Münster, and moved there on 12 September. The Prince de Soubise, with the bulk of the army, was continually on the left bank of the Lippe; only a few detachments of light troops go from there to the region of Nordkirchen and Dülmen, to forage.

Moreover, that the Erbprinz always trusted and placed special value on the informants drafted by the Major of Monkewitz. Such is evidenced by a letter of this prince, dated Beckum, 9 September, at ten

---

[391] Translator's note: Beckum is a town in the northern part of North Rhine-Westphalia, Germany. It is about 20 km (12 miles) north-east of Hamm and 35 km (22 miles) south-east of Münster. It gives its name to the nearby Beckum Hills. Falsheim may refer to Fehlheim which is a village in Regierungsbezirk Darmstadt (Hesse).

o'clock in the morning, reads as follows: "It is said that Prince Condé marched yesterday against Dorsten against Waltrup; Are you looking for positions to find out if there is still a warehouse on this side of the Lippe or not? Scheither is in Lüdinghausen, with whom you will be in communication."

Add to that the fact that Scheither evidently knew the direction which the enemy must have taken to the Lippe, and to get closer to Major von Monkewitz in Notteln as well.

As a matter of this fact, both the present original papers, and, hopefully, the facts cited, show that the Major von Monkewitz was a very distinguished leader of light troops, and that his value as such was fully recognized by Duke Ferdinand of Brunswick and Count Wilhelm. It is striking, then, not to mention his name once in the many writings of the Seven Years' War, for he would surely deserve to be named alongside many of the celebrated partisans of the day.

On 19 September, Major von Monkewitz made a reconnaissance of Schapdettem against Dülmen, and learned that Soubise had gone to the right bank of the Lippe near Haltern and was moving toward Kösfeld. On the 21st of September, Lieutenant von Berk went with 30 horse, a detachment composed of men from various commands, again into the area of Dülmen, then turned right against Notteln and met before Havisheck an enemy outpost of about 40 horses, which was immediately attacked and thrown back. Some enemy riders were cut down and three made prisoners.[392]

The Prince of Soubise stood in and around Kösfeld, with his forces spread from there to the East Frisian border and shortly after took also the small Meppen fortress near Münster.[393] As there were few worthy troops back in Münster, the enemy had thus gained a free hand

[392] Translator's note: Havixbeck is a municipality situated on the north-east edge of the Baumberge in the district of Coesfeld, in northern North Rhine-Westphalia, Germany. It is located approximately 15 km west of Münster. This may be an engagement commented on by William Todd. See The Journal of Corporal Todd 1745-1762. Andrew Cormack and Alan Jones eds. (Gloucestershire: Sutton Publishing Limited, 2001): 199.

[393] Tranlator's note: Meppen is a town in and the seat of the Emsland district of Lower Saxony, Germany, at the confluence of the Ems, Hase, and Nordradde rivers and the Dortmund-Ems canal. At this time, it was a fortress town.

to take up the whole of the bishopric, together with a part of Osnabruck and East-Germany, whereupon he made himself master.

Battle at Lüdinghausen

Between the light troops on each side there were some insignificant clashes, of which the most important was Captain Baum with 80 horse from mixed commands, in the area of Lüdinghausen on the 12th of October, when he surprised a hostile convoy and took part of the covering force consisting of 4 loaded enemy carriages. In addition, he left one lieutenant colonel, 2 subalterns and 23 riders killed or wounded. He himself lost only 2 dragoons from the Bock regiment (Hanoverian); 2 Carabinier were wounded.

Toward the end of October, after the land was so completely picked over that there was almost nothing left of food or forage in it, the Prince de Soubise returned with the greater part of his army across the Rhine. The General von Oheimb moved to the area of Drensteinfurth, and the campaign in Westphalen was completed for this year.[394] Duke Ferdinand was at this time with the bulk of the army in the area of Eimbeck; Duke de Broglie in Göttingen and around Kassel.

On 5 December the Hereditary Prince of Brunswick arrived with part of the army in Münster and took over the command in Westphalen. The Carabinier and Jäger, along with three squadrons of the Legion, moved from Münster to Hesse on December 11 into the winter quarters, as well as to observe the Lippe against Hamm and Lünen, and occupied from here to Werne. Formed in Westphalia, the cordon of winter posts went from Lippstadt to Olphen along the Lippe, then right on Haus Seithen, Dülmen, Kösfeld, Geschen, Aahaus, Nienburg and Bentheim to the Ems. The enemy army under Soubise drew a cordon from Wesel along the Ruhr through the Bergische and a part of the County Mark to Avensberg. The headquarters of the Hereditary Prince remained in

---

[394] Translator's note: Drensteinfurt is a town in the district of Warendorf, in North Rhine-Westphalia, Germany. It is situated approximately 15 km north of Hamm and 20 km south of Münster.

Münster; That of Duke Ferdinand was relocated to Hildesheim at the beginning of December.

On the orders of the hereditary prince, Major von Monkewitz went to Lünen to talk to a familiar person from the Wesel area, who had been given a rendezvous, and to pay her 150 ducats on behalf of the prince. On the 24th the Major received orders to come to Münster, who gave him various assignments, especially to get acquainted with the area on the left bank of the Lippe down to Wesel. This assignment occupied him until 1 January 1762, on which day Monkewitz returned to Hesse, without having encountered anything of the enemy during this expedition.

Chapter 6

Campaign from 1762 to 1763

Assault and capture of the castle of Arensberg. Reconnaissance against Wesel. The cavalry fight at Westerhole. Battle
at Amelsbüren. The French attack the castle of Bentheim. The
French bombard Hamm. Lieutenant von Berk falls into a hiding place and is caught again. Last battle of the Carabinier.
The peace is closed. Remarks on the Carabinier Corps; Conclusion.

On January 3 Monkewitz met again met with the hereditary
prince for a long conversation at the Fortress of Wesel, which, however,
was later unfortunately given up, by the prince.[395]

Everything was quiet until the month of March; but during this
month, the enemy sent strong detachments to the areas of Bockholt and
Stadtlohn, as well as against Schermbeck.[396] Their only purpose was to
disturb the respective posts. In the meantime, Major von Monkewitz
patrolled through the County of Mark almost constantly, in order to gain
news of the enemy, and on the 2nd of April, like the Major in the diary,
sent to the hereditary prince by express a wordy message. The prince
replied the following evening: "I have received your letter directly, and
I will take it as I have only one from you, the sooner the better to be in
person all together. I am your most humble servant. "

On the 3rd of April, von Monkewitz went to the Crown Prince,
and there among others he was commissioned to familiarize himself

---

[395] Translator's note: The Wesel citadel is the largest intact fortification system of the Rhineland
and was built 1688–1722 in Wesel according to plans by Johan de Corbin, in the form of a pen-
tagonal star, with each point of the star being a bastion. The citadel was the core of the fortress
of Wesel.
[396] Translator's note: Stadtlohn is a town in the north-west of North Rhine-Westphalia, Germany,
part of the district Borken. The Berkel river flows through it on its way to the Netherlands.

with the paths and districts of Arensberg.

Bombardment and Capture of the Castle of Arensberg

After the major had disposed of this order, the Crown Prince, with a part of the army and a train of heavy artillery, under the Hessian Major General Huth, set out from Münster on the 14th of April to undertake the capture of Arensberg. Major von Monkewitz, on the Prince's orders, took over the command of Prussian Hussars, three squadrons of the Legion Britannique (which the major Bischer always had with him), two battalions of infantry and the Karabiner and Jäger Corps.

The march went quickly from Hamm to Werl and Neheim.[397] On the night of 17 April, the advanced guard crossed the Ruhr and advanced to Hachem. There they were abolished by General von Bock the following day, and now advanced further towards Iserlohn, to visit the Vergische and the Dusseldorf area.[398] The Hanoverian general von Freitag moved at the same time via Sundern to Stockum in order to visit the Köllnische Sauerland.[399]

On the 19th of April they began firing at the castle of Arensberg, and soon afterwards it was on fire. The enemy commander did not even have the time to surrender, but jumped with the whole crew, panicked, from the castle down and asked for pardon. However, as the enemy had concentrated considerable forces in the area of Dusseldorf, and even his light troops were already moving against Iserlohn, where the Prussian Hussars had a rather close battle on 19 April. All the troops gathered at

---

[397]Translator's note: Neheim is a district of Arnsberg in the Hochsauerlandkreis. The village was fortified in the 13th century and served the border protection first of the county of Arnsberg and later of the Duchy of Westphalia opposite the county of Mark.

[398] Translator's note: Iserlohn is a city in the Märkischer Kreis district, in North Rhine-Westphalia, Germany.

[399] Translator's note: Sundern is a town in the Hochsauerland district. Stockum today is an urban borough of Düsseldorf. It is located north of Unterrath and Golzheim, east of Kaiserswerth, west of Lohausen. Also given as Freytag, he was a leader of light troops in the Hanoverian service. See James R. Mc Intyre, 'The Freytag Jäger Corps in the Seven Years' War: Their Organization and Employment', Journal of the Seven Years War Association, 22:4 (Summer 2019), pp.13–21 and 'Field Marshal Freytag's Records', Journal of the Seven Years War Association, 22:4 (Summer 2019), pp.30–66.

Arensberg on 21 April; a part of the castle was blown up, and the hereditary prince retreated over the Lippe without being troubled by the enemy. On 24 April, everyone moved back into their old quarters.

Although the enemy had attempted from Wesel to divide and gain the rear of the Crown Prince. During this expedition, he was very worried about his outpost line; but at the great speed with which this blow had been carried out and the Crown Prince returned to the Münster, the enemy gave up his plan and withdrew to Wesel.

On 5 May, von Monkewitz with the corps, 3 squadrons of the Legion and a battalion of infantry moved to Heinrichenburg via Hamm and Lünen, not far from Recklinghausen, to visit Wesel from this side, while the hereditary prince crossed the Ruhr at Hattingen. Meanwhile the enemy withdrew from Elberfeld and threw in the Bergisch, because of an unpaid contribution, which was soon exacted, whereupon the Prince with all troops on the Ruhr and Lippe went back into their previous quarters.[400]

Major von Monkewitz kept the reinforcements assigned to him and occupied Kappenberg on 17 May. The hereditary prince drew the troops nearer this time and took his headquarters to Buldern, on the road from Münster to Dülmen.[401] On 19 May, Monkewitz, accompanied by Major General Huth, made a reconnoitering of Lünen and Recklinghausen along the Imster.

Meanwhile, in the course of this month, the enemy moved his troops together near Düsseldorf and Wesel. The order was given to Prince Condé. Soubise had replaced the Duke de Broglie in the command of the army in Hesse.

Count William left on 24 May for Portugal as Generalissimo. The Lieb-Carabinier followed him.

Major von Monkewitz was in Kappenberg until 18 June; the enemy's light troops began to strike heavily against his outposts, so the major asked the hereditary prince to send another detachment of hussars to Kappenberg. Lieutenant-Colonel von Jeanneret stood with 4 squad-

---

[400] Translator's note: Heinrichenburg is situated in Recklinghausen, Münster
[401] Translator's note: Buldern is a suburb of Coesfeld, in Münster

rons in the area of Reckum.

On 16 June, von Monkewitz crossed the Lippe with eight Carabinier and passed through Recklinghausen towards Märle, where it was reliably learned that the enemy was camped at Wesel, on the right bank of the Lippe, with the largest number of its troops.[402] Upon the announcement made to the Hereditary Prince, he immediately sent all the troops to three different camps, one of which was at Buldern, the second at Lüdinghausen, and the third at Werne; the headquarters of the princes were transferred to Dülmen.[403] On this day the hereditary prince wrote to Major von Monkewitz:

> *The requested Hussars will arrive in Kappenberg this afternoon. From the 15th of June a message is sent from beyond the Ruhr that the battalions at Dusseldorf had passed the Rhine that day and were marching on Wesel. On 14 June, the great Conflans on the Tönnies Haide have contracted.[404] Jeanneret announces that they have bridges between Schermbeck and Dorsten; my people have not reported anything to me. Before the 20th of June, they can not start anything properly, because their bread wagons are only expected on this day; meanwhile their intention is to mislead us; Then from Rees the men are also gone and marched up behind the Rhine, but not yet engaged in Wesel; Anholt and Werth are still busy.*

On the 17th of June Major von Monkewitz was ordered to go as far as possible on the left side of the Lippe to the vicinity of Wesel, to find out how strong the enemy was here, and at the same time to direct

---

[402] Translator's note: Marl is a town and a municipality in the district of Recklinghausen, in North Rhine-Westphalia, Germany. It is situated near the Wesel-Datteln Canal.

[403] Translator's note: Werne or Werne an der Lippe (Westphalian: Wäen) is a town in the Federal state of North Rhine-Westphalia in the Unna district in Germany. It is located on the southern edge of the Münsterland region near the Ruhrgebiet.

[404] Translator's note: Tönnies Haide refers to a region in the Dithmarschen district of Schleswig-Holstein.

a detachment against the Ruhr from there to collect messages.

"I left," says von Monkewitz,

> *Captain Baum with 20 horses at Lünen to go over the*
> *Lippe with the command against the Ruhr to forage.*
> *After he was gone a few hours, I took six excellently*
> *well-mounted Carabinier, who had to leave all the lug-*
> *gage behind to be more mobile, and whom I had secretly*
> *ordered to fasten an empty sack of food under the mate-*
> *lines. So, I rode out of Kappenberg, as if, as usual, I*
> *wanted to go every day, I moved against Olphen.*[405]
> *Quickly I moved, on paths and footpaths I knew exactly,*
> *after I had passed the Lippe at Flasheim, against Dor-*
> *sten. It was already night when I arrived there; Now I*
> *had the oats that I had taken in Flasheim hidden in a*
> *grove, and after a few hours sat down again. At dawn*
> *I reached the hill of Hingsen, from where I could very*
> *clearly overlook the hostile camp and determine that it*
> *consisted of 16 battalions. The enemy's cavalry was not*
> *there. In Hingsen I learned that they were still cantoned*
> *on the other side of the Rhine, near Wesel. Now I started*
> *the march back and arrived in Kappenberg the follow-*
> *ing morning before dawn, after marching back through*
> *Recklinghausen and Lünen, because I had designated*
> *the first place as the rendezvous for unforeseen cases,*
> *and myself almost at the same time with him arrived.*[406]
> *Captain Baum had been fortunate enough to find an en-*
> *emy patrol of Conflans composed of eight horses near*

---

[405] Olphen, also rendered as Olfen is a town in the Coesfeld district in the North Rhine Westphalia area of modern Germany. It is sometime called the "Gate to the Ruhr," and is known as the most horse-friendly town in Westphalia.

[406] Recklinghausen is the northernmost city in the Ruhr district and the modern capital of the area of the same name. Recklinghausen was the site of over 100 witchcraft trials between 1514 and 1710 as well. Lünen is a town in the same district and is located north of Dortmund. The modern town spans both sides of the Lippe River.

*Bockum; he fell upon them so unexpectedly and impetu-
ously that he captured all eight men, three of whom were
severely wounded. I was sorry for this, because people
could barely sit on their horses, but I could not leave
them alone.*

*Buldern's camp had moved to Dülmen during my ab-
sence, and those at Werne and Lüdinghausen to Olphen,
my detachment, however, had remained at Kappenberg.*

The Hereditary Prince replied to the Major's report on the evening of 19 June:

*The report of this noon I have received as well, and I
am especially attached to the trouble given, all my news
coincides with yours. In Rees 5000 men are to stand. E.
assures that nothing of Düsseldorf marches on Wesel;
the same is reported by B. to me. If you find it expedient
to march with your cavalry and infantry to Rauschenberg, Dalen, or Heinrichenburg, I am content if you believe that you can better observe movements of the enemy from there. In that case you should deal with Major
von Sebo, who is at Dalen[407], and warn Jeanneret, who
is portrayed to courtiers and not to retainers, and has
order to place his patrols against Recklinghausen and
Märle.[408] Knowing whether anything really has marched
from Dusseldorf to Wesel is most important to me; from
Rees they left Bockholt to the right, marching hard for
the Dutch border. But this may be a deception, you will*

---

[407] Seems and yet a somewhat unique way of giving an order! If Sebo wanted to stay in Dalen
and the Major wanted to stand there as well? - In the meantime, no such appointments would
take place. Tranlator's note: Dalen (Dutch Low Saxon: Daoln) is an old village and a former
municipality in the northeastern Netherlands, in the province of Drenthe. Since 1998, Dalen has
been part of the municipality of Coevorden.

[408] Translator's note: Marl is a town and a municipality in the district of Recklinghausen, in
North Rhine-Westphalia, Germany. It is situated near the Wesel-Datteln Canal, approx. 10 km
north-west of Recklinghausen.

*see how things are going on our left wing on the Weser
and then we will have it.*

That same night, Major von Monkewitz crossed the Lippe against Heinrichenburg, and found out at once that the enemy had passed the Ruhr at Mühlheim that very night from Düsseldorf. This induced the hereditary prince to pass the Lippe on the same day with the greater part of the troops, and to encamp at Horneburg. [409] Lieutenant von Berk was sent with four Carabiner in the area of Bockum to collect news. He had, however, the misfortune to encounter a strong enemy division and to be caught with three of the Carabiner. The fourth was cut down by the enemy as Berk tried everything to escape.

The hereditary prince, accompanied by General Huth, came to Heinrichenburg on the same day to make a reconnaissance along the Imster, with Major von Monkewitz being assigned to accompany him. However, Captain Baum was sent to Dortmund with 60 horses to ascertain whether the enemy was marching in this direction. At the same time Lieutenant von Müller had to move from Horneburg with a strong detachment to Menegede to cover Hamm, where the bakeries were located. [410]

The prince stayed overnight in Jekern House. The reports which had been collected along the Imster, in connection with the report of the Captain Baum arriving the next morning, "that nothing of the enemy can be found beyond Dortmund and Hörde," made it certain that this was counteracting at the Ruhr, the Muhlheim Corps went against Wesel. The hereditary prince therefore decided to surprise as much as possible the enemy troops between Imster and Lippe. The Carabiner and Jäger Corps on 21 June remained under the command of Captain Baum and moved to Heinrichenburg. [411] Major von Monkewitz was commissioned

---

[409] Translator's note: Horneburg is a municipality southwest of Hamburg in the district of Stade in Lower Saxony. Horneburg is also the seat of the Samtgemeinde Horneburg.

[410] Translator's note: Menegede (now Mengede) is a suburb of Dortmund in North Rhine-Westphalia.

[411] Translator's note: Heinrichenburg is a town in modern Westphalia. It is famous for the boat lift which serves as a key juncture on the Dortmund-Ems Canal.

to remain for the time being with the Erbprinzen. In the afternoon the prince set off in the direction of Recklinghausen, Westerholte, and Buer against Essen to attack the corps that had passed through the Ruhr at Mühlheim. The latter, however, had received news of the prince's crossing of the Lippe, and had speeded up his march on Wesel so that only a few hussars of Conflans were to be seen. The hereditary prince moved on 22 June again to the position of the Horneburg. General von Oheimb camped at the height of Flasheim, opposite Haltern, with 6 battalions and 6 squadrons. Prince Condé moved on this day on the right bank of the Lippe into the camp between Dorsten and Damm.

On 24 June, Monkewitz was sent off with some hussars to reconnoiter the camp near Dorsten; he found that the enemy had not changed his position. Since it was not yet possible to discover whether it would pass over the Lippe or agitate on the right bank, the hereditary prince decided to change his position that very day. If the enemy advanced on the right bank of the Lippe; one could pass this river more swiftly and attack them, or, if the enemy passed through the Lippe, in order to try something against the general von Oheimb, the hereditary prince would be ready to support him. The army therefore took a position at Datteln; the Carabiner and Jäger Corps were replaced by the Legion Britannique and moved there as well.

Cavalry fight at Westerholte

On the 25th of June, before the dawn, when part of the army moved from the abandoned camp of Horneburh to Datteln, Captain Baum went with 20 horses to reconnoiter the enemy camp at Dorsten. Major von Monkewitz was ordered to act against Recklinghausen by announcing the news that there had been an enemy patrol there. When he came to Hornburg von Monkewitz learned with certainty that General Conflans was quite close to Westerholte, and with that message he hurried back to the prince. He immediately took 300 horses from the army, among which were 50 Carabinier, and moved quickly to Westerholte to surprise the enemy wherever possible.

When we were told by Monkewitz, the enemy had passed Recklinghansen, everything had to be opened up; a detachment was sent off; on the other hand, the vanguard of the advanced guard was drawn in. His Highness had the intention of throwing himself at him as if one were aware of the enemy. A field guard stood in front of Westerholte, who escaped when they saw us.

The detachment set to work to meet us, and we were at a loss for reasons, since they occupied the heights, and wondered at the intention of General Conflans, who, with 800 horses, who seemed to be waiting for us.

The prince saw at once that it was too late to turn back, and therefore silently signaled orders to attack. The most exhausting cavalry battle I witnessed in my life now took place. In vain we tried to cut through the squadrons of the enemy, but in vain did he try to bring us apart for a long time! - So, the fuss may have lasted over half an hour when the prince's horse was shot dead. This caused some disorder, from which the enemy immediately sought to pull Votheil, and with several detachments rushed towards the place where the prince was being dragged out from under the horse and remounted. Everyone now fought their hardest to save the general, which was also happy; but now we had to give way to the crush of troops. Blood turned cold, however, when nothing had happened, and the prince gave the order to retreat, which was now carried out by the four divisions of both wings, with such order, that the enemy could do nothing against us. The retired squadrons always found an opportunity to position themselves in such a way that the enemy ventured to strike at the center when they went back; they always maintained such good composure when the wings went down, for the enemy, as small as

our little group, had to content themselves with an enter-
taining an insignificant banter.
The pursuit stopped at Recklinghausen. This battle cost
us 4 dead and wounded and in prisoners 4 officers and
83 horsemen. Of the Carabiner 4 men had remained
and 6 of the enemy fell into our hands. On returning to
the camp the Hereditary Prince received the news that
Duke Ferdinand had beaten the Prince of Soubise at Wil-
helmsthal and had returned to Kassel.[412]

On 26 June, the Prince of Condé set off for Dorsten and advanced to Haltern. This prompted the hereditary prince to go over the
Lippe early on 27 June to take a position at Kappenberg. Major von
Monkewitz was sent with 100 horses against Ludinghausen, in order
to find out whether the enemy would let someone march against Münster. But since everything was quiet here, in the evening he returned
to Kappenberg. The Carabinier and Jäger Corps stood under Baum at
Nordlkirchen.

On the 28th of June the prince left the position of Kappenberg
and crossed Werne to Herben, where Prince Condé had marched on that
day from Haltern to Dülmen.[413] The corps was posted to the Gottendorf
post to consider the road from Dülmen to Münster, as the enemy's light
troops roamed to Appelhülsen.[414]

On 29 June Major von Monkewitz was posted with 150 horses
and a battalion of infantry to Nordkirchen, in order to keep an eye on
the area between Haltern and Lünen, and to strike as far as possible

---

[412] The battle of Wilhelmsthal, fought on 24 June 1762.

[413] Haltern am See (*Haltern at the lake*, before December 2001 only Haltern) is a town and
a municipality in the district of Recklinghausen, in North Rhine-Westphalia, Germany. It is
situated on the Lippe and the Wesel–Datteln Canal, approx. 15 kilometres (9 miles) north of
Recklinghausen.

[414] Translator's note: Gottendorf is the contemporary name for the modern town of Otterndorf,
which is located on the southwest side of the Danish peninsula near its base. The town is at the
mouth of the river Medem on part of the Elbe delta in the district Cuxhaven in the state of Lower
Saxony. Appelhülsen, a suburb of the municipality of Nottuln, in the district of Coesfeld in the
German state of Nordrhein-Westfalen.

against Dülmen. By 3 July, nothing happened. On this day it was reliably learned that the Prince of Condé was moving from Dülmen towards Kösfeld. Major von Monkewitz had this reported immediately and was ordered to advance as far as possible along the Lippe, in order to know with certainty whether the Prince of Condé had made any movements across the river.

The major broke out in the evening when it was dark, went down on the left bank of the Stever, and occupied the bridges near Olphen and Hültern with infantry. The same thing happened to Haltern, when the Major moved in with the retreat, and learned with certainty that the enemy had let four infantry and three cavalry regiments near Dorsten cross the Lippe, marching in the direction of Westerholte against the Ruhr. The enemy was no longer in Haltern, and without being disturbed, the Major returned to Nordkirchen.

The information collected prompted the Prince to send the Hanoverian General von Bock over the Lippe with a detachment of troops near Hamm, to watch over the enemy's detachment, while the prince remained with Herbern until 7 July. But as the enemy's light troops below Münster touched the canal and the Ems, the prince changed his position both to cover Münster and to see his position closer to the advance of the Prince of Condé across the Ems. He went in the end on 8 July to the Wera and camped at Wolbeck. The light troops followed this movement. Captain Baum stood with the corps to Angelmudde.[415]

On the 9th of July came news that enemy light troops had crossed the Ems and were burning the counties of Lingen and Tecklenburg. The hereditary prince therefore sent a strong detachment there. On 10 July, the Jäger from the corps occupied the castle Schönflöth and the Ems to observe the area between the channel of the Ems. The Carabinier under Captain Baum arrived in Münster. The enemy, however, had sent several troops to the counties of Tecklenberg and Lingen, which dwelt dreadfully there. This prompted the hereditary prince to set out for this area on 12 July with a few battalions and squadrons in rapid marches. But when the prince arrived in the area of Ladbergen, the enemy was

---

[415] Translator's note: Angelmudde or Angelmodde is a part of Munster.

already in full retreat.[416] All his detachments went to Rhine Über den Ems, whereupon the prince also returned to Wolbeck.

The enemy seemed to have made the prowling on the other side of the Ems with the sole intention of drawing the attention of the hereditary prince, while the Prince of Condé let a large section of his army pass Haltern over the Lippe. Von Monkewitz undertook a reconnaissance on the 14th of July with 100 horses and scouted the area about Venne and Lüdinghausen against Olphen safely.[417]

Battle at Amelsbühren

The Prince de Condé himself set out again from Kösfeld on the 15th of July, and marched back to Dülmen, but detoured a strong detachment against Münster and Wolbeck to mask this march.[418] On the 16th of July, Captain Baum, near Amelsbühren, succeeded in cutting down several men of the hussars of Conflans' and arresting a captain with 13 men.[419] The Carabinier lost 4 dead.

Since the Crowned Prince wished to gather certain news of the further movements of the Prince of Condé, he commissioned Major von Monkewitz with this business. "I rode, says the same, with two Carabinier, crept on all the way to Buldern, and from there all the way forward against Dülmen. Here I learned with certainty that Prince Condé had moved out early in the morning from Dülmen and had gone over the Lippe at Haltern. In a hurry, I returned to the Crowned Prince, who was very satisfied with the news and immediately gave orders to leave the following day."

On 19 July, the hereditary prince of Hamm crossed the river Lippe to see the army of Prince de Condé moving through the Köllnische Sauerland to rendezvous with Soubise. General-Major Huth re-

---

[416] Translator's note: Ladbergen is a municipality in the district of Steinfurt, in North Rhine-Westphalia.

[417] Translator's note: Venne was a village in the principality of Osnabrück.

[418] Translator's note: Wolbeck is a section of Münster

[419] Translator's note: During the Seven Years' War, Amelsbühren was an independent village on the outskirts of Münster. Today, it composes part of the Hilltrup district of that city.

mained as head of all troops in Westphalia. Major von Monkewitz was hired by the Erbprinzen to serve as his chief of staff.

The enemy had left some 6,000 men near Wesel, who continued to disturb the connection with Holland and strike against the Ems. Major-General Huth was first and foremost anxious to put a stop to these raids against the Ems, and to secure as far as possible the connection along the Dutch frontier. He used the time until July 29 and took his headquarters in Münster on this day. Lieutenant von Zerßen had occupied the castle of Bentheim with his foot-Jäger. Captain Baum stood with the Carabinier in Rheine, under the Hanoverian colonel von Hohnstädt, who had been posted here with a strong detachment to secure the crossings over the Ems and had occupied Ohme and Shüttorf to the end.[420]

On the night of 3 August, Lieutenant von Zerßen was attacked by the enemy in the castle of Bentheim, but stubbornly resisted. Colonel von Hohnstädt had been informed of this attack by his patrols, and arrived at Bentheim at noon, whereupon the enemy withdrew on his approach. The Carabiner were ordered to pursue enemy but could no longer reach him and only brought in a few stragglers as prisoners, who had been delayed in Ochtrup. One man was shot dead by the Jäger and 2 wounded. Lieutenant von Berk received his certificate of exchange and returned to the corps.

On the 12th of August General Huth was ordered to send the greater part of the troops he commanded in Münster to Hesse, so that his force was so weakened that the post along the Ems had to be abandoned, and all troops were drawn to Münster. Hamm retained a garrison of two battalions. The enemy took advantage of these circumstances at once and occupied Dülmen and Kösfeld, interrupted the trade with Holland, and marched until 17 August against and over the Ems.

---

[420] Translator's note: Ohme is a town in North Rhine Westphalia. Today it is the name of a famous brand of China as well. The town of Schüttorf lies in southwestern Lower Saxony and in the westernmost part of the Federal Republic of Germany. It is roughly 10 km to the Dutch border. With regards to the cultural makeup and to the natural environment, it lies in a transitional zone between the Emsland and Westphalia. The surroundings may be characterized as settled countryside. Middle centers in the area are, among others, Nordhorn and Rheine.

On that day Major von Monkewitz made a reconnaissance from Rorel to Alten Bergen and learned that the enemy had recalled his patrols from the Ems and had gone to Dorsten.

Major von Monkewitz went with the corps and 50 cavalry from Münster on 19 August via Herbern and Werne to Old Lünen, where he arrived at daybreak on 20 August and learned that the enemy General Danett was at Lünen on the left bank of the Lippe. The major took post at Alt Lünen and gave a report to General Huth.

On 23 August General Danett set off again and camped near Hamm. Major von Monkewitz occupied Werne with 100 grenadiers sent to support Münster, and moved to Hövel, where on the same day General Huth arrived. On the morning of the 24th of August, the enemy was busy establishing a battery against the Lunen Gate at Hamm, and on the 25th of August began to burn the city with heated shot. A part of Hamm soon went up in flames, but the besieged managed to regain control of the fire almost immediately. The enemy continued the bombardment throughout the day and demanded that the post be handed over in the evening. But when an abusive answer came, the enemy retreated to Lunen at night after 25 houses had been burned into ashes. Major von Monkewitz moved back to Alten Lünen and on 28 August General Danett marched to Recklinghausen. Major von Monkewitz retired to Werne on the orders of General Huth.

Battle of Olphen

On 29 August, Lieutenant von Berk was sent down on the right bank of the Lippe with thirty cavalrymen, a mixed force from various commands, to collect news on the enemy, but had the misfortune to fall into an enemy mounted patrol on 30 August at daybreak in the Olphen area again with a Carabinier and 3 heavy riders in captivity. The remainder of the command succeeded in punching through, leaving a Carabinier and 5 heavy riders in the square.

G. W. *During*

Last Battle of the Carabinier at Ober Wisch[421]

On 30 August, Major von Monkewitz was commanded to go with the Carabinier, 100 heavy horse, and 100 grenadiers against Lunen, to find out which route General Danett had taken. The enemy had occupied Lunen with a division of cavalry, who, however, when von Monkewitz suddenly appeared on the scene at daybreak on the 31st of August, this force withdrew hastily from Waltrup and Horneburg towards Recklinghausen.[422] The cavalry went down quickly, caught up with the enemy at Oder Misch, ran at him, cut down several, and made five prisoners, who were told, as in other ways, that General Danett had marched back to Dorsten. On his return to Werne, the Major decided to recombine with the entire detachment in Münster.

This was last battle of the Carabinier in the Seven Years War! At this time, captain Baum switched over to the service of Brunswick.

On 8 September, General Huth left for Hesse, with about half of the troops still in Westphalia, for the siege of Kassel. This move weakened the army in Westphalia so that it was necessary to confine itself to the possession of Münster, Lippstadt, and Hamm. The cavalry left in Münster, about 300 horses; under Major von Monkewitz and maintained the link between these three places. The enemy, on the other hand, did nothing about it, but contented himself with the county of Mark, like the districts of Werne, Dülmen, Haltern, Koesfeld, and others. To mock our weak forces and engage in plunder, they sent out small detachments to Nötteln and Drensteinfurth. The Jäger of the Corps clashed with one of these near Herbern on the 12th of October and the enemy took 8 prisoners.

Everything remained in that situation until the end of October. Kassel was taken and Duke Ferdinand withdrew the English General Lord Cavendisch with a corps to Westphalia to stop the enemy's quar-

---

[421] Translator's note: Ober Wisch or Wisch (Danish: Visk, North Frisian: Väsk) is a municipality in the district of Nordfriesland, in Schleswig-Holstein, Germany.

[422] Translator's note: The moder spelling is Waltrop. Waltrop is a town in the district of Recklinghausen, in North Rhine-Westphalia, Germany. Horneburg is a municipality southwest of Hamburg (Germany) in the district of Stade in Lower Saxony.

rels. Major von Monkewitz was ordered to join the Lord Cavendisch with the Carabinier and Jäger Corps, who arrived at Nordkirchen on 7 November and the Major with the Corps, 100 Grenadiers and 50 heavy horses, to the post at Old Lünen, with the assurance that Duke Ferdinand specifically instructed him; "After all, in difficult cases, it is best to use the Herr von Monkewitz's Corps."

Until 15 November, von Monkewitz stood in Old Lünen. On that day, the armistice was declared, and the Carabinier and Jäger moved into winter quarters in Bork and Kappenberg, where they stayed until 18 January 1763.

The Allied army meanwhile demobilized as the peace between the Crown of England and France was concluded around this time. Major von Monkewitz was ordered to lodge the corps in Münster. Count Wilhelm was, as you know, in Portugal and so von Monkewitz was instructed by the government in Bückeburg to return with the corps. General Major la Chevallerie, who commanded in Münster, did not want to express his consent to the march until the order was received by the Hannöverian government and there were some delays, which led to the march of the corps being delayed until the end of February.

As a reason for the refusal of General la Chevallerie to have the corps demobilized, Major von Monkewitz states:

> *The peace between Prussia and France had not yet been completed, and between the English and Prussian cabinets some jealousies seemed to take place. The garrison of Münster was very weak and the Legion Britannique in administered the area of Münster. Hordes of the same roamed the area, allowing themselves terrible debauchery. Major von Monkewitz was commissioned to protect the area from this, which he did very vigorously.*

The English Colonel Beckwith had meanwhile entered Prussian service, recruited the dismissed legion for this power, established himself in Munster, and began to play the Lord, as the Legion became stronger than the Hanoverian occupation, much of Hanover from two infantry regiments and 150 horses went there for reinforcements. The Peace of Hubertsburg took place, and Major von Monkewitz entered Bückeburg on 1 March 1763 with his small troop.

Concluding Remarks

The results of what these brave riders performed as light troops is here well documented. The corps served in six successive campaigns, and was always to be found in the advanced posts which is the true warrior's highest pride, at the post of danger! Even in times when all the rest of the heavy riders were quiet in the winter quarters, these men lay on the extreme outpost of the winter camps. The concept of heavy and light is so fused in the individuality of this little group that the ideas of some of the theorists fail to explain the skillful rider who, like the Hungarian and Pole, easily rides his horse like the Hussar and Ulan, boldly undertakes rambles, which the theoretician trusts only the above-mentioned weapons, and indeed undertakes them exclusively, and where horse steps on man, jumps from the Gaule, with his sword in his fist to pave the way through the gunfire into the castle!

Now neither Harnisch nor Stahlhelm, nor any other man is to blame. No! All these apparitions are based on the spirit that animates the troop, and this spirit was breathed into our Carabinier by the Count Wilhelm early on their first appearance! They awoke, cherished, and cultivated by our energy, and bore fruits which corresponded to the expectations which Count Wilhelm had for this little cavalry.

As for the protective armor, the exploits, we are so informed, by decisive opinion, that many of the coups carried out by the Carabinier would not have occurred or been less brilliant if they were not armored, and boldly ridden into the enemy. He who knows the soldiers well, knows how many times a small thing can happen! The riders did not think that the cannon fire was as effective as the small rifle-they only had to clear the rifle at 100 paces and learn from experience-a teacher to whom all theories are silenced that in the melee of the armor many a saber-hedgehog, as well as some, though clumsily led, held a bayonet, and it was precisely this that inspired the Carabinier with a certain belief in invincibility, who, nourished sorely by their leader, fortified in the curriculum of boldness; which prevailed in the corps.

Of the audacity with which these horsemen rode, and how they were masters of their horses, still more tell the story of the old men who were part of this glittering period of the Carabinier. Yet the stranger, who is interested in such things, can be shown two places. Where a pair of Carabinier dared to leap for a mere farce with a Frenchman (the legend goes), whom he now probably tasted bile, who would remember, and author confesses that he, too, puts himself in this category. In one of the cases a Carabinier in full armor passed through a not-so-narrow window, the two wings of which were open, into one room, the other, likewise from the pavement, where two gallop-jumps formed the whole approach, over the almost three-foot-high railing of a staircase from four steps away into the house, with the horse snapping off the back trunnion. The house where this happened is incidentally just opposite the royal Prussian post office.

The loss figures for the corps in the six campaigns, in which the same fought in the Allied Army, yield, according to the diaries we have in Seblemen, 160 men in front of the enemy, and 152 men wounded. Horses lost by the corps, both remaining and taken by the enemy, total 109, and 71 wounded.

Once returned to Bückeburg, the Peace establishment of the Carabinier was set at 100, then at 50 horses, all black stallions, and again, at Count William's return from Portugal, all Andalusian upper barbs, that gentleman in Spain and on the coast bought from Africa. The Jäger Corps was dissolved completely.

Already during the Seven Years' War some of these horsemen and Jäger, who had become incapacitated, had been supplied in an upright manner, and employed by their qualities as foresters, Jäger, coachmen, and pioneers in the Marstalle or in other civilian operations. A similar thing happened now with the reduction of the corps. All the people without exception, who had fought in the corps, were given an occupation or a pension, which certainly protected them from want and gave them a carefree life; or Count Wilhelm granted them special privileges. Thus, for example, he gave to the Carabinier Stahlhuth, who had attended all campaigns, a brave soldier, an excellent rider, and was one of those who raided Tecklenburg in 1757 and stormed the castle, the privilege of creating a distillery on his estate. Since the distillery is definitely an asset, it is easy to see that the privilege for the recipient was advantageous. A Franconian Carabinier, who had also attended all the campaigns, and involved in the affair in Tecklenburg as well was later hired as a forester. He provided Count Wilhelm with considerable capital for the purchase and repair of a small town near the fortified houses.

Count Wilhelm was distinguished as a man, as a general and as regent, with acts of princely generosity. He repaid acts distinguished by blood, exile, and bravery. He granted many of his warriors particular estates along with furnishings for them, cattle, and the like, at his expense. These estates were referred to as the New Colonies. He thereby showed to the sons of the Fatherland that it beheld glory to defy death when the war-trumpet resounded, but equally glorious to be a useful diligent nourisher of the state as soon as the goddess of peace returns and the state no longer needed the Arms of the Man to fight for the veteran.

Above the door of each such house was a sign on which was written the name of the Crusader, whose property it now became, as the deed for said property. About a quarter of an hour from the town of Bückeburg, on the northern slope of the Har Mountains, we can still see the signs of the homes of the so-called New Colonies, and cannot help but announce their inscriptions here, convinced that they belong to the public to which these sheets are dedicated, i.e. to the Honorable admirers:

Nr. 1. Grenadier Wilhelm Brand bestowed, because he emerged in a splendid manner by courage and service leader. 1772.

Nr. 2. Gifted to the sergeant Woebbeking, because of the hearty and meritorious acts done as a city junker. 1772.

Nr. 3. Gifted to the Karabiner Wilhelm, because of proven bravery and remarkable loyalty. 1772

Count William did not forget his officers after peace returned, however, no mention is made. Some of them later joined the militaries of other states. Such was the fate of Baum, who ended his days far away in America. But as we wrote only the story of the Carabiners and Jäger, we must here deal with the fate of those officers of this corps, whom we met in the course of this account.

Several times Major von Monkewitz proffered the most honorable requests to enter Prussian or Brunswick services, however, various reasons of gratitude persuaded him to complete his earthly career in the Bückeburg service. Captain Reipe, who commanded the Lieb Carabinier, was at the same time adjutant of Count Wilhelm, whom he accompanied twice to Portugal and died as a colonel in the local service. Captain Baum has served in Brunswick services, as we have shown, and died heroic death as colonel in the American war. Lieutenant von Berk served as captain lieutenant in the Carabinier until 1778, when he was transferred to the Grenadier Regiment as captain, and subsequently became a major in Electoral Hesse. Lieutenant von Gerstein bid farewell after the first campaign. His fate is unknown. The same is true of the Jäger Lieutenants Hoffmann and von Zersen as the master lists of the Jäger Corps are no longer available.

Truly esteemed and loved by his monarch, Major von Monkewitz continued to command the Carabinier. In fact, he enjoyed the special distinction that every time Duke Ferdinand or the hereditary prince of Braunschweig traveled to the troop exercises in Westphalia and came through Bückeburg, these princes always honored the brave Monkewitz with their high visits.

According to Count Wilhelm's estimates, the state of finances urgently demanded a reduction of the military, and it was determined that the Carabinier Corps should consist of only thirty mounted men. In December 1785 von Monkewitz was appointed lieutenant colonel. When, later on, several necessary reductions had to be made in the military, the horses were also taken from the Carabinier, and their numbers diminished as they died out. From then on, they served as bodyguards inside the castle, and thus they still exist under the ruling Count.

In memory of the great founder of this cavalry formation, their uniform as a whole remained the same as it was in the Seven Years' War. The uniform was made of black cloth. However, because of the delicate nature of the leather collars; the cuirass was discarded. The former helmet now represents a lighter head covering - a helmet of burnt leather with a white tail - which seems more elegant to some than the old one. Quite frankly, we do not like it for the reason that we ought not have changed anything about a uniform that was worn with so much glory. For once the uniform was changed, would tropers continue to remember the glorious deeds done by their predecessors in the old one? Also, after some years for reasons we were not able to discover, the looped W on the sabretache disappeared.[423]

The father of the now ruling prince, a regent who had to appreciate every oath, inherited William's benevolent sentiments towards Monkewitz, and made him both stand out as a hero of the Seven Years' War. The now ruling serene prince ordered von Monkewitz image to be painted from life and to display this portrait at Wilhelmstein next to that of their great lord and guide.

Lieutenant Johann Kasimir von Monkewitz died in the first days of February 1789, sincerely mourned by his comrades and all the nobles who knew him.[424] He was a truly noble man, that is still the opinion of all those who knew him personally. What he did as a warrior is shown clearly in the preceding pages. What he was as a human, we gather from the testimonies of his contemporaries. They say of him: "he crowned all his merits by modesty and unpretentiousness."

Monkewitz was tall and well built, a handsome soldier, as can be seen from his portraits. Until the last day of his life he maintained military elegance and dignity in his suit, and he was always dressed as a black rider officer, on solemn occasions with the black and silver cuirass, which was his companion in many a heated battle. Dressed as a black cavalry officer, his earthly cloak was handed over to Mother

[423]Translator's note: It is likely that the W was removed as it specifically referred to Count Wilhelm. His successors may have removed the emblem in order to present the Carabiniers as a more national force.

[424] For a short biography of Monkewitz, see appendix one.

Earth.

The officers' corps of the Royal Prussian regiment of Wolbeck, which was garrisoned at Minden at that time, closed its doors to the funeral procession. The Consistorial Councilor Froreip says about this in connection with the speech in Fruck, which he adduced to the grave of the immortal: "There are certain acts which one may only call to make the taste felt in them, and to them certainly belongs the above-mentioned action of the brave sons of Lithuania!"[425]

The friends of the Fatherland are certainly interested in getting to know the glorious deeds of worthy countrymen, and their applause alone would be sufficient reward for the author. If, however, he had at the same time attained that his account of it appeals to the state to which he belongs and does nothing but contribute to the narrative of the historical facts described above, in kindling in the breast of the young warrior the feeling of the blazing flame: indefatigable and desperate to beat, when the Prince and the Fatherland shake his arm, but without calculating the danger according to numbers! "then, truly, the author would have been happy to undertake this work!

The ideal of a light cavalry, according to the author's modest views, was described here. Although the little group was small, the services rendered by it speak loud and clear to the present and the future: "what a well-practiced, well-guided and well-mounted cavalry can do in small numbers, if the heart does not believe in impossibility, and fist and thighs do their duty at the right time."

---

[425] Translator's note: Monkewitz was Lithuanian by birth.

Appendix I

Maps of the Area of Operations for the Carabinier and Jäger Corps

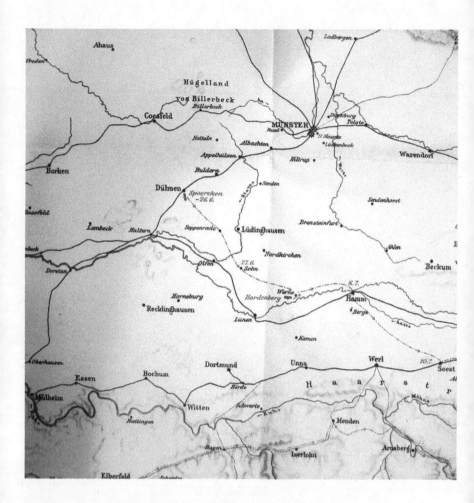

Figure 1 Map of the area of Munster and the towns to the south from the German General Staff History.

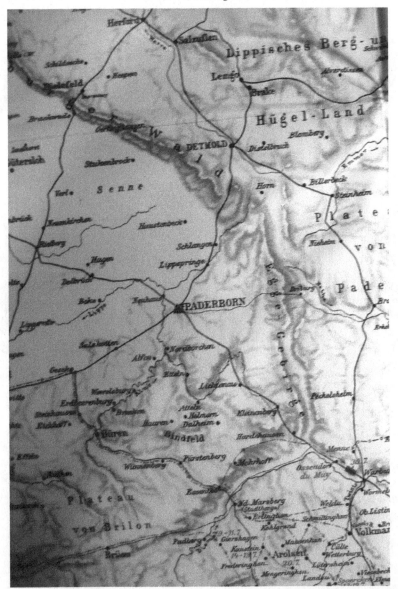

*Figure 2 Map of Paderborn and surrounding areas form the German
General Staff History.*

Figure 3 Towns and Municipalities in Kries Lippe

Appendix II

The Life of Lieutenant Colonel Joachim Kasimir von Monkewitz

Johann Kasimir von Monkewitz was a Schaumburg-Lippescher lieutenant colonel, born in August 1722 at Keydan in Lithuania. He served in the War of the Austrian Succession as a Prussian freicorporal. In this role he participated in the battles of Hohenfriedberg (4 June 1745), Soor (30 September 1745) and Kesselsdorf (15 December 1745). He next served Countess Bentinckschen Schloßcompagnie zu Knyphausen as ensign from 1751–1755 and entered the service of Count Wilhelm von Bückeburg as a lieutenant with the infantry in July 1755.

On the outbreak of the Seven Years' War, Count Wilhelm appointed him as the captain and commander of his Carabinier corps, which he established in 1753. At the head of this troop, the "black men", or the "diables de Bückeburg," he made a fearsome name among his enemies and his friends as a bold and prudent partisan leader. If this fact is little mentioned in the larger historical works, it is partly because the achievements of the smaller contingents in these works are often pushed back and overshadowed, but due partly to Monkewitz's undemanding and humble personality as well. Nevertheless, he and his troops' accomplishments are unforgettable. Right at the beginning of the campaign of 1757, when the Allies drove the bulk of the Allied army to Westphalia, Monkewitz's Carabinier emerged favorably. Later, when Duke Ferdinand of Braunschweig took command after the Battle of Hastenbeck, in which the Carabiner played only a minor role they would now make significant contributions.

Beginning at the end of Winter 1758 when Duke Ferdinand initiated his triumphal flight from the Elbe to the Rhine, they were - as with the rearguard the year before - now with the advanced guard. On 25 February von Monkewitz entered Bremen, on 26 March he attacked an important enemy transport near Bentheim. For his brave behavior in the clash at See, on 5 August, Count Wilhelm honored him with a saber. He took part in the campaign in 1759 in the "small" army of General von Spörcken in Westphalia. In a raid on Buer on 4 May, he fooled the enemy with counterfeit guns and caused him great harm using the terror created. The preceding was one of his best exploits.

At the battle Klein-Dortmund on 30 September he was commended by Duke Ferdinand for his conduct once again. In the autumn of that year he was given the command of a larger division, this time of 2 battalions and 3 squadrons, for the first time, at the Duke's express command. Next, Monkewitz received orders to cover the siege of Münster during which he repulsed the enemy's attempt at relief on 19 November in a battle near Notteln. Later such commands often fell to him. Winter passed with marches and outposts. Promoted to major at the beginning of 1759, he took part in the campaign of 1760 under Spörcken again. In the course of the same he had the misfortune to be taken prisoner in a skirmish near Wolfhagen on 26 July, when his horse, a young irrepressible stallion - the Carabinier only rode stallions - went through with him. The Duke de Broglie immediately paroled him on his word of honor, and Duke Ferdinand ensured that he would be exchanged soon, whereupon he again took part in the hostilities in Westphalia and in the troubled winter postings on the Lippe.

The year 1761 saw a brilliant but losing battle at Darfeld, where, without being guilty of any mistake, he struggled through a strong hostile force on 9 April. It turned out to be particularly useful for scouting and intelligence gathering. He was, therefore, often posted with the Hereditary Prince of Braunschweig, with whom he carelessly entered into the stubborn cavalry battle at Westerholt on 26 June 1762. When the hereditary prince marched to Hesse soon thereafter, Monkewitz as chief of the staff, was added to General von Huth's command. The force remained in Westphalia. When Huth later went to the siege Cassel and the English general Lord Cavendish was sent to Westphalia for reinforcement, the Duke recommended that "in difficult cases use the council of the Lord von Monkewitz." After the peace was concluded, Monkewitz remained, although his corps, which at the beginning of the war had only 75 men on horseback and 50 on foot, but was brought to a strength of 100 men in the course of the war, was considerably reduced. Soon the mounted contingent was no longer financially viable. He refused an offer to move to Prussia or Braunschweig. He died on 1 February, 1789 in Bückeburg.

Appendix III

List of Major Engagements in which the
Schaumburg-Lippe-Bückeburg Carabinier and Jäger Corps Took Part

Battles:

Hastenbeck- 26 July 1757

Krefeld-23 June 1758

Combat of Mehr-5 August 1758

Lutterberg- 10 October 1758

Attempt on Lippstadt-1 July 1759

Warburg-31 July 1760

Vellinghausen-15-16 July 1761

Combat at Albachten 24 August 1761

Wilhelmsthal-24 June 1762

Second Battle of Lutterberg-19 July 1762

Grüningen-25 August 1762

Sieges:

Siege of Minden-1-15 March 1758.

Siege of Münster- 2 October-20 November 1759

Siege of Wesel-10-18 October 1760

Double Siege of Kassel- 17 February-28 March 1761

Siege of Meppen-30 September-3 October 1761

Bibliography

Bibliography

Books:

Primary Sources:

Archenholz, Johann Wilhelm von *Prussia and the Seven Years' War, 1756-1763*. Translated from German by F.A. Caty. Frankfort: C Jugel, 1843.

Clausewitz, Carl von *Clausewitz on Small War*. Christopher Daase and James W. Dais, eds and trans. Oxford: Oxford University Press, 2015.

Ewald, Johann *Treatise on Partisan Warfare*. Robert A. Selig and David Curtiss Skaggs, trans. New York: Greenwood Press, 1991.

Simcoe, John Graves *Simcoe's Military Journal: A History of the Operations of a Partisan Corps, called The Queen's Rangers, Commanded by Lieutenant Colonel J.G. Simcoe, During the War of the American Revolution*. 1781.

Tempelhoff, George F. Geschichte des siebenjährigen Krieges in Deutschland. 6 vols. Berlin: Nach. D. Ausg.,1783-1801.

Todd, William *Journal of Corporal Todd, 1745-1762*. Andrew McCormack and Alan Jones, eds. Gloucestershire: Sutton Publishing Limited, 2001.

Tory, John *A Journal of the Allied Army's Marches, from the first arrival of the British troops, in Germany, to the present time; with an accurate account of all the particular battles and skirmishes they have had with the French army*. Osnabruck: J.W. Kisling, 1762.

Secondary Sources:

Anderson, M.S. *The War of the Austrian Succession 1740-1748*. London: Longman, 1995.

Black, Jeremy *The British Abroad: The Grand Tour in the Eighteenth Century*. Stroud, Gloucestershire: The History Press, 2003.

_____ *France and the Grand Tour*. Basingstoke: Palgrave Macmillan, 2003.

Browning, Reed *The War of the Austrian Succession*. New York: St. Martin's Griffin, 1995.

Carmichael, Ewan *Like a Brazen Wall: The Battle of Minden, 1759, and its Place in the Seven Years War*. Warwick, England: Helion and Company, 2021.

Duffy, Christopher, *Frederick the Great, A Military Life*. New York: Routledge, 1985.

_____ *The Military Experience in the Age of Reason 1715-1789* New York: Hippocrene Books, 1987.

_____ *The Army of Frederick the Great*. 2nd ed. Chicago, IL: E The Emperor's Press, 1996.

_____ *Instrument of War vol. 1 The Austrian Army in the Seven Years' War*. Chicago:The Emperor's Press, 2000.

_____ *By Force of Arms vol. II The Austrian Army in the Seven Years' War*. Chicago: The Emperor's Press, 2008.

Düring, G. W. von *Geschichte des Schaumburg-Lippe-Bückeburges-chen Karabinier– und Jäger– Korps im Siebenjährigen Kriegs*. Berlin: Graf Sigfried Mittler, 1828.

Fonblanque, Edward Barrington de, ed. *Political and Military Episodes in the Latter Half do the Eighteenth Century: Derived from the Life and Correspondence of the Right H. John Burgoyne, General, Statesman, Dramatist*. London: MacMillan, 1876.

Froriep, Justus Friedrich *Zur Erinnerung an den Herrn Oberlieutenant Joh. Casimir von Monkewitz, ehemaligem Befehlshaber des Bückeburgischen Karabiniers- u. Jäger-Korps*. Bückeburg 1789.

Kapp, Freidrich *Der Soldatenhandel deutscher fürsten nach Amerika. Ein Beitrag zur Kulturgeschichte des Achtzehnten Jahrhunderts*. Berlin: Verlag von Julius J. Springer, 1874.

Knötel, Richard, Herbert Knötel, and Herbert Seig, *Uniforms of the World: A Compendium of Army, Navy and Air Force Uniforms 1700-1937*. New York: Charles Scribners and Sons, 1980 reprint of 1956 translation.

Lapray, Olivier *Hastenbeck 1757: The French Army and the Opening Campaign of the Seven Years War*. Warwick, England: Helion and Company, 2021.

Mc Intyre, James R. *The Development of the British Light Infantry, Continental and North American Influences, Mc Intyre, 1740-1765*. Point Pleasant, NJ: Winged Hussar Publishing, 2015.

_____ *Light Troops in the Seven Years War: Irregular Warfare in Europe and North America, 1755-1763*. Warwick: England: Helion and Company, 2023.

O'Shaughnessy, Andrew J. *The Men Who Lost America: British Leadership, the American Revolution and the Fate of Empire*. New Haven: Yale University Press, 2013.

Reid, Stuart *Frederick the Great's Allies*. Gery and Sam Embleton, illus. Oxford: Osprey Publishing, 2010.

_____ *The Battle of Minden: The Miraculous Victory of the Seven Years' War*. Havertown: Frontline, 2016.

Savory, Sir Reginald *His Britanic Majesty's Army in Germany during the Seven Years' War*. Oxford: Clarendon Press, 1966.

Smith, Digby *Armies of the Seven Years War: Commanders, Equipment, Uniforms and Strategies of the 'First World War'*. Stroud, Gloucestershire: The History Press, 2013.

Szabo, Franz J. *The Seven Years War in Europe 1756-1763*. New York: Longman, 2008.

Tempelhof, Georg Friedrich von *Geschichte des siebenjährigen Krieges in Deutschland zwischen dem Könige von Preussen und der Kaiserin Königin mit ihren Alliirten als eine Fortsetzung der Geschichte Lloyd*. 6 vols. Berlin: J.F. Unger, 1783-1801.

Articles:

Gadue, Col. Michael R. "Lieutenant Colonel Friedrich S. Baum, Officer Commanding, the Bennington Expedition A Figure Little Known to History." in *The Hessians: Journal of the Johannes Schwalm Historical Association*. Vol. 11 (2008):37-54

McIntyre, James R., 'Field Marshal Freytag's Records', *Journal of the Seven Years War Association*, 22:4 (Summer 2019): 30–66.

McIntyre, James R., 'Heavyweight of the Lights: Andreas Count Hadik von Futak', *Journal of the Seven Years War Association*, 22:3 (Spring 2019): 5–19.

Poten Bernhard von: *Monkewitz, Johann Kasimir von.* In: *Allgemeine Deutsche Biographie* (ADB). (Band 22, Duncker & Humblot, Leipzig 1885): 169–171.

Patrick J. Speelman, "Field Marshal Friedrich Wilhelm Ernst, Graf zu Schaumburg" in Daniel Coetzee and Lee Eystrulid eds. *Philosophers of War: The Evolution of History's Greatest Military Thinkers*. 2 vols., Santa Barbara, CA: Praeger, 2013, 92.

White, Charles E. "Scharnhorst's Mentor: Count Wilhelm zu Schaumburg-Lippe and the Origins of the Modern National Army." in *War in History*. 24, 3 (2017): 258-285.

Wilson, Peter H. "The German "Soldier Trade' of the Seventeenth and Eighteenth Centuries: A Reassessment." *The International History Review*. 18, 4 (November 1996): 757-792.

An example of the Schaumburg-Lippe double barreled pistol

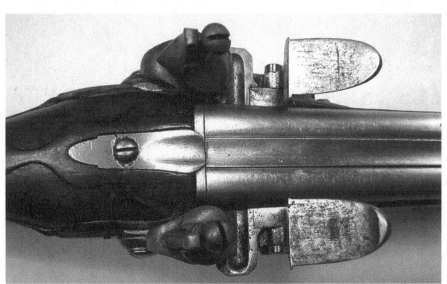

Close-up of the firing mechanism of the double barreled pistol

Top view of the double barreled pistol

Index